D0442665

Spatial Price Theory
O F
Imperfect Competition

Number Eight:
Texas A&M University Economics Series

Spatial Price Theory

O F

Imperfect Competition

BY HIROSHI OHTA

TEXAS A&M UNIVERSITY PRESS

COLLEGE STATION

LIBRARY OF CONGRESS CATALOGING-IN-PUBLICATION DATA

Ohta, H. (Hiroshi), 1940–
    Spatial price theory of imperfect competition / by H. Ohta.— 1st
ed.
        p.   cm. — (Texas A & M University economics series ; no. 8)
    Bibliography: p.
    Includes index.
    ISBN 0-89096-372-X
    1. Prices.   2. Space in economics.   3. Competition, Imperfect.
I. Title.   II. Series.
HB221.0385   1988
338.5′2—dc19   87-22333
                                                CIP

To Y. O.
and, most gratefully,
to the late Professor K. Shibata

Contents

\

Acknowledgments

The author is grateful to Professor R. Sato for repeated encouragement and helpful comments on the present study; to Professors M. L. Greenhut, J. Greenhut, M. J. Hwang, and the editors of *American Economic Review, Econometrica, Environment and Planning, Journal of Regional Science, Regional Science and Urban Economics,* and *Review of Economic Studies* for permission to use some of our results published either independently or jointly in their journals. In addition, some materials from M. L. Greenhut and H. Ohta, *Theory of Spatial Pricing and Market Areas* (Durham, N.C.: Duke University Press, 1975) have been used with permission.

The author's special thanks go to Martin Bronfenbrenner, Mel Greenhut, Janet Kohlhase, Chao-cheng Mai, and Joel Sailors, who read earlier drafts of this monograph and provided deep insights and invaluable suggestions. The author is also indebted to those individuals who spotted technical and mathematical errors in various stages of the manuscript. These sharp-eyed graduate students include T. Wako, Waseda University; D. Greenstreet, University of Pennsylvania; and M. Naito, Aoyama Gakuin University.

This work has been partly supported by a Grant-in-Aid for Scientific Research from the Japan Ministry of Education, Science, and Culture. Chapter 3 is based on M. L. Greenhut and H. Ohta, *Theory of Spatial Pricing and Market Areas* (Durham, N.C.: Duke University Press, 1975) and M. L. Greenhut, H. Ohta, and J. Greenhut, "Derivation of Optimal Spatial Prices under Spatial Monopoly," *Environment and Planning A* 6 (1974): 191–98. Chapter 5 is based on H. Ohta, "On the Neutrality of Freight in Monopoly Spatial Pricing,"

Journal of Regional Science 24 (1984): 359–71. Chapter 6 is based on a paper presented at the Pacific Regional Science Conference, Molokai, Hawaii, 1985. This study was supported by the Ganjoh Kosaka Memorial Scholarship, Aoyama Gakuin University. For Chapter 7, I am indebted to M. L. Greenhut for the use of part of an unpublished paper we had the pleasure of writing, titled "A General Method for Determining Output and Welfare Effects of Discriminatory Pricing." Chapter 11 is a revised version of H. Ohta, "Agglomeration and Competition," *Regional Science and Urban Economics* 14 (1984): 1–17.

Finally, this book is the product of a bilateral monopoly between myself and my wife in her capacity as irreplaceable PC operator. Whether or not the monopolist input supplier dominated, or the monopsonist husband took advantage of his wife's willing assistance, or both colluded for a Pareto optimum is irrelevant. In any case, the book is virtually our joint work.

PART I

Nonspatial versus Spatial Theory of Pricing

1.

Introduction

I. The Fundamental Objective and Significance of Study

Economic space, defined as the distance that separates economic agents by imposing time and other costs upon their trades, is an important analytical variable. Nevertheless, this distance variable has long been a neglected element in orthodox economics; economic distance was thought only to complicate the argument unnecessarily. However, the theoretical impact and the implications of the assumption of economic space are major and cannot be ignored despite the oft-claimed notion that the cost of distance has increasingly become negligible in the world of modern technology. The drastically reduced time cost of commuting by automobile and airplane along with instant telecommunication seems to make the globe appear a "small world"; however, "the very development of modern technology along these lines simply reflects man's quest for minimizing/overcoming the significant cost of distances; it does not prove the *insignificance* of economic space" (Ohta [20, p. 1]).

The firm in economic space differs from its nonspatial counterpart in diverse ways. For one thing, as stressed by M. L. Greenhut [7], the very postulate of distance as a cost places the theorist outside the fundamental context of the purely competitive framework, unless one assumes all buyers to be at one point so that only sellers are differentiated by the varying distances between them and the buyers. Indeed, in any nontrivial assumption of distances (i.e., where both buyers and sellers are distributed over space), an oligopolistic market arises, in which behavioral uncertainty is intrinsic. Moreover, the distance that separates economic agents may be considered a benefit as well as a cost. Because scarce inputs are needed to transport goods and services over economic distance, distance may protect separate agents from one another by serving as a barrier to the entry of competitors.

In light of these observations, this study endeavors to answer the question of why and in what ways the firm in economic space behaves differently from the classical nonspatial firm. Specifically, what is the impact of economic space on the pricing practices of the firm? Of particular interest in this connection are some analytical features of spatial pricing that lead to theorems which seem to run counter to those of nonspatial price theory.

For example, one would probably be surprised if the effect of greater entry of firms in a given industry were to raise, not lower, industrial prices, but this apparent paradox can exist in fairly general and well-defined conditions of spatial competition (see, for example, Benson [2], Ohta [18, 19] and Greenhut, Hung, and Norman [8]). Moreover, the apparent paradox can be resolved readily with the aid of elementary microeconomic analysis of the firm in economic space. Thus, the meaning or theoretical implication of competition could be radically different, depending on whether the scope of microeconomic theory is open to the nontrivial concept of economic space.

As a related note on the meaning of competition, consider two alternative pricing practices for the firm to choose: discriminatory and nondiscriminatory pricing. In classical nonspatial theory, the selection of a pricing policy depended in part on the existence (or absence) of competition in the market. But even given the market type, for example, given monopoly, the question of pricing policy was not immediately resolved. Price discrimination might or might not prevail under conditions of nonspatial monopoly and was not even considered for competitive markets. In contrast, price discrimination is intrinsic to the space economy; it may even be triggered or intensified by spatial competition, as a model presented by G. Norman [15] suggests.

Related to the pricing pattern of firms over economic space is the question of which pricing system yields greater outputs. The classical (nonspatial) economists' answer to this question again was indefinite. Their common contention has been that discrimination typically yields more output than does nondiscrimination. In space economics, the output and other welfare effects of discrimination are revealed more clearly—and more generally. See, for example, Ohta [16], Holahan [13], and Greenhut and Ohta [9].

II. Two Fundamental Assumptions

These and other unconventional results of spatial pricing are based typically on two fundamental assumptions:

Assumption A. Costs of transportation are significant.

Assumption B. Buyers with identical tastes or demands are distributed uniformly over a landscape.

These two assumptions are intended to make other things equal, aside from spatial differences, in identifying the impact of economic space on the pricing patterns of the firm.

The significance of the first assumption should be manifest. Without this assumption, the significance of *economic* space cannot be understood; costless space is *not economic space*.

The second assumption is significant only in connection with the first. Assumption B alone yields, for example, the conclusion that no price discrimination should be expected when elasticities of demand for separate submarkets are identical.

Assumption A changes the results completely, however. This combination of the two assumptions implies demand curves falling as distance increases, as seen by the spatial firm. These curves, in turn, indicate that the firm will necessarily practice price discrimination, unless somehow restricted. We can go further and contend that discrimination could even prevail under conditions of spatial competition. Moreover, the greater are the costs of distance, the more likely is the prevalence of discriminatory pricing under zero profit competitive equilibrium, ceteris paribus. (See Greenhut and Ohta [10], chapter 8, p. 140, in particular.) As indicated previously, greater outputs are coterminous with spatial price discrimination.

III. Scope and Plan of the Book

The introduction of economic space, via assumptions A and B, thus gives rise to considerable impacts on (i.e., changes in) the classical nonspatial theory of the firm.[1] It is no wonder that a change in atmosphere has taken place belatedly since the beginning of the 1970s, putting an end to what Dorward [5] calls the "historic neglect of spatial variables, or distance costs, in the analysis of economic relationships." In fact, an increasing number of contributions have recently been made to the subject of economic space and its theoretical implications. Moreover, many of the contributions reviewed by Dorward in 1982 have been followed by still others.[2] This work, however, is not intended to be a follow-up review of all the latest important contributions to the literature. Instead, I attempt a sort of stock-taking and maintenance of my work published elsewhere (often with M. L. Greenhut or other coauthors). In short, updating, coordinating, and extending selected parts of the previous book [10] is the main task of the present one. However, the present work, although going beyond [10], is but a small step along the developmental path of a theory of the firm in economic space.

The subject of this book is primarily the determination of prices, outputs, and market areas for the firms under conditions of spatial competition (oligopoly) subject to various behavioral assumptions. The problem of locational choice is neglected in the parametrical treatment of firms' locations throughout the present study, except in Chapter 11, where we extend the classical (Weberian) theory of location under conditions of monopolistic competition.

The book consists of four parts. Part I has only one chapter beyond this introduction, and it presents the fundamental frame of reference for later chapters. It shows, in particular, how to represent mathematically a given population of consumers *either* concentrated at a point *or* dispersed over a landscape. The aggregate demand perceived by the firm is then derived for comparison under alternative popula-

---

[1]A third assumption, namely the existence of at least partial scale economy, is sometimes stressed in this connection. Without this assumption the neoclassical paradigm resurges, rendering spatial analysis redundant. Under conditions of strict constant returns to scale and the underlying assumption of perfect divisibility, goods can be produced most cheaply at any and every market point of consumption, an obvious trivium to be disregarded throughout the present study.

[2]Examples include Benson and Hartigan [3]; Gee [6]; Greenhut et al. [8]; Greenhut et al. [11]; Hsu [14]; Ohta [20, 21]; Phlips [22]; and Schöler [23]. Also, a timely and important review by Stevens [24] on location theory, with a scope much wider than the present one, provides the most up-to-date, comprehensive references to the literature, even though they are limited mostly to papers published in *Journal of Regional Science*.

tion distributions. The focal point of this chapter is to show how to formally and most simply analyze the impact of costly distance upon the general form and elasticities of the demand that the firm faces.

Part II considers conditions of spatial monopoly. The first two chapters set forth alternative models of spatial monopoly, followed by three chapters on related subjects. Chapter 3 shows how the optimal spatial price schedule can be derived from varying consumer demand or taste conditions, when the monopolistic firm is under no institutional or legal constraint upon its pricing policy.

Chapter 4, in turn, develops and compares two alternative price policies of the monopolist, who is constrained to practice either FOB mill or uniform CIF pricing.[3] The two alternative models to be examined in Chapter 4 are based on the most general assumptions regarding the consumer distribution over an economic space, the form of consumer demand and costs of production and transportation. In this sense, Chapter 4 is an extended analysis of spatial monopoly pricing along the lines of Beckmann [1], Heffley [12], Hsu [14], and so forth.

Chapter 5 is taken from Ohta [21] with few alterations. It deals with basically the same models of spatial monopoly as in Chapter 4. However, whereas Chapter 4 is concerned mainly with the general comparison of the two alternative constrained price policies, Chapter 5 raises a particular question of comparative statics. Consider a technological improvement in the transport industry. This would cause freight rates to decline. Would it accordingly cause product prices to fall in a space economy? The answer is, it depends. That is, prices may fall, or even rise, under certain conditions. Moreover, somewhat paradoxically, although the *existence* (vis-à-vis nonexistence) of economic distance (i.e., freight costs) has no insignificant impact upon industrial pricing, rather broad conditions also can be shown to exist under which *changes* in freight rate cause *no* changes in FOB mill (or uniform) prices!

Chapter 6 is an extended analysis of spatial price discrimination

---

[3] The FOB (free on board) mill pricing requires buyers to pay a unique mill price plus relevant costs of insurance and/or transportation. The cost to a buyer thus includes not only *cost* at the mill but also *insurance* and *freight* costs. This total cost, called CIF (cost, insurance, and freight) *price,* normally is a monotonically increasing function of freight, as it is under FOB mill pricing. However, under *uniform* CIF pricing, the CIF price is constant; mill price is required accordingly to vary inversely with the costs of distance.

along the lines of Chapter 3 and previous works by Greenhut and Ohta [9; 10, chapter 4]. In addition to the output effects of spatial price discrimination, of particular interest in the chapter will be the question of who gains from discrimination and under what conditions. Although Chapter 6 is self-contained, some background knowledge of spatial price discrimination would be desirable for a deeper understanding of the subject. The final chapter of Part II, Chapter 7, is devoted to this purpose.

Part III relaxes the fundamental assumption of spatial monopoly and considers conditions of spatial competition. Several alternative models of spatial competition are reviewed tersely. Chapter 8 examines four of these. While each model is predicated on a distinct "conjectural variation," one feature is common to all: each firm monopolizes its own market area with no part shared with rivals. The spatially separated firms of Chapter 8 are thus described as creating local monopolies, so that each enjoys an exclusive market area. However, such a result seems to be in conflict with, at least, casual empiricism. In fact, we often observe apparently overlapping market areas. Insofar as we consider this to be a stylized fact, a theory is needed to explain it. The spatial version of the Cournot oligopoly model fills this need, as in Chapter 9. This chapter shows, in particular, how the original Cournot model may be converted to a spatial version and may preserve an analytical continuity as well as contrast with the previous chapter.

Chapter 10 is a direct extension of Chapter 8, as we examine alternative types of short-run and long-run price and output effects of spatial competition and related market areas monopolized by spatially separated competitors. Sections of Ohta [18, 19] are reorganized for this examination.

Chapter 11 revisits, as a digression, the classical Weberian location theory by assuming in effect a "point" market rather than an "area" market in dealing with the problem of plant location. A major question addressed in this chapter is under what conditions a representative firm may move toward the market site or toward an input site. Although most of the text of this chapter is taken from Ohta [20], a new section has been added. This new section ponders the division of labor *and* vertical integration as additional factors of spatial agglomeration, in addition to competitive factors stressed previously.

The fundamental difference between Chapter 11 and the rest of the book is that whereas Chapter 11 assumes a "point" market (demand) in dealing with locational choice, the rest of the book assumes an "area" market in dealing with price, output, and market boundary determination when location is fixed.

After this groundwork for these models of spatial monopoly and competition has been laid, Part IV attempts an analytical extension of previous chapters, by making the models of spatial competition appear more realistic and by asking new as well as the questions previously posed that are of interest in the book. The welfare implications of spatial competition and of growth are a focal point of the analysis.

Going back to the basic postulate of the "area" market, Chapter 12 proposes a further extension of Chapter 10 using the background of Chapters 8 and 9. Although all these background chapters postulate that competing firms are spatially separated from one another, Chapter 12 is based on the observation that in some industries a number of firms are located virtually at one point. An example is a shopping area, called Akihabara, in downtown Tokyo, in which "hundreds" of stores specializing in electric equipment and appliances such as TV sets and air-conditioners, are located side by side, like sardines. These stores appear to be subject not only to *inter*local competition but to *intra*local competition as well (Ohta [17]). Chapter 12 deals with this locational complexity of competition in connection with the normative conditions under which the social welfare is maximized.

Chapter 13 develops a model of spatial pricing with specific reference to the spatial labor market, in addition to the product market. This last chapter is thus an attempt to widen the theoretical scope to take into consideration the interdependencies of the related markets. The prime problem of the chapter concerns the impact of innovation upon the spatial labor market as well as the product market under conditions of spatial competition in the short run and in the long run. Selected findings on the impact of innovation (summarized in a table of the chapter) include a higher mill price, lower real wage rate, decreased aggregate employment, and increased aggregate output in the long run as compared with the equilibrium values before innovation.

The model presented in the main text of Chapter 13, however, is not formulated as a general equilibrium system in the strictest sense. Theoretical purism calls for an appendix to the chapter to purify further the model toward a strict one-product, one-factor model of spatial general equilibrium. The appendix confirms that the main conclusions of the text remain unchanged.

One possible objection to the scheme of spatial analysis just proposed is that the impact of economic distance may be analyzed more simply by a model à la Chapter 11, which assumes only one node, or two at best, of demanders, who in the real world are *not* spread evenly along a line or over an area. Would this model, with innumerable nodes or market points, be *sufficiently* more realistic than the one- or two-node conventional model (as in Chapter 11) to be worth the extra trouble? In response, we certainly are not pursuing realism for the sake of realism. Many or infinite nodes of demanders are assumed in the model not because they represent the real world more closely than one or two nodes, but to ascertain if and how the number of nodes or market areas served by the firm is affected by the price policy of the firm itself. The assumption of fixed numbers of nodes, therefore, is methodologically unacceptable. The market area is—and will be treated so herein—an endogenous variable among other key variables, such as regional prices, outputs, and welfare levels, whereas location will be treated as an exogenous parameter.

References

[1] Beckmann, M. "Spatial Price Policies Revisited." *Bell Journal of Economics* 7 (1976): 619–30.

[2] Benson, B. L. "Löschian Competition under Alternative Demand Conditions." *American Economic Review* 70 (1980): 1098–1105.

[3] Benson, B. L., and J. C. Hartigan. "Tariffs Which Lower Price in the Restricting Country: An Analysis of Spatial Market." *Journal of International Economics* 15 (1983): 117–33.

[4] Capozza, D. R., and R. Van Order. "Pricing under Spatial

Competition and Spatial Monopoly." *Econometrica* 45 (1977): 1329–38.

[5]   Dorward, N. "Recent Developments in the Analysis of Spatial Competition and Their Implications for Industrial Economics." *Journal of Industrial Economics* 31 (1982): 133–51.

[6]   Gee, J. M. A. "Competitive Pricing for a Spatial Industry." *Oxford Economic Papers* 37 (1985): 466–85.

[7]   Greenhut, M. L. *Plant Location in Theory and in Practice.* Chapel Hill: University of North Carolina Press, 1956.

[8]   Greenhut, M. L., C. S. Hung, and G. Norman. *Economics of Imperfect Competition.* Cambridge: The University Press, 1987.

[9]   Greenhut, M. L., and H. Ohta. "Monopoly Output under Alternative Pricing Techniques." *American Economic Review* 62 (1972): 705–13.

[10] ———. *Theory of Spatial Pricing and Market Areas,* Durham, N.C.: Duke University Press, 1975.

[11] Greenhut, M. L., H. Ohta, and J. Sailors. "Reverse Dumping: A Form of Spatial Price Discrimination." *Journal of Industrial Economics* 34 (1985): 1–15.

[12] Heffley, D. "Pricing in an Urban Spatial Monopoly." *Journal of Regional Science* 20 (1980): 207–25.

[13] Holahan, W. L. "The Welfare Effects of Spatial Price Discrimination." *American Economic Review* 65 (1975): 498–505.

[14] Hsu, S. K. "Pricing in an Urban Spatial Monopoly: A Generalized Analysis." *Journal of Regional Science* 23 (1983): 165–75.

[15] Norman, G. "Spatial Competition and Spatial Price Discrimination." *Review of Economic Studies* 48 (1981): 97–111.

[16] Ohta, H. "Aspects of Spatial Pricing." Ph.D. dissertation, Texas A&M University, 1971.

[17] ———. "On Efficiency of Production under Conditions of Imperfect Competition." *Southern Economic Journal* 43 (1976): 1124–35.

[18] ———. "Spatial Competition Concentration and Welfare." *Regional Science and Urban Economics* 10 (1980): 3–16.

[19]   ———. "The Price Effects of Spatial Competition." *Review of Economic Studies* 48 (1981): 317–25.

[20]   ———. "Agglomeration and Competition." *Regional Science and Urban Economics* 14 (1984): 1–17.

[21]   ———. "On the Neutrality of Freight in Monopoly Spatial Pricing." *Journal of Regional Science* 24 (1984): 359–71.

[22]   Phlips, L. *The Economics of Price Discrimination.* Cambridge: The University Press, 1983.

[23]   Schöler, K. "The Welfare Effects of Spatial Competition under Sequential Entry." *Southern Economic Journal* 52 (1985): 265–73.

[24]   Stevens, B. H. "Location of Economic Activities: The JRS Contribution to the Research Literature." *Journal of Regional Science* 25 (1985): 663–85.

2.
Impact of Economic Space on Monopoly Pricing: A Preliminary View

I. Introduction

This chapter presents, along the lines of Greenhut and Ohta [1, chapter 2 in particular], a preliminary analysis of a firm that faces a given population of consumers, concentrated at a point or dispersed along a line or over a landscape. The firm to be examined is a "simple" (i.e., nondiscriminatory) monopolist firm, whereas the consumers as well as competitive buyers are assumed to be homogeneous.

The model we will set forth in Section II disregards the costs of distance as we examine some fundamental relationships that underscore simple monopoly pricing. Section III examines the impact of economic distance on the aggregate demand that the monopolist faces when customers are assumed to be dispersed along a line or over a plane (landscape) and, in any case, away from the plant site. Section IV makes some general as well as specific comparisons of the nonspatial demand presented in Section II and the spatial demand derived in Section III. The concluding Section V presents some selected findings on spatial pricing in contrast with nonspatial pricing under conditions of simple nondiscriminating monopoly.

II. Nonspatial Monopoly Pricing

Assume a homogeneous set of n buyers with identical demand functions. Aggregate as well as individual demand may then be defined as

$$Q = f(p), \qquad \text{or its inverse}$$

$$p = f^{-1}(Q), \qquad Q = nq \tag{1}$$

where p stands for price, Q for quantity of aggregate demand, and q for quantity of individual demand.

If we assume further that the cost of distance that separates buyers from the monopolistic seller is negligible, or that all n buyers are located at the seller's location, the classical theory of simple monopoly requires the firm to equate the additional cost dC of producing the last units of output with the corresponding additional revenue $d(pQ)$. However, the last unit of output dQ must be divided equally and purchased by homogeneous buyers; that is, $dQ = ndq$, since $Q = nq$. It follows that

$$\frac{dC}{dQ} = \frac{d(pQ)}{dQ} = \frac{d(pq)}{dq} \tag{2}$$

Thus, marginal cost MC as a function of total output Q must be equated with the corresponding additional revenue, which we call total marginal revenue TMR. TMR must be equated, in turn, with the additional individual revenue derived from each buyer; this we call individual marginal revenue MR_i. In short, the firm's marginal cost must be equated with the marginal revenue it obtains in total and from each buyer.

This fundamental relation may be illustrated in Figure 2-1. Specifically, the figure indicates that total equilibrium output Q is determined at the intersection of the MC curve and the TMR (total marginal revenue) curve. It is also apparent that the equilibrium level of MC, that is, MC_0, determines the equilibrium level of individual marginal revenue ($MR_i = TMR_0$) and the equilibrium sales ($q = q_0$) to each buyer. It follows further that sales to each buyer are not determined in general by the intersection of the MC and MR_i curves. If they were determined at such an intersection, the firm would produce the quantity n times this individual demand; but this total clearly implies disequilibrium, namely, $MC > TMR$, when the MC curve is rising to the right, as in Figure 2-1.

On the other hand, if MC is falling with increasing output,

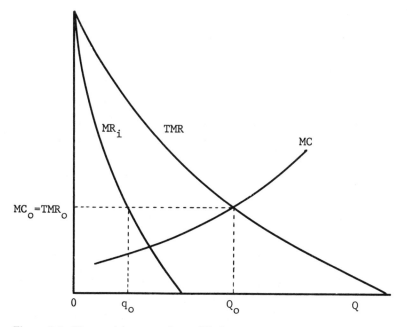

Figure 2.1. Nonspatial monopoly equilibrium.

$MC < TMR$. If MC is horizontal, $MC = TMR = MR_i$. Only in this last special case may attention be focused on the individual marginal revenue curve in deriving the equilibrium relations in the market. In the other cases, the equilibrium level of MC at its intersection with TMR must be determined first, not MC with MR_i.

III. Spatial Demand Function

Let us change assumptions by positing an even distribution of n buyers along a street so that no buyer is located at the same site as the seller, the first (two) buyers are located one unit of distance away (in opposite directions) from the seller, the second buyers are two units of distance away from the seller, and so on. Also, assume the freight rate per unit of distance is a positive constant. Other assumptions being the same, the following set of equations is identifiable:

$$q = \frac{1}{n} f(p) \tag{3}$$

$$p = m + tx \tag{4}$$

where q is the quantity demanded at any buying point on the line, p is the delivered price, m the mill price, t the freight rate, and x the distance units from origin; that is, from the seller's location to the given buying point.

Equations (3) and (4) can be reduced by simple substitutions to the general form:

$$q = \frac{1}{n} f(m + tx) \tag{5}$$

which establishes the quantity of demand in terms of m at any distance x from the seller's site. Equation (5), therefore, may be referred to as the *derived net individual* demand function at a location x distance units from the seller.

Aggregate (market) demand can be obtained, in turn, from Equation (5). This derivation requires summation of individual demands as in

$$Q = \frac{2}{n} \sum_{x=1}^{x_0} f(m + tx) = \frac{2}{nt} \sum_{x=1}^{x_0} f(m + tx)t$$

$$[f^{-1}(0) - tx_0 \geq m > f^{-1}(0) - t(x_0 + 1),$$

$$x_0 = 1, 2, \ldots , n/2] \tag{6}$$

where x_0 is the firm's market radius when mill price m falls within the specified domain. This Equation (6) depicts a discrete distribution in which the freight rate per unit of distance t is relatively high and n small.[1]

Of course, if n relates to many buyers evenly distributed along

---

[1] The particular value assumed for t signifies that the mill price plus the freight rate applicable to locations greater than x_0 units of distance from the seller exceeds the price intercept value of the demand function. It also signifies that the maximum number of buyers the firm can supply with the line market is n.

a line, and t is a very small positive constant, for example, $t = 2f^{-1}(0)/n$, then letting $u = tx$,[2] observing the approximation of t by du, and noting that $tx_0 = f^{-1}(0) - m$, Equation (6) can be rewritten as

$$Q = \frac{2}{nt}\int_0^{tx_0} f(m + u)du = \frac{2}{nt}\int_0^{f^{-1}(0)-m} f(m + u)du$$

$$= \frac{2}{nt}\int_m^{f^{-1}(0)} f(u)du = \frac{-2}{nt}\int_{f^{-1}(0)}^m f(u)du$$

$$[f^{-1}(0) > m \geqslant 0] \quad (6)'$$

where $2/nt$ may further be rewritten as $1/f^{-1}(0)$ insofar as the "natural" market radius x_0^* (which may be defined by $f(tx_0^*) = 0$ or $x_0^* = f^{-1}(0)/t$) is assumed to be equal to $n/2$; that is, $x_0^* = f^{-1}(0)/t = n/2$. Note that this assumption requires the net demand to vanish at this critical distance x_0^* *even if mill price is kept as low as zero.*

When consumers are assumed to be dispersed evenly, though discretely, over a plane as illustrated by scattered points in Figure 2-2, the number of buying points at a location x distance units from the firm site is seen to be equal to $4x$. The net aggregate demand is then given by

$$Q = \frac{4}{n}\sum_{x=1}^{x_0} xf(m + tx) = \frac{4}{nt^2}\sum_{x=1}^{x_0} txf(m + tx)t$$

$$[f^{-1}(0) - tx_0 \geqslant m > f^{-1}(0) - t(x_0 + 1), \qquad x_0 \leqslant x_0^*] \quad (7)$$

where x_0^* stands for the critical distance at which the net demand may be assumed to vanish even if mill price is zero; that is, $f(tx_0^*) = 0$ or $tx_0^* = f^{-1}(0)$. Assuming that all n buyers are evenly distributed within this critical distance or "natural" market radius x_0^*, we obtain the following relationship between them:

---

[2] Note that u approaches a continuous variable as n approaches infinity in the light of the following variable transformation $u = tx = f^{-1}(0)Y$, $Y = x/(n/2)$ ($x = 1, 2, \ldots, n/2$).

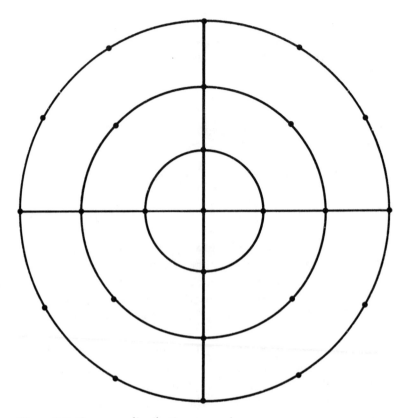

Figure 2.2. Consumer distribution over a plane.

$$n = 4 \sum_{x=1}^{x_0^*} x = 4x_0^*(x_0^* + 1)/2 \tag{8}$$

Substituting this into Equation (7) yields the limiting formula (7)′ for the aggregate demand counterpart to (6)′:

$$Q = \frac{4}{2u_0^* (u_0^* + t)} \sum_{x=1}^{x_0} txf(m + tx)t \quad (u_0^* = tx_0^*)$$

$$= \frac{2\pi}{\pi f^{-1}(0)^2} \int_0^{u_0} uf(m + u)\, du \quad (u = tx) \tag{7′}$$

where $u_0 = f^{-1}(0) - m$ and divisor $\pi f^{-1}(0)^2$ stands for the firm's market area with the "natural" dollar-term radius $f^{-1}(0)$; that is, the critical distance cost tx_0^*.

IV. Spatial Compared with Spaceless
Demand Functions

The aggregate *spatial* demand function (6)', henceforth referred to as the *free spatial demand*, following the convention, may be compared with the *spaceless* aggregate demand function (1), henceforth the *basic demand*. But, first note that the integral Q of (6)' is related to the area of a particular portion of the basic demand (1) divided by $nt/2$. Specifically, it equals the shaded area of the curve given in Figure 2-3. This constant divisor must be assumed to be equal to or greater than $f^{-1}(0)$; that is, $t \geq 2f^{-1}(0)/n$. This follows, in turn, from the basic assumption that no more than n buyers are part of the monopolist's market.[3]

Curvature of the free spatial demand curve differs sharply from that of the basic demand curve. To understand this important relationship, assume for the moment the linear basic demand:

$$p = a - bQ, \text{ or alternatively,} \tag{9}$$

$$Q = \frac{(a - p)}{b} \tag{9'}$$

Then via (6)' the free spatial demand takes the form:

$$Q = \frac{2}{nt} \int_m^a \frac{a - u}{b} du = \int_m^a \frac{a - u}{ba} du = \frac{(a - m)^2}{2ba} \tag{10}$$

provided $nt = 2a$. This particular result signifies that when mill price is a, no sale can be made to any distant buyer(s). It follows that

---

[3] If the freight rate t per unit of distance is assumed to be less than $2f^{-1}(0)/n$, the seller could sell a product to more than n buyers provided that the mill price is very low. However, we have assumed n buyers in total. (See note 1.)

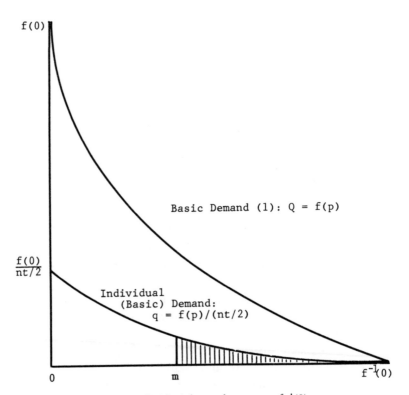

Figure 2.3. Integrating individual demand over m to $f^{-1}(0)$.

the free spatial demand coincides with the basic demand at the price intercept point. But, if the spatial mill price m is zero, the spatial quantity intercept, via the linear basic demand function $Q = (a - p)/b$, equals $a/2b$ rather than a/b. The spatial impact thus becomes increasingly distinctive as mill price is lowered from a to 0.

The relation derived earlier between a linear basic demand and the corresponding free spatial demand is illustrated in Figure 2-4. The convex curve in the figure depicts the free spatial demand under the assumption that buyers are distributed along a *line* market; the basic demand is described by the linear curve. Clearly, the former is smaller in magnitude than the latter.

When n buyers are distributed evenly over a *plane*, the free spatial demand is

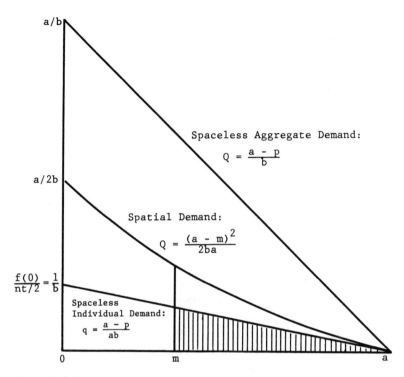

Figure 2.4. Deriving spatial demand from spaceless demand.

$$\frac{1}{b\pi a^2} \int_0^{2\pi} \int_0^{u_0} (a - m - u)u \, du \, d\theta \tag{11}$$

where u_0 is the freight cost limit and πa^2 is the area of a circle. Thus πa^2 is the counterpart to a; that is, the area of a *line* market. By elementary manipulations, we obtain

$$Q = \frac{1}{b\pi a^2} \int_0^{2\pi} \int_0^{a-m} [(a - m)u - u^2] du \, d\theta$$

$$= \frac{2\pi}{b\pi a^2} \left[\frac{(a - m)^3}{6} \right] = \frac{(a - m)^3}{3ba^2} \tag{12}$$

When mill price is a, $Q = (a - m)^3/3ba^2 = 0$. When mill price is 0, it follows that $Q = a/3b$. The quantity demanded is just one-third of the basic demand and two-thirds that of the free spatial demand for the *line* market case. Also, it is clear again that the free spatial demand is convex.

Thus far, we have assumed a linear basic demand and derived a convex free spatial demand. It should be stressed, however, that the convexity of the free spatial demand does not require the linearity of the basic demand. In fact, the form of the free spatial demand can be shown to be strictly convex regardless of the form of the basic demand f.[4]

The fundamental reason why the form of the free spatial demand tends to be convex is that it is the horizontal sum of the vertically shrinking individual demands (on the Marshallian quadrant) with increasing distances. As the price is successively lowered at the mill, an increasing number of buyers will be enticed to purchase along their successively shrinking demands, as indicated, for example, by Equation (6). This successive increase in the number of buyers in response to price reductions causes a convex downward slope of the free spatial demand.[5] This is important information leading to a strong, if not a necessary, implication that free spatial demand tends to be more elastic than nonspatial basic demand regardless of the latter curve.

[4] The first and second derivatives of (6)' with respect to m are

$$\frac{dQ}{dm} = \frac{-2}{nt}f(m) < 0$$

$$\frac{d^2Q}{dm^2} = \frac{-2}{nt}\frac{df(m)}{dm} > 0$$

provided that the assumed gross demand f^{-1} is negatively sloped.

Differentiating (7)' with respect to m likewise yields $dQ/dm < 0$ and $d^2Q/dm^2 > 0$, regardless of the form of f provided $f' < 0$. Thus, the free spatial demand is always convex regardless of the form of the nonspatial basic demand curve. See Greenhut, Hwang, and Ohta [2].

[5] The free spatial demand *can* be a concave curve under certain, unusual conditions. If, for example, the population density degenerates exponentially with distance, the individual demands shrink not only vertically but also horizontally; accordingly, the shrinking demand virtually disappears very rapidly. The horizontal sum of these fairly negligible curves therefore could yield a curve virtually the same as the basic demand in its curvature. Similar results apply to a case in which freight rate increases exorbitantly (exponentially) with distance. Both cases, of course, are irrelevant to the space economy and should be ruled out accordingly.

The cost of distance, ceteris paribus, thus provides the firm in economic space with incentives to lower, rather than raise, its mill price. Economic distance can be at least a mixed blessing to all consumers, insofar as part of the distance cost is absorbed by the firm. Moreover, to consumers located in the neighborhood of the firm's plant site, a lower mill price is always a full blessing. Different elasticities of spatial and nonspatial demand thus are important in evaluating welfare implications of spatial pricing.

As a preliminary to fully appreciating this important relation let us reexamine our example of linear basic demand. The price elasticity of the basic demand e_B is given by

$$e_B \equiv -\frac{dQ}{dp}\frac{p}{Q} = \frac{p}{a - p} \tag{13}$$

where a is the price intercept value and along with p is a major determinant of e_B. Note further that the higher this price intercept a is, the lower will be the elasticity of demand e_B. To be compared with e is the elasticity of the free spatial demand e_F evaluated at the same price level p. For this purpose, consider a straight auxiliary line tangent to the spatial demand at any price p under consideration. The resultant line will be a pseudo-spatial demand with a price intercept value a' that, under conditions of *demand convexity*, will stay strictly below a. It is to be noted that the elasticity of free spatial demand e_F evaluated at a given p is exactly equal to the elasticity of the pseudo-spatial demand evaluated at the same p. Thus, it follows

$$e_F = \frac{p}{a' - p} \tag{14}$$

Comparing Equations (13) and (14) readily yields the strict relation $e_F > e_B$ simply because $a > a'$.

The same inequality relation can readily be derived from a *concave* basic demand as well. Starting from the common price level $p = f^{-1}(0)$, the slope of the concave basic demand becomes increasingly steep as price goes down while the slope of the corresponding free spatial demand, being convex, becomes increasingly flat. The result will be that the price intercept value of the pseudo basic demand always exceeds that of the pseudo free spatial demand evaluated for any price below $f^{-1}(0)$. Thus, the free spatial demand is more elastic than a basic demand that is either linear or concave.

What of the case in which the basic demand itself is convex? Even in this case, it should be clear that insofar as the slope of the derived free spatial demand is flatter than that of the basic demand, the former curve remains more elastic than the latter. Although more general conditions under which the free spatial demand becomes less elastic than the basic demand will be examined in Chapter 10, suffice it to say for the time being that the free spatial demand generally tends to be more elastic than the basic demand unless the latter is extraordinarily convex.

The class of basic demands that are *not* extraordinarily convex includes the form of f such that

$$p = (a - bQ)^{1/\alpha} \qquad (a,b,\ \alpha > 0) \tag{15}$$

Note that the form of the basic demand in the case of Equation (15) is convex, linear, or concave according to $\alpha < 1$, $\alpha = 1$, or $\alpha > 1$. In all these alternative conditions, the free spatial demand can be, and later will be, shown to be more elastic than the basic demand.

V. Spatial versus Nonspatial Monopoly Pricing

Market demand in the space economy has been shown to be derivable from nonspatial market demand. It goes without saying that the spatial monopolist will equate *spatial* marginal revenue *SMR* derived from the free spatial market demand with the marginal cost of production *MC* to determine the profit-maximizing mill price m. Since the marginal revenue is uniquely related to the elasticity of demand, the formula for profit maximization can be given by

$$SMR = m\left(1 - \frac{1}{e_F}\right) = MC \tag{16}$$

where $SMR \equiv d(mQ)/dQ = m + (dm/dQ)Q = m(1 + (dm/dQ)Q/m)$ and therefore $e_F \equiv -(dQ/dm)(m/Q)$, which is to be evaluated on the spatial demand functions (6)′ and (7)′. This formula for spatial monopoly can be compared directly with the formula for spaceless monopoly:

$$TMR = p\left(1 - \frac{1}{e_B}\right) = MC \qquad\qquad (17)$$

where $TMR \equiv d(pQ)/dQ$ and $e_B \equiv -(dQ/dp)(p/Q)$ are evaluated on the spaceless basic demand (1). Thus it follows that insofar as $e_F > e_B$ while MC remains constant, the equilibrium spatial FOB mill price m is strictly lower than the nonspatial price p.

It is certainly possible, when MC is declining rapidly, for the equilibrium spatial price to be higher than the equilibrium spaceless price. This special result stems from the upper intersection of a falling MC curve with the spatial aggregate marginal revenue curve; in this event, its intersection with the spaceless aggregate marginal revenue curve occurs at a much lower level.

The fall (rise) in equilibrium spatial price below (above) the spaceless price is illustrated in Figure 2-5 by the values p, m_0, and m_1. The heavy lines in Figure 2-5 represent the (inverse) spaceless aggregate demand curve and its corresponding marginal revenue curve; the two light curves, also originating at a, apply, respectively, to some spatial aggregate demand curve (in the figure, that applicable to the line distribution) and its associated marginal revenue curve. Observe that the alternative marginal cost curves, MC_0 and MC_1, cut the spatial marginal revenue curve at different points. These intersections yield different equilibrium price levels, namely, m_0 and m_1, besides spaceless equilibrium price p.

It thus is clear that the price effects of space depend, in general, on cost conditions, namely, the shape of the MC curve. If substantial economies of scale prevail and the MC curve falls rapidly, the effect of economic space is an increase in prices. In the more likely case of a horizontal or rising MC, the spatial price tends to be lower than the spaceless price. The cost of distance, in other words, can provide the monopolist with incentives to lower, not raise, mill price to entice otherwise remote customers in his own market territory. In this sense, the cost of distance has distinctively different implications than does the nonspatial cost of, say, a tax. Moreover, the analytical relations

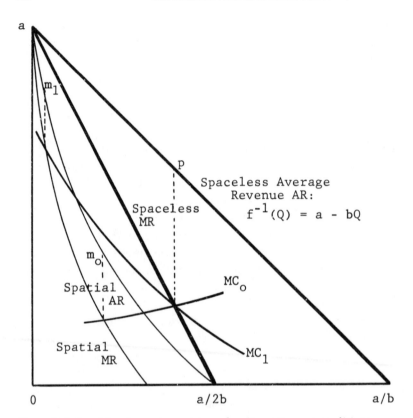

Figure 2.5. Spatial and spaceless prices under alternative cost conditions.

derived already for spatial monopoly can be and will be used later
to derive even more startling implications underscoring spatial
competition.

References

[1]   Greenhut, M. L., and H. Ohta. *Theory of Spatial Pricing and
      Market Areas.* (Durham, N.C.: Duke University Press,
      1975).

[2]   Greenhut, M. L., M. J. Hwang, and H. Ohta. "Observations
      on the Shape and Relevance of the Spatial Demand Func-
      tion." *Econometrica* 43 (1975): 669–82.

PART II

Fundamentals of Spatial Monopoly Pricing

3.
Unconstrained versus Constrained Spatial Monopoly Pricing

I. Introduction

The price of a good prevailing at some local market point may or may not be identical to the price of that same good at another market point. Price differentials over regions depend in part upon the number and locations of firms that sell in these regions and upon regional differences in the population density and consumer tastes. But, more fundamental, if not intuitively obvious, are regional price differentials despite an identical preference pattern of homogeneous consumers uniformly distributed over the regions. Even under these homogenized spatial market conditions, a spatial monopolist may find it profitable to subdivide the market into several submarkets, utilizing nondiscriminatory pricing for some submarkets and discriminatory pricing for others. These are some of the conclusions drawn in this chapter in determining the optimal price policy of the spatial monopolist.

Section II sets forth some fundamental assumptions under which we derive the optimal spatial price schedule for the monopolistic firm. Depending upon the form of the assumed basic demand function, the monopolist may find it profitable to raise delivered prices, because of greater transport costs, by amounts greater than the increments of freight costs involved in shipping the good. The firm is then said to extract "phantom freight" charges or discriminate against more distant buyers in favor of nearby ones.

In practice, however, phantom freight may invoke repackaging and reselling of goods by buyers. Such resale possibilities are disre-

garded in this section, and because of the absence of exogenous constraints, the spatial prices derived here will be called *unconstrained
optimal prices*.

The possibility of reshipment by proximate buyers to more distant
buyers is considered in Section III, where we derive optimal prices
over space subject to the constraint that no phantom freight may be
extracted. It thus will be shown how, in principle, the spatial monopolist may determine the constrained optimal prices to avoid resale
(arbitrage).

Section IV concludes the chapter by summarizing the major findings of the initial inquiry into spatial monopoly pricing.

II. Unconstrained Optimal Spatial Prices

Assume the following.[1]

    Assumption A. A monopolist firm is located at an arbitrary point
        of an unbounded linear market.

    Assumption B. The local demand density is a monotonically de-
        creasing function f of the delivered (or CIF) price and is distrib-
        uted uniformly and continuously along the line market. The
        function f is called, as before, the *basic demand function*.

    Assumption C. The basic demand f is subject to the constraint
        that demand vanishes at some critical finite level of price.

    Assumption D. The freight rate per unit of distance per unit of
        quantity is constant.

    Assumption E. The marginal cost of production is also constant.

    Pursuant to Assumption B, the spatial monopolist faces the fol-
lowing demand density function:

$$q(x) = f[p(x)] \qquad (f' < 0,\ x \geqslant 0) \tag{1}$$

where $p(x)$ stands for the delivered price, $q(x)$ for the demand density,
at any point x in the market, respectively, and f' stands for the

---

[1] In contrast, a location model by Hotelling [8] restricted Assumption B to the
infinitely inelastic demand case with Assumption A being replaced by a duopoly market.
The Hoover-Smithies model [7] and [11] and the Hotelling model also are different in
design. The latter is concerned with the locations of duopolists, the former with spatial
prices.

derivative of f with respect to p. In addition to its negative slope an economically relevant demand function requires the following condition subject to Assumption C:

$$f^{-1}(0) < \infty \tag{2}$$

The economic meaning of (2) is that the consumer will not pay an infinitely high price for an economic good, so that demand vanishes as price approaches a critical level.

The total revenue R for the monopolist selling over distances ranging from zero to x_0 is given by

$$R = \int_0^{x_0} p(x)q(x)dx \tag{3}$$

Costs of transportation can be specified by reformulating Assumption D as Equation (4):

$$t = \frac{T'(x)}{xq(x)} \qquad [T'(x) = txq(x)] \tag{4}$$

where $T'(x)$ stands for the cost of shipping q over distance x. The total cost of transportation T therefore may be given by

$$T \equiv \int_0^{x_0} T'(x)dx = \int_0^{x_0} txq(x)dx \tag{5}$$

Production cost C, in turn, is given below by reference to Assumption E:

$$C = F + cQ \qquad (F, c \geqslant 0) \tag{6}$$

where F stands for fixed cost, c for marginal cost, and Q stands for the total quantity produced and sold. Thus, Q is defined by Equation (7):

$$Q = \int_0^{x_0} q(x)dx \tag{7}$$

Pursuant to the revenue and cost conditions set forth above, monopoly profit Π and the related maximizing conditions are given by Equations (8) and (9), respectively:[2]

$$\Pi = R - T - C \tag{8}$$

$$\frac{\partial \Pi}{\partial q(x)} = \frac{\partial \Pi(x)}{\partial q(x)} = R_m(x) - tx - c = 0 \tag{9}$$

where $R_m(x) = \partial[p(x)q(x)]/\partial q(x)$ represents marginal revenue obtained on sales to any consuming point x, $\Pi(x)$ is profit at x, and tx stands for the marginal cost of shipping q over distance x. Equation (9) demonstrates that the marginal revenue derived from any point x must be equated with the marginal cost of producing and shipping the last unit of output to that point. (The marginal cost of *transport* is an increasing function of x, whereas the marginal cost of production is independent of x.)

Marginal revenue is redefined in terms of the delivered price p and demand elasticity e at any point x in the market. Equation (9) therefore applies:

$$R_m(x) = p(x)\left[1 - \frac{1}{e(p)}\right] \qquad (e > 1) \tag{10}$$

where $e(p)$ stands for elasticity of the basic demand as a function of price p (at market point x; i.e., $p \equiv p(x)$).[3]

Substitution of Equation (10) into Equation (9), and the assumption $c > 0$, yield

$$p(x) = \frac{e(p)}{e(p) - 1}(tx + c) \qquad (e > 1) \tag{11}$$

---

[2] The alternative condition equivalent to Equation (9), of course, is $\partial \Pi / \partial p = 0$, where $(x_0 \geqslant x \geqslant 0)$. Optimization with respect to p is equivalent to optimization with respect to q as long as p and q are uniquely related, as via Equation (1).

[3] Although the basic demand elasticity in the previous chapter was denoted by e_B for distinction from e_F, the subscript B is deleted here and dependence on p is stressed by $e(p)$ in the present chapter, which deals only with $e(p) = -f'(p)p/f(p)$.

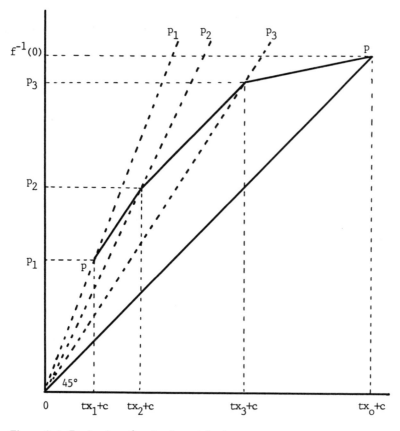

Figure 3.1. Derivation of optimal spatial prices.

The right-hand side of Equation (11) can be represented in Figure 3-1 as a set of dashed straight lines OP_i with angle $e(p)/[e(p) - 1]$, which is greater than $45°$. This follows because demand elasticity e is a single function of price, given any specific demand function. (Note, accordingly, that any specific line OP_i is associated with a specific price p, which in turn is given by the left-hand side of Equation (11). Thus, equating the two sides of Equation (11) yields a specific relation, or function, in effect, from p to x.) This relationship may be understood more fully after reading the following discussion.

Related to a demand function and a specific level of p is a particular value of e. This value e, in turn, is specifiable via Equation (11) as a line like OP_1, OP_2, OP_3 of Figure 3-1. These may be called the elasticity identification lines, the slopes of which are $e(p_1)/[e(p_1) - 1]$, $e(p_2)/[e(p_2) - 1]$, and $e(p_3)/[e(p_3) - 1]$, respectively. Note that a unique $e(p)$ is identifiable on any elasticity identification line. For example, if the slope of this line is 2, then $e(p)/[e(p) - 1] = 2$, and $e(p) = 2$ at any point on the line. Thus, demand elasticity $e(p)$ is identified by the slope of an elasticity identification line, whereas $e(p)$ itself is determined by price p, given the form f of the basic demand.

The optimal delivered price schedule pp over the firm's market space is now readily identifiable via Equation (11). For example, the distance at which the optimal price p_1 applies is determined by the intersection of the horizontal line $p(x) = p_1$ and the related identification line OP_1 over the horizontal axis of Figure 3-1, whose axis measures a transform of distance x, that is, $tx + c$, and thus may be called an *economic distance*. Remember that the slope of OP_1 identifies, and is determined by, the demand elasticity $e(p_1)$ to be evaluated at p_1 on the basic demand function. Thus, the intersection of the horizontal price line p_1 and the elasticity identification line OP_1 points to the underlying economic distance or its transform $tx_1 + c$ along the horizontal axis of Figure 3-1, yielding the following result:

$$p_1 = \frac{e(p_1)}{e(p_1) - 1}(tx_1 + c) \tag{12}$$

The ordered pair of distance and price (x_1, p_1) therefore confirms the profit-maximizing condition given in Equation (11). Identification of the particular x_i's with the lines OP_i and prices p_i thus establishes the equilibrium points in Figure 3-1, which constitute a locus or schedule pp of optimal prices over the seller's market space.

The general form of the curve pp may be given by differentiating Equation (11) with respect to x, applying the chain rule, and effecting appropriate substitutions. Thus,

$$\frac{dp}{d(tx)} = \frac{e}{\varepsilon - (1 - e)} \qquad \varepsilon = \left(\frac{de}{dp}\right)\left(\frac{p}{e}\right) \tag{13}$$

where ε defines how elasticity e responds to a percentage change in price p. A specific relation therefore exists between the slope of the curve pp and the elasticity of demand. Thus,[4]

$$\frac{dp}{d(tx)} = 1 \qquad \text{iff } \varepsilon = 1 \tag{14a}$$

$$1 > \frac{dp}{d(tx)} > 0 \qquad \text{iff } \varepsilon > 1 \tag{14b}$$

$$\frac{dp}{d(tx)} > 1 \qquad \text{iff } 1 > \varepsilon > 1 - e \tag{14c}$$

$$\frac{dp}{d(tx)} < 0 \qquad \text{iff } 1 - e < \varepsilon < 0 \tag{14d}$$

Let us now consider the meaning of these relations. Suppose that for some range of price p on an assumed demand curve, elasticity e increases (decreases) proportionately with p; that is, $\varepsilon = 1$. This condition, applied to Equation (14a), shows that any regional price differential dp is completely explained by an equal change in the cost of transportation $d(tx)$. The rate of freight absorption, defined as $[d(tx) - dp]/d(tx)$, is zero in regions observing equilibrium prices that yield the condition $\varepsilon = 1$. The spatial monopolist thus is willing to sell FOB mill in these regions. In Figure 3-1, the unitary ε is assumed for prices such that $p_3 > p > p_2$. The slope of the optimal price schedule for the relevant region $\{x_2, x_3\}$ accordingly is unity.

Suppose that another part of the demand curve is subject to the conditions of Equation (14b). Then, the freight cost will be absorbed partly by the seller, the rate of freight absorption being positive but less than unity. Accordingly, the delivered price increases less rapidly than the cost of delivery for the assumed range of prices; for example, $f^{-1}(0) > p > p_3$ in Figure 3-1.[5] This means that price discrimination is applied increasingly to more distant buyers in terms of differentiated mill prices.

---

[4] For further details, see Greenhut et al. [4; 5], and cf. Hoover [7], Smithies [11], Dewey [1], and Stevens and Rydell [12].

[5] As price approaches the price intercept value $f^{-1}(0)$, elasticity e approaches infinity so that by (12) price also approaches marginal costs of production and transportation over the limiting point x_0.

Conditions of Equation (14c) can be partitioned into three cases, namely, $1 > \varepsilon > 0$, $\varepsilon = 0$, and $0 > \varepsilon > 1 - e$. When $1 > \varepsilon > 0$, elasticity e increases or decreases less rapidly than price p. In any case, the condition $\varepsilon > 0$ requires these two variables to move in the same direction. In contrast, the two variables are required to move in opposite directions when $\varepsilon < 0$. Thus $0 > \varepsilon > 1 - e$ requires elasticity to decrease (increase) as price increases (decreases), with the rate of change being greater than the $1 - e$ algebraic value. When $\varepsilon = 0$ for any assumed range of prices, demand elasticity clearly remains constant. In each of these cases, the rate of freight absorption is seen to be negative. Thus, under the conditions of (14c), a price schedule can be derived by which prices increase more rapidly than the related transport costs, for a market radius (x_1, x_2) illustrated by Figure 3-1.

For this reason, in its monopolistic pricing, the firm may absorb part or none of freight or even extract phantom freight in its market area. It is important to note, however, that while a positive freight absorption can be applied to the *entire* market area, only a part of it can be subject to negative or no freight absorption. Positive freight absorption, in other words, must always apply to the rest of the market areas—toward the market extremity in particular. Directly related to this requirement, of course, is our basic postulate $f^{-1}(0) < \infty$ in (2); that is, vanishing demand as the price approaches a *finite* maximum.

Note finally that the last case, Equation (14d), appears to require a negative slope of the optimal price schedule pp. However, this case involves instability, because marginal revenue derived from any local market point x under the conditions of $1 - e < \varepsilon$ can be shown to intersect the marginal cost $tx + c$ from below.[6] This unstable case of a decreasing pp henceforth will be disregarded.[7]

---

[6] To see this only requires differentiating (10) with respect to $q(x)$ to obtain

$$\frac{dR_m}{dq(x)} = \frac{\varepsilon - (1 - e)}{e} \frac{dp(x)}{dq(x)}$$

This expression clearly is positive insofar as $1 - e > \varepsilon$, since $dq/dp (= f')$ is negative, ε negative, and e positive. Thus, marginal revenue increases with quantity of sales to market point x, while the marginal cost to this point is constant.

[7] A stable case of a decreasing pp curve will be evaluated later, however, in connection with conditions of spatial competition.

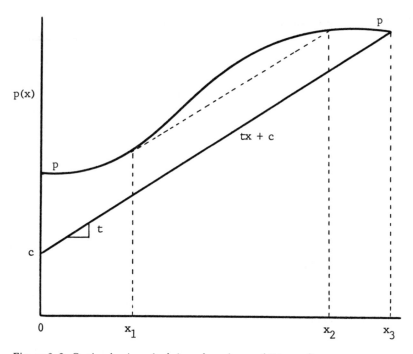

Figure 3.2. Optimal price schedule and resale possibility at distance x_1.

So far we have ignored the possibility of resale by nearer customers to more distant ones when the firm extracts phantom freight under conditions of Equation (14c). If the monopolist is to avoid such a resale possibility, some constraint may be imposed upon the optimal price schedule.[8] Two related questions arise accordingly: How would the constrained price schedule over space compare with the unconstrained? And, how would it be derived vis-à-vis the optimal unconstrained prices that would exist otherwise?

Before considering these queries, recall that a curve pp in Figure 3-1 can be mapped into the (x, p) plane, since $tx + c$ is a simple linear function of x. In turn, visualize a new wavy curve pp on the $(x,$

___

[8]See, for example, Hoover [7] and Smithies [11], who consider that a monopolist may not find it practical to discriminate against more distant customers in favor of proximate buyers because of resale possibilities. However, Olson [10] rules out those possibilities on grounds of the costs of repackaging and so forth, which may help yield phantom freight imposed upon distant customers.

p) plane, as in Figure 3-2; let this be an optimal spatial price schedule. But then, ceteris paribus, a customer located at x_1 would be able to resell the purchased commodity at a profit to any (or all) buyer(s) located between x_1 and x_2. The price he would receive by reselling the commodity clearly would be greater than the purchase price plus freight cost. If, however, the seller was constrained by such resale possibilities, the price schedule of Figure 3-2 could not be followed. The resulting schedule and the queries related to it, as set forth earlier, warrant our attention in the section that follows.

III. Constrained Optimal Spatial Prices

Suppose that some of the buyers, at greater distances from the seller than others, possess generally less elastic *net* demands for the good than the more proximate buyers, even though all customers may be assumed to possess identical demands. The concave part of the wavy pp schedule in Figure 3-2 reflects this situation compared to other distances. However, in anticipation of resale possibilities, the monopolist (instead of discriminating in net mill prices over the whole domain of his market) may either (a) sell FOB mill between such points as x_1 and x_2 in Figure 3-2 or else (b) constrain the buyers in the environs of x_1 from reselling to the more distant buyers, against whom discrimination is taking place. (This latter policy is likely to be in violation of antimonopoly and antitrust laws, hence, might be impractical.)

A third alternative exists for the monopolist's price policy, which is superior to either strategy. To understand this additional alternative, note that any FOB pricing practice that is also designated for points more proximate than x_1 reduces the monopolist's profit on sales to customers in the environs of x_1 below that which otherwise would be obtainable. Under the FOB price schedule, prices on sales made to customers located between 0 and x_1 will deviate from those indicated by the price line pp between these points in Figure 3-2. Deviation from the optimal price line (by definition of the word *optimal*) implies a decrease in profits. However, by following the wavy portion of pp for nearer customers and also pricing FOB mill beginning at a point before x_1, the monopolist's actual delivered price schedule now may be both higher and closer to the *unconstrained* optimal prices. The firm would gain greater profits on sales to the majority of its more distant buyers, located beyond x_1, even if a loss may be incurred by the customers in the neighborhood of x_1. The question then is at which point(s) the monopolist should begin to price FOB mill and at which point(s) such pricing should be terminated.

The answer to this question requires precise specification of the monopolist's profits over each subdivided (partitioned) market; that is, profits between points 0 and x_1, x_1 and x_2, x_2 and x_0. In this regard, note initially that the net mill price m pertaining to any point x may be defined as the difference between the delivered price and the applicable costs of transport tx and production c. These costs are independent of $q(x)$, and hence they are constant with respect to $q(x)$.[9] The difference defined earlier stands for the net mill price or unit profit that, in turn, can be multiplied by quantity $q(x)$ to calculate total profits. Thus,

$$m(x) = p(x) - (tx + c) \qquad (15)$$

The profit $\Pi(x)$ received from sales at point x is definable as

$$\Pi(x) = m(x)q(x) = [p(x) - (tx + c)]f[p(x)] \qquad (16)$$

Now let the function $g(x)$ in Equation (17) stand for the optimal unconstrained price schedule $p(x)$ over space, as depicted by the wavy pp schedule in Figure 3-2.

$$p(x) = g(x) \qquad (x \geqslant 0) \qquad (17)$$

Then the constrained price schedule $p_c(x)$ over selected distances may be defined as

---

[9]Note, however, that c is not required to be independent of the aggregate output $\Sigma_x q(x)$.

$$p_c(x) = g(x) \qquad (0 \leqslant x < x_1)$$

$$= g(x_1) - tx_1 + tx \qquad (x_1 \leqslant x < x_2)$$

$$= g(x) \qquad (x_2 \leqslant x < x_0) \qquad (18)$$

where x_0 is given by $p(x_0) = c + tx_0$. Substitution of Equation (18) into Equation (16) then yields the related constrained profit density function:

$$\Pi(x) = [g(x) - tx - c]f[g(x)] \qquad (0 \leqslant x < x_1)$$

$$= [g(x_1) - tx_1 - c]f[g(x_1) - tx_1 + tx]$$

$$(x_1 < x < x_2)$$

$$= [g(x) - tx$$
$$- c]f[g(x)] \qquad (x_2 \leqslant x < x_0) \qquad (19)$$

Integration of Equation (19) with respect to x yields the related total constrained profits:

$$\Pi = \int_0^{x_1} \phi(x)dx + \int_{x_1}^{x_2} \psi(x)dx + \int_{x_2}^{x_0} \phi(x)dx \qquad (20)$$

where $\phi(x) = [g(x) - tx - c]f[g(x)]$ and $\psi(x) = [g(x_1) - tx_1 - c]f[g(x_1) - tx_1 + tx]$.

It follows that Π is a function of x_1 alone, because x_2 is given once x_1 is known along with $g(x)$, and x_0 also is given by $p(x_0) = c + tx_0$. Thus, Equation (20)$'$ applies.

$$\Pi = h(x_1) \qquad (20)'$$

The conditions for maximization can then be specified as

$$\frac{dh(x_1)}{dx_1} = 0, \text{ and } \frac{d^2h(x_1)}{dx_1^2} < 0 \qquad (21)$$

Note that it is unnecessary to locate x_1 at the point where $(dp/dx_1) = t$ on the wavy curve pp in Figure 3-2. However, it is necessary that the solution x_1^* for (21) be subject to the locational condition

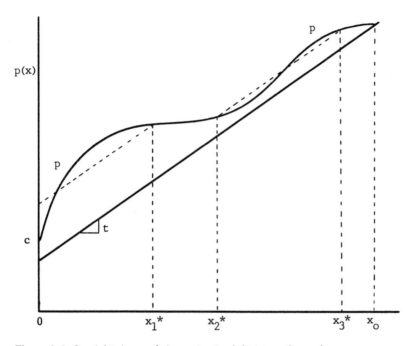

Figure 3.3. Spatial prices and the optimal subdivision of a market.

$$x_1{}^* < x_1 \tag{22}$$

where x_1 is the smallest solution for $dp(x)/dx = t$.

This analysis can be extended readily to the more general case of a multiwaved spatial price schedule, as is presented in Figure 3-3. As seen in the figure, the spatial monopolist may price FOB mill between 0 and $x_1{}^*$ and also between $x_2{}^*$ and $x_3{}^*$. The problem now is that of optimization with respect to two variables, since the profit Π is now a function of $x_1{}^*$ and $x_2{}^*$, as $x_3{}^*$ clearly depends upon the location of $x_2{}^*$ and hence cannot constitute an independent choice variable. Thus, Equations (23) and (24) apply respectively as the profit function and its maximization conditions.

$$\Pi = h(x_1{}^*, x_2{}^*) \tag{23}$$

$$h_i = 0, \ h_{ii} < 0, \ \text{and} \ \begin{vmatrix} h_{11} & h_{12} \\ h_{21} & h_{22} \end{vmatrix} > 0 \tag{24}$$

where h_i and h_{ij} $(i, j = 1, 2)$ stand for partial derivatives pursuant to usual convention.

IV. Summary and Conclusion

Under the specified set of assumptions, the optimal spatial price schedule was shown in Section II to be uniquely derived diagrammatically as well as mathematically. Section III indicated how the *constrained* price schedule may be derived given the *unconstrained* optimal spatial price schedule and demonstrated how the monopolist can (a) subdivide his market into economic submarkets, (b) set forth different FOB mill prices for these different submarkets, and (c) follow the optimal price schedule over the remaining submarket.

It should be pointed out in conclusion that the spatial monopolist generally discriminates in the mill price against customers located nearer to the mill, in effect charging more distant buyers lower mill prices. However, a fixed mill price (by definition) must apply to particular FOB submarkets. The mill price applicable to the nearest FOB mill submarket then would have to be higher than the mill prices for the more distant submarkets, as illustrated in Figure 3-3. Thus, mill prices necessarily decrease as distance increases; otherwise one would have to assume that (a) buyers at greater distances from the seller have lower demand elasticities and, in effect, that (b) in none of these increasingly distant submarkets does demand vanish, no matter how high the delivered price might be, in violation of constraint (2). The seller's market thus would have to be unbounded under constraint (2). Ruling out this unlikely event supports the use of monotonically (though not smoothly) decreasing mill prices over space whenever sellers cannot constrain their buyers against the simple resale of their goods.

Some related final notes are warranted. While the demand curve can be of any type such that $\varepsilon > 1$ at practically all points; that is, for practically all p over the whole domain of the assumed demand function, $\varepsilon \leq 1$ cannot be true for the whole domain given constraint (2). In particular, elasticity must increase more rapidly than price, at least as one approaches the neighborhood of the price intercept subject to (2). This condition alone is sufficient for the spatial monopolist to absorb freight with respect to the most distant buyers, even if FOB mill pricing is applied to (some groups of) nearer buyers.

In neoclassical spaceless economics, price discrimination appears as an arbitrary "take-advantage-of-some-buyers" policy, which only a few monopolists might adopt. In spatial economics, price discrimination does not have the same antisocial connotation. Moreover, in neoclassical spaceless economies, arbitrage can exist in general. But insofar as spatial price discrimination favors the most distant buyers in terms of mill prices and yet the delivered prices to these buyers are still greater than those paid by nearer buyers, no arbitrage profit via resale of goods is possible.

In order for price discrimination to occur in the world of classical spaceless monopoly, the buyer's demand curves must be intrinsically different from those of others. In economic space, the basic demand curve of buyers (i.e., the basic tastes and incomes of spatial buyers) may be identical, and yet the net demand curves viewed by the seller may differ, thus encouraging price discrimination. These relations yield the fundamental proposition of this chapter, which may be stated very simply in summary form: Spatial monopolists who are rational profit-maximizers always discriminate against nearer buyers if not constrained by antitrust laws or consumer-public recognition of and objection to this discrimination. Neoclassical spaceless monopoly price discrimination theory, in effect, requires taste and income differences among consumers in order for discrimination to take place.

References

[1]   Dewey, D. "A Reappraisal of F.O.B. Pricing and Freight Absorption." *Southern Economic Journal* 22 (1955): 48–54.

[2]   Greenhut, M. L. *Plant Location in Theory and in Practice.* Chapel Hill: University of North Carolina Press, 1956.

[3]   Greenhut, M. L., and H. Ohta. *Theory of Spatial Pricing and Market Areas,* chapter 5. Durham, N.C.: Duke University Press, 1975.

[4]   Greenhut, M. L., H. Ohta, and J. Greenhut. "Derivation of Optimal Spatial Prices under Spatial Monopoly." *Environment and Planning A* 6 (1974): 191–98.

[5]   Greenhut, M. L., H. Ohta, and M. Hwang. "Price Discrimination by Regulated Motor Carriers: Comment." *American Economic Review* 64 (1974): 780–84.

[6]   Holahan, W. L. "The Welfare Effects of Spatial Price Discrimination." *American Economic Review* 65 (1975): 498–505.

[7]   Hoover, E. M., "Spatial Price Discrimination," *Review of Economic Studies* 4 (1937): 182–91.

[8]   Hotelling, H. "Stability in Competition." *Economic Journal* 39 (1929): 41–57.

[9]   Ohta, H. "Aspects of Spatial Pricing." Ph.D. dissertation, Texas A&M University, 1971.

[10] Olson, J. "Price Discrimination by Regulated Motor Carriers." *American Economic Review* 62 (1972): 395–402.

[11] Smithies, A. "Monopolistic Price Policy in a Spatial Market." *Econometrica* 9 (1941): 63–73.

[12] Stevens, B. H. and C. P. Rydell. "Spatial Demand Theory and Monopoly Price Policy." *Papers Regional Science Association* 17 (1966): 195–204.

4.
Two Alternative Systems of Constrained Spatial Monopoly Pricing

I. Introduction

We have assumed so far no legal or institutional constraint *exogenously* imposed upon the firm as it behaves as a spatial monopolist. In the last chapter, we did consider a self-imposed constraint, which, however, is set forth *endogenously,* to the firm's own advantage. This chapter alters this basic assumption and posits that the firm is constrained by, for example, antitrust laws, to set forth either a unique FOB mill price or uniform CIF price for *all* customers. These two alternative pricing systems are examined comparatively along the lines of—and going beyond—the classics of Beckmann [1] and a contribution by Hsu [5].

Section II introduces some fundamental assumptions for analysis. A related special note also is briefly entered on an interchangeable representation of consumer distribution over a plane and along a line market. Section III, in turn, sets forth two alternative models of spatial pricing under the most general conditions regarding the consumer density over an economic space, the form of consumer demand, and costs of production and transportation. Results of prices, outputs, and market areas most generally derivable from these conditions are presented in Section IV. The most general assumptions and corresponding results are partly particularized in Section V to feature some selected relationships to be observed between the two alternative pricing techniques. The specific findings of Section V are used as a departure point for a more general and yet definitive analysis presented briefly in the concluding Section VI.

II. The Fundamental Assumptions

Assume the following:

   Assumption A. The individual consumers possess the identical
     demands of the form $f(p)$, where p stands for the CIF price of
     the commodity under consideration.
   Assumption B. The monopolist firm is located at a point of a
     spatially extended market (line or plane).
   Assumption C. The consumer density $n(x)$ at a point x distance
     units from the seller is known to the seller and is a continuous
     function of distance x.

Before we start formulating the two models of spatial pricing
pursuant to these assumptions, a special note about the nature of
Assumption C is warranted. This assumption allows us to conceive of
any form of the consumer density along a linear economic space.
Moreover, although $n(x)$ is expressed in terms of the linear distance
x, it may be interpreted readily or simply transformed back to represent a two-dimensional topology. The consumer density at a point of
the circumference of a circular market area with radius x is then
defined as $n(x)$ divided by $2\pi x$. Conversely, if $n(x)$ is assumed to
represent the consumer density at a point x distance units from
the center in a two-dimensional space, then the same topology can
be transformed readily to or represented by $2\pi x n(x)$ in a one-
dimensional space. Thus, for example, an even (i.e., uniform) distribution of consumers *over a plane* is analytically equivalent to, and
therefore can be transformed to, the consumer density that *increases
linearly along a line market,* and vice versa. In other words, $n(x) = n$
(constant) *over a plane* is equivalent to $n(x) = 2\pi x n$ along a line
market. (See Ohta [6] for further details.)

   Unless otherwise specified, therefore, attention will be confined to
the linear economic space for simplicity, that is, to avoid double
integrations required for the two-space analysis.

III. The FOB Mill vs. Uniform Pricing Systems

We are now in a position to set forth basic models of spatial pricing.
Consider first the spatial demand the monopolist can exploit from

an individual consumer located at a point x distance units from the firm site:

$$q_x = f(p_x) \qquad (1)$$

where q_x stands for the quantity of individual demand at distance x as a function f of the CIF price p_x applicable to that distance point x. The f is assumed, as it should, to be a nonnegative nonincreasing function of p_x. The profit Π for the spatial monopolist may then be defined pursuant to Assumptions A, B, and C as

$$\Pi = \int_0^{x_0} p_x f(p_x) n(x) dx - C(Q)$$
$$- \int_0^{x_0} T_x [x,\, f(p_x)] n(x) dx \quad [Q = \int_0^{x_0} f(p_x) n(x) dx] \qquad (2)$$

where $n(x)$ stands for the consumer density as a function of x; x_0 for the critical distance or the market radius for the firm; $C(Q)$ for the total cost of production as a function of total output Q; and $T_x(x, f(p_x))$ for the cost of transporting the quantity demanded q_x over the distance x. It is to be noted that $T_x[x,\, f(p_x)] n(x)$ stands for the total cost of transportation of all goods consigned (without freight consolidation) to a given distance x. Note further that while the total cost of production depends on total output alone, the total cost of transportation over the firm's market radius depends on each $T_x[x,\, f(p_x)]$ for each market point x, and T_x on both the shipping distance x and the quantity shipped over that distance.

Consider now the constraints imposed on the mill pricer and the uniform pricer, constraints which may be expressed as, respectively,

$$p_x = m + \tau(x) \qquad \left\{ \tau(x) = \frac{T_x[x,\, f(p_x)]}{f(p_x)} \right\} \qquad (3)$$
$$p_x = p \qquad (4)$$

where m stands for a unique FOB mill price, τ for transport rate (cost per unit quantity), and p is a unique CIF price. Subject to these constraints, the profit for the mill pricer and the uniform pricer can be respecified readily via (2) as, respectively,

$$\Pi_m = g(m, x_{0m}) = mQ_m - C(Q_m)$$

$$\left\{ Q_m = \int_0^{x_{0m}} f[p(m, x)]n(x)dx \right\} \quad (5)$$

$$\Pi_p = h(p, x_{0p})$$

$$= \int_0^{x_{0p}} \{pf(p) - T_x[x, f(p)]\}n(x)dx - C(Q_p)$$

$$\left[Q_p = \int_0^{x_{0p}} f(p)n(x)dx \right] \quad (6)$$

where $p(m, x)$ stands for the CIF price at market point x under FOB mill pricing, a price that is clearly p_x defined implicitly by (3) and is dependent upon mill price m and distance x; that is, $p_x = p(m, x)$.

IV. The General Comparison of the Alternative Pricing Systems

The spatial monopolist chooses mill price m or uniform price p to maximize profit. The first-order conditions for profit maximization for the mill pricer and the uniform pricer, respectively, are [1]

$$g_1 = 0 \tag{7}$$
$$g_2 = 0 \tag{8}$$
$$h_1 = 0 \tag{9}$$
$$h_2 = 0 \tag{10}$$

where g_i and h_i are the partial derivatives of the profit function g and h with respect to the ith argument. Thus, for example, Equation (7) refers to the partial optimization condition to find mill price m, given the firm's market radius x_{0m}, whereas Equation (8) refers to the partial condition to find the firm's optimal radius x_{0m}, given its (optimized)

---

[1]The second order conditions for optimization are given by $g_{ii} < 0$, $(g_{11}g_{22} - g_{12}g_{21}) > 0$ and $h_{ii} < 0$, $(h_{11}h_{22} - h_{12}h_{21}) > 0$, respectively.

mill price m. In principle, the two partial optimization conditions are solved simultaneously for optimal m and x_{0m}.

Likewise the optimal set for (p, x_{0p}) is to be obtained from Equations (9) and (10).

Let us consider first the solution for Equations (7) and (8), which can be reduced readily to

$$m\left(1 - \frac{1}{e_{F_0}}\right) = C'(Q_m) \qquad \left(e_{F_0} = -\frac{\partial Q_m}{\partial m}\frac{m}{Q_m}\right) \qquad (11)$$

$$f^{-1}(0) = p(m, x_{0m}) \qquad (12)$$

where e_{F_0} (distinct from e_F) stands for the partial (i.e., given x_{0m}) elasticity of free spatial market demand in terms of mill price, $C'(Q)$ for marginal cost of production, $f^{-1}(0)$ for the maximum price at which demand quantity vanishes; that is, $q = f(p) = 0$, and $p(m, x_{0m})$ for the CIF price at the market boundary point. Equation (12) defines the optimal market radius x_{0m} implicitly in terms of mill price whereas Equation (11) simply points to the $MR = MC$ principle, where MR stands for marginal revenue in terms of either mill price m or aggregate quantity of demand Q_m, given x_{0m}. The solution set (m^*, x_{0m}^*) for Equations (11) and (12) in general depends on the form of consumer distribution $n(x)$, consumer demand f, and the transport cost function T_x, as well as on the form of the production cost function C. This follows because underlying the function form p in (12) are T_x and f in (3), whereas (11) depends on C' and also on Q, which in turn depends on f and $n(x)$.

In contrast, the optimality conditions for the uniform pricer, Equations (9) and (10), can be reduced to

$$p\left(1 - \frac{1}{e_B}\right) = C'(Q_p) + E(T_{x2}), \qquad e_B = -f'p/f$$

$$E(T_{x2}) = \int_0^{x_{0p}} T_{x2}[x, f(p)]n(x)dx \div \int_0^{x_{0p}} n(x)dx \qquad (13)$$

$$p = C'(Q_p) + \tau, \qquad \tau = \frac{T_x[x_{0p}, f(p)]}{f(p)} \qquad (14)$$

where e_B stands for the elasticity of basic or individual demand in terms of CIF price p, T_{x2} for the marginal cost of transporting q_x (equal to $f(p)$, not Q,) over the distance x, and $T_x[x_{0p}, f(p)]$ for the total cost of transporting $q_{x_{0p}}$, equal to $f(p)$, over the market limit x_{0p}. Thus, Equation (13) posits the balancing of the marginal revenue (accruing from each individual consumer) in terms of CIF price p and the unique marginal cost of production *plus the expected value of all marginal costs of transportation T_{x2} applicable to all market points over a given market radius x_{0p}*. Given p, the market radius in turn is to be determined optimally via Equation (14), where the sum of the marginal cost of production and the unit freight cost reaches the given CIF price p. The solution set (p^*, x_{0p}^*), as before, depends on $T_x, f,$ C, and n. This result may appear, however, to reveal no definite relationships between p^* and m^*, or x_{0p}^* and x_{0m}^*, much less between Q_p^* and Q_m^*. Fortunately, some fundamental features of the two alternative pricing systems readily can be derived pictorially, as will be illustrated.

The left-hand side of Figure 4-1 pictures the optimality condition of Equation (11) to determine, via an $MR = MC$ intersection, the optimal mill price m^* on the spatial demand SD. The m^* in turn is transmitted to the right-hand side to yield, via Equation (12), the optimal market radius x_{0m}^*. The curve monotonically increasing to the right shows the CIF price schedule, which need not be linear *unless the freight rate per unit quantity per mile is assumed to be constant.* Figure 4-2(a) correspondingly illustrates the optimality condition (13) to determine the optimal uniform price p^*. A warning is needed here on the measurement scale: Q in $MC(Q) \equiv C'(Q)$ is required to be scaled down to the quantity of individual demand in terms of which the other marginal quantities are defined. Since $Q = \int_0^{x_{0p}} f(p)n(x)dx$, the rate of scale reduction r is $r \equiv Q/f(p) = \int_0^{x_{0p}} n(x)dx$. The MC curve in terms of Q therefore is required to be reduced horizontally to the right by this reduction rate r as in Figure 4-2(a). The resultant MC, labeled $MC(rq)$ in Figure 4-2(a), is the marginal production cost arising from any single shipment decision q_x that, in turn, is linked to all the others by the multiplier r.[2] Added

---

[2] This concept should not be confused with the marginal cost of producing q_x or dC/dq_x, which is distinct from the present MC that defines dC/dQ, not dC/dq_x, as a function of q_x.

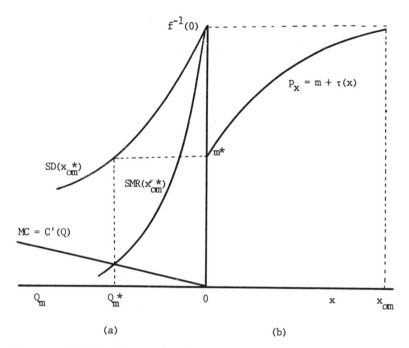

Figure 4.1. FOB mill monopoly pricing.

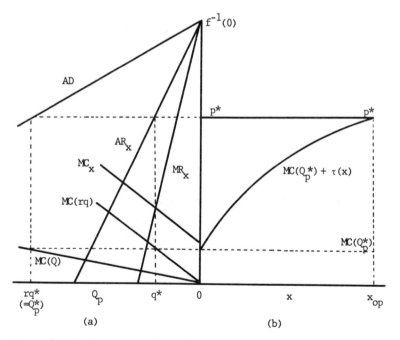

Figure 4.2. Uniform monopoly pricing.

to this is the expected marginal cost of transportation $E(T_{x2})$ to obtain the relevant MC_x, which in turn is to be equated with the individual marginal revenue MR_x as in Figure 4-2(a). The subject equilibrium yields the optimum (p^*, q^*) on the average revenue AR_x and the aggregate output Q_p^* on the aggregate demand curve AD (in terms of CIF price) and also on the $MC(Q)$ curve. Correspondingly, Figure 4-2(b) shows how the transport rate τ (or average transportation cost in effect) may increase with distance x until $MC(Q) + \tau$ is equated to p^* at the market boundary x_{0p}^*.

V. Relationships between the Two Pricing Systems: Some Specific Analyses

We have so far assumed no specific forms of the consumer demand f, the cost function C, or the transport function T_x. The cost of generalism, however, is an analytical intractability often encountered in the search for some definitive results. In order to make the prior analysis more tractable, this section initially follows the usual convention in assuming a very specific form of the transport cost function T_x:

$$T_x[x, f(p_x)] = txf(p_x) \tag{15}$$

Note that the present form of T_x is so specific as to yield a "constant" marginal cost of transportation with respect to quantity T_{x2}, and it also yields a "constant" freight with respect to distance T_{x1}. The functional forms of consumer demand f and production cost C are assumed to remain general, as earlier.

Pursuant to the form of T_x specified by Equation (15), the optimization conditions of Equations (11) and (12) and Equations (13) and (14) can be rewritten as

$$MR(Q_m) = C'(Q_m) \tag{16}$$

$$f^{-1}(0) - m = tx_{0m} \tag{17}$$

$$MR(Q_p/r) - t\bar{x}_p = C'(Q_p)$$

$$(r = \int n(x)dx, \ \bar{x}_p = \int xn(x)dx/\int n(x)dx) \quad (18)$$

$$p - tx_{0p} = C'(Q_p) \quad (19)$$

where $MR(Q_m)$ stands for the marginal revenue from the sales quantity Q_m under the mill pricing, $MR(Q_p/r)$ for the marginal revenue from each individual customer under the uniform pricing, r for the effective number of buyers, and $\bar{x}$ for what Hsu [5] calls the "average distance," following Beckmann [2].

Observations of these equations readily establish the following consecutive propositions. From (18) and (19) follows:

Proposition I. The net marginal revenue, net of freight, obtainable from a customer located at the average distance $\bar{x}$ from the uniform pricer is equal to that pricer's marginal cost of production, and both are equal to the net price (average revenue), net of freight, to the market boundary point. In symbols, $MR(Q_p/r) - t\bar{x}_p = C'(Q_p) = p - tx_{0p}$.

Comparing Equations (16) and (18) in turn yields:

Proposition II. Provided that the marginal cost of production curve slopes upward, the mill pricer's output is greater (less) than the uniform pricer's output if and only if (iff) the former's net marginal revenue is greater (less) than the latter's net marginal revenue from the average buyer. In symbols, given $C'' > 0$, $Q_m \gtrless Q_p$ iff $MR(Q_m) \gtrless MR(Q_p/r) - t\bar{x}_p$.

It goes without saying that Proposition II is reversed if the marginal cost curve slopes downward with $C'' < 0$. Thus, given $C'' < 0$, $Q_m \gtrless Q_p$ iff $MR(Q_m) \lessgtr MR(Q_p/r) - t\bar{x}$.

The firm's market areas x_{0m} and x_{0p}, which are assumed to be fixed in Proposition II, can now be optimized and compared via Equations (17) and (19). Proposition III is thus established, based on fixed outputs Q_m and Q_p (given by Proposition II).

Proposition III. The market radius is greater (less) under mill pricing than it is under uniform pricing if and only if the maximum price the consumer would be willing to pay in excess of mill price is greater (less) than the uniform price is in excess of the marginal cost of production. In symbols, $x_{0m} \gtrless x_{0p}$ iff $f^{-1}(0) - m \gtrless p - C'(Q_p)$.

While these propositions are predicated upon a specific form of T, the forms of f and C are assumed to be fully general. To probe still deeper into these propositional relationships, however, the functional forms need to be specified concretely, for example, linearly for the time being at least, as follows:

$$f = (a - p_x)/b \qquad (a, b > 0) \tag{20}$$

$$C = cQ \qquad (c \geqslant 0) \tag{21}$$

where (21) has appeared already in an unspecified form but only as part of Equation (2), not as an independent equation. These specific assumptions are needed to derive some of the results set forth by Hsu [5], used as our departure point.

Subject to the conditions of Equations (20) and (21), the optimization conditions (16) and (17) can be solved readily for m^* as

$$m^* = a/2 + c/2 - t\bar{x}_m^*/2 \tag{22}$$

where $\bar{x}_m^*$ is the optimal "average distance" under the mill pricing to be solved simultaneously with the corresponding market radius x_{0m}^* via Equations (23) and (24) below.

$$\bar{x}_m = \int_0^{x_{0m}} xn(x)dx \Big/ \int_0^{x_{0m}} n(x)dx \tag{23}$$

$$x_{0m} = (a - c)/2bt + \bar{x}_m/2 \tag{24}$$

The counterpart results for the uniform pricing can be obtained from Equations (18) and (19) as

$$p^* = a/2 + c/2 + t\bar{x}_p^*/2 \tag{25}$$

where $\bar{x}_p^*$ is determined along with x_{0p}^* via the following equations.

$$\bar{x}_p = \int_0^{x_{0p}} xn(x)dx \Big/ \int_0^{x_{0p}} n(x)dx \tag{26}$$

$$x_{0p} = (a - c)/2t + \bar{x}_p/2 \tag{27}$$

It is to be noted that the functional forms of Equations (23) and (24) are identical with (26) and (27), respectively. Based on these observations, the following two identities are readily established.

$$\bar{x}_p^* = \bar{x}_m^* \tag{28}$$

$$x_{0p}^* = x_{0m}^* \tag{29}$$

In words, the mill pricer's optimal market area is equal to that of the uniform pricer in terms of the market radius x_0^* and the average distance $\bar{x}^*$ as well.

These results, in turn, point to the identical outputs optimally produced by the mill pricer and the uniform pricer:

$$Q_m^* = Q_p^* \tag{30}$$

The derivation of Equation (30) is straightforward. Substituting (22) in (5) and (25) in (6) yields

$$Q_m^* = \int_0^{x_{0m}} (a/2 - c/2 + t\bar{x}_m^*/2 - tx)(1/b)n(x)dx$$

$$= (a/2 - c/2 - t\bar{x}_m^*/2)(1/b)\int_0^{x_{0m}^*} n(x)dx$$

$$- (t/b)\left[\int_0^{x_{0m}^*} xn(x)dx - \bar{x}_m^*\int_0^{x_{0m}^*} n(x)dx \right] \tag{31}$$

$$Q_p^* = (a/2 - c/2 - t\bar{x}_p^*/2)(1/b)\int_0^{x_{0p}^*} n(x)dx \tag{32}$$

Note that the bracketed term in (31) vanishes in light of (23). The forms of (31) and (32) thus are identical; the preceding result $Q_m^* = Q_p^*$ immediately follows from the conditions $\bar{x}_m^* = \bar{x}_p^*$ and $x_{0m}^* = x_{0p}^*$ accordingly.

Although the monopoly profits also are the same under the two alternative pricing systems, that is, $\Pi_m^* = \Pi_p^*$, the aggregate (marketwide) consumer surplus is greater under mill pricing than it is under uniform pricing regardless of the consumer density $n(x)$. The proof of $\Pi_m^* = \Pi_p^*$ is obtainable by simply substituting Equations (22) and (25), respectively, in (5) and (6). The comparison of consumer surpluses, however, requires the definition of the aggregate consumer surplus CS, which, subject to linear demand, is given by[3]

$$CS = \int_0^{x_0} (a - p_x)^2 (1/2b)n(x)dx \tag{33}$$

The result of $CS_m > CS_p$ readily follows from substituting Equations (3) through (15), (22) and (25), selectively, in p_x of (33) and effecting proper manipulations to obtain (asterisks deleted):

$$CS_m = \int_0^{x_{0m}} (a/2 - c/2 - t\bar{x}_m/2)^2 (1/2b)n(x)dx$$
$$+ (t^2/2b)\int_0^{x_{0m}} (x - \bar{x}_m)^2 n(x)dx \tag{34}$$

$$CS_p = \int_0^{x_{0p}} (a/2 - c/2 - t\bar{x}_p/2)^2 (1/2b)n(x)dx \tag{35}$$

where, to recall, $x_{0m} = x_{0p}$ and $\bar{x}_m = \bar{x}_p$. For an intuitive interpretation of this result, remember that the nearby customers benefit from the mill pricing markedly more than the distant buyers lose from it in terms of the "triangular" surplus areas a mill or uniform price yields.

These definitive relations among x_{0m}, x_{0p}, Q_m, Q_p, and so forth, have been derived by Hsu and are predicated on an unspecified consumer density $n(x)$. Moreover, the constancy of MC as assumed earlier is not even needed in derivation of these identical relations, since it is the equilibrium level, not the form, of MC that counts in solving for these equilibrium values (cf. Figure 4-3 *infra*). It therefore should be the assumed linearity of the basic demand that may be responsible for these specific results.

[3] A more rigorous definition of consumer surplus requires the use of the Hicksian (utility constant) demand curve rather than the Marshallian (income constant) demand unless marginal utility of income (or money) is assumed to be a given constant. See Greenhut and Ohta [3, appendix to chapter 3]; cf. Willig [7], who argues that the Marshallian measure is a close approximation of the correct measure of consumer surplus, whereas Hausman [4] shows how to obtain the latter directly.

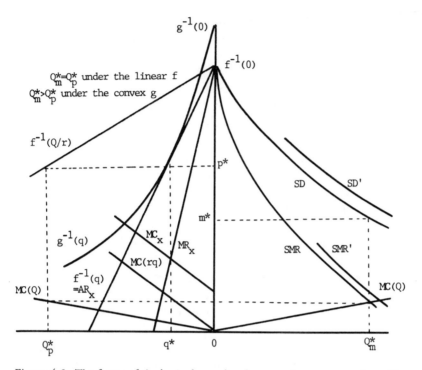

Figure 4.3. The forms of the basic demand and monopoly outputs under mill versus uniform pricing.

VI. General and Definitive Results

In what follows, the linear demand assumption is relaxed to examine changes, if any, in conclusions just obtained. Consider initially the basic demand g, which is convex to the origin. Without loss of generality, the convex demand is assumed to be tangent to a linear basic demand at the point of equilibrium uniform price p^*, as in Figure 4-3. This means that the two distinct forms of the basic demand yield the same equilibrium price p^* and quantity of individual demand $q(p^*)$ as well as market demand Q_p^* under conditions of uniform pricing regardless of the form of $MC(Q)$.[4]

---

[4] The uniqueness of the identical solution is guaranteed if the form of f is assumed to be of monotonically increasing elasticity with price p.

Remember now that the linear basic demand that yields $Q_p{}^*$ also yields the same market demand quantity $Q_m{}^*$ along the spatial market demand under conditions of mill pricing. The question is now one of what happens to spatial market demand if the basic demand is assumed to be convex and tangent to the linear basic demand. The answer is that the spatial market demand SD is invariably enlarged SD' for any mill price below the critical one $g^{-1}(0)$.[5] Insofar as the marginal revenue SMR is pulled correspondingly outward SMR', the optimal output of the monopolist mill pricer generally will be larger under the assumed convex demand than under the linear demand tangent to it.

The opposite relations hold for the concave basic demand.

In any case, remember that both the convex (concave) demand and the linear demand tangent to it yielded the same $Q_p{}^*$. By the law of transitivity, we thus have established the following proposition.

Proposition IV. When the basic demand is convex (concave), the mill pricer produces more (less) output than does the uniform pricer, regardless of the assumed consumer density and/or cost conditions.

Welfare implications of the present relations should be manifest insofar as the producer is concerned. In particular, the superiority of mill pricing over uniform pricing in terms of producer surplus is reinforced (weakened) under conditions of the convex (concave) demand to the extent of the shift in SMR and the related output effect it yields relative to the linear demand.

It is not clear, however, if the same relationships hold for the aggregate consumer surplus because of the two offsetting welfare effects that a nonlinear basic demand yields. On the one hand, a convex (concave) basic demand shifts the spatial market demand outward (inward) relative to the one derived from a linear basic demand (tangent at p^* as defined earlier) and increases (decreases) con-

---

[5]This follows readily from the definition of the spatial market demand Q_m as an integral in effect of the basic demand $g(p)$ with respect to p (from $p = m$ to $p = g^{-1}(0)$ under the simplified assumptions, though not needed, of constant density and constant freight rate) and the convexity of $g(p)$, which exceeds the linear tangent $f(p)$ for all prices other than the optimal uniform price p^*. See Figure 4-3 for the relationships among $g(p)$, $f(p)$, and p^*. Thus, if p^* happened to be the optimal uniform price associated with the convex basic demand $g(p)$, then the linear $f(p)$ tangent to $g(p)$ at p^* also yields the same optimal uniform price p^*.

sumer surplus accordingly. On the other hand, equilibrium mill price may be higher (lower) under the convex (concave) basic demand than it is under the linear basic demand for two reasons. First, the spatial market demand shifted outward (inward) presumably may be less (more) elastic because of an upward (downward) shift in its price intercept value.[6] Second, in the absence of scale economy, the mar-

---

[6]This presumption is a sheer speculation, however. In fact, if the basic demands are assumed to take alternative algebraic forms but are tangent to one another at a common optimal uniform price p^*, then the corresponding elasticities of the spatial market demands happen to be all equal at the optimal mill price m^* derivable from the "linear" basic demand. For proof of this surprising result, consider the following basic demand:

$$p = a\left(1 + \frac{1 - \alpha}{\alpha}\theta\right) - (b^\alpha/\alpha)(a\theta)^{1-\alpha}q^\alpha \tag{N-1}$$

where a, b, $\alpha > 0$ and θ is a sufficiently small fraction $(1 > \theta > 0)$ to ensure a common tangency at p^* under uniform pricing. Note that (N-1) becomes a convex, linear, or concave basic demand, accordingly as α is assumed to be less than, equal to, or greater than unity. Note further that these alternative basic demands are tangent to one another at $(q^*, p^*) = [\theta a/b, (1 - \theta)a]$.

Assuming constant population density and unitary freight rate, the spatial market demand from (N-1) is obtained as follows:

$$Q = \int_0^{x_0} \left\{\frac{a[1 + \theta(1 - \alpha)/\alpha] - m - x}{(b^\alpha/\alpha)(a\theta)^{1-\alpha}}\right\}^{1/\alpha} dx$$

$$\{x_0 = a[1 + \theta(1 - \alpha)/\alpha] - m\}$$

$$= \frac{b^\alpha(a\theta)^{1-\alpha}}{\alpha + 1}\left\{\frac{a[1 + \theta(1 - \alpha)/\alpha] - m}{(b^\alpha/\alpha)(a\theta)^{1-\alpha}}\right\}^{(1+\alpha)/\alpha} \tag{N-2}$$

The elasticity of this spatial market demand e_F then is given by

$$e_F = \frac{1 + \alpha}{\alpha}\frac{m}{a[1 + \theta(1 - \alpha)/\alpha] - m} \tag{N-3}$$

Clearly, e_F appears to take different values depending on the convexity α of the basic demand for any given mill price m. It turns out, however, that e_F becomes independent of α when m approaches a particular value, namely, $m = (1 - 2\theta)a$. Moreover, this m value, which yields $e_F = (1 - 2\theta)/\theta$, can be shown to be optimal mill price derivable from the linear basic demand (with $\alpha = 1$) when the level of marginal cost of production MC is given by $MC = (1 - 3\theta)a$, which requires θ to be less than $1/3$. This particular MC is the equilibrium MC that underscores the common optimum uniform price p^* assumed at the outset of this note. Substituting this MC value and (N-1) back in Equations (18) and (19) in the text, we can readily confirm that $p^* = (1 - \theta)a$.

ginal cost of production MC will be increased (decreased) as output is increased (decreased). Equilibrium mill price tends to be higher (lower) in any case and consumer surplus lower (higher), accordingly. The net effect of the basic demand form upon the consumer surplus thus is unknown. However, under conditions of footnote 6 and constant returns to scale, that is, constant MC, the equilibrium mill price remains constant and the net welfare effect of the basic demand convexity (concavity) turns out to be definitely positive (negative).

No definitive relationships can be predicted either between the market radii x_{0m} and x_{0p} under the two alternative pricing systems when the basic demand is nonlinear. Related to this indeterminacy is a shift in the price intercept value and the optimal mill price m^* relative to those associated with the linear tangent. It nevertheless can be concluded that, if the basic demand is convex (concave), then x_{0m} tends to exceed (fall short of) x_{0p} unless its price intercept value in excess (short) of the intercept value of the linear tangent yields an equal amount of difference in mill price and in price intercept value (see Proposition III).

References

[1] Beckmann, M. *Location Theory*. New York: Random House, 1968.

[2] ————. "Spatial Price Policies Revisited." *Bell Journal of Economics* 7 (1976): 619–30.

[3] Greenhut, M. L., and H. Ohta. *Theory of Spatial Pricing and Market Areas*. Durham, N.C.: Duke University Press, 1975.

[4] Hausman, J. "Exact Consumer's Surplus and Deadweight Loss." *American Economic Review* 71 (1981): 662–76.

[5] Hsu, S. K. "Pricing in an Urban Spatial Monopoly: A Generalized Analysis." *Journal of Regional Science* 23 (1983): 165–75.

[6] Ohta, H. "Some Passing Notes on Spatial Pricing." *Aoyama Journal of Economics* 33 (1981): 71–81.

[7] Willig, R. "Consumer's Surplus without Apology." *American Economic Review* 66 (1976): 589–97.

5.
Impact of Freight on Monopoly Spatial Pricing

I. Introduction

The prior belief that economic space has a significant impact upon the microeconomic theory of pricing has been affirmed by the study of spatial relationships. Thus, we have seen that freight cost will likely lower equilibrium price rather than raise it (Chapter 2). However, one would be surprised, and even confused, if told that "changes" in freight rate caused no change in FOB (or uniform) price. Yet, these somewhat paradoxical and seemingly contradictory propositions are, in fact, all readily derivable from a certain set of assumptions conventionally set forth in the literature of spatial pricing. These assumptions set forth by, for example, Greenhut [3] and Beckmann [1], include

Assumption A. Uniform consumer distribution over a plane or a linear market.

Assumption B. Identical consumer demand as a linear function of price.

Assumption C. A monopolist firm located at a point on the spatially extended market area.

Greenhut and Ohta [4; 5] have shown that the independence of monopoly mill price from changes in freight rate does not require Assumption B of linearity in demand.

Heffley [6] recently demonstrated, however, that the mill price independence no longer holds if Assumption A is replaced by a negative exponential consumer density assumption. It is specifically argued that, within the general context of an urban economy, the mill pricer will raise prices when the uniform pricer lowers prices in response to a reduction in freight rate. Hsu [7], in turn, claims to have shown more general conditions on consumer distribution under which a spatial monopolist will raise or lower the mill (or uniform) price. The findings by Hsu are given in terms of what he calls *elasticity of the average distance,* which is shown to be functionally related to the form of consumer distribution. However, no exact relationship between the two seems to have been established in his paper.

This chapter is based on Ohta [9] and shows a rather broad class of consumer distributions that yield the price independence result regardless of changes in freight rate. The population density function of this class includes not only constant but also increasing and decreasing functions of distance from the firm. Thus, the findings disprove the conventional notion that population decay has something to do with an inverse relationship between optimal price and freight rate. The present chapter, of course, goes beyond a mere critique and probes deeper into the general conditions under which changes in freight may have a negative, positive, or neutral impact on optimal monopoly pricing in economic space.

Section II reviews the paper by Hsu to demonstrate the nature of its fundamental findings. Part of Chapter 4, Section V, is redeveloped as a departure point for the present chapter. Section III sets forth examples of consumer distribution corresponding to Hsu's unitary elasticity of the average distance. These examples provide a rather broad case for the neutrality of freight rate changes to spatial monopoly pricing. Section IV, in turn, examines the general conditions for nonneutrality of freight rates in spatial monopoly pricing. Section V concludes this chapter by revisiting conditions for freight neutrality. Conditions, seemingly more general than those set forth in Section III but more tractable than those found in Section IV, are presented and related to the Section III conditions.

II. The Two Fundamental Propositions by Hsu

Relaxing the foregoing Assumption A while holding Assumptions B and C intact and further assuming marginal cost of production to be constant, one can set forth the spatial demand, Equation (1), and the profit function, Equation (2), for the spatial monopolist. Thus,

$$q_x = f(p_x) = (a - p_x)/b \qquad (a, b > 0) \tag{1}$$

where q_x stands for the quantity of local demand as a linear function of price p_x, which the consumer at x is required to pay. The profit Π in turn is

$$\Pi = \int_0^{x_0} (p_x - tx - c)(a - p_x)(1/b)n(x)dx \tag{2}$$

where $n(x)$ stands for the consumer density as a function of x, t for freight rate, c for constant marginal cost of production, and x_0 for the critical distance at which either demand quanity or additional profit vanishes. Although $n(x)$ is used by Hsu to represent consumer distribution along a line market, it may be reinterpreted to represent a two-dimensional topology (see Beckmann [2]). The consumer density at a point on the circumference of a circular market area with radius x then is defined as $n(x)$ divided simply by $2\pi x$. Conversely, the consumer density $n(x)/2\pi x$ over a plane readily can be transformed back to $n(x)$ to represent the original density along a line market. Without loss of generality, henceforth we will follow Hsu to consider the one-dimensional topology only.

The constraints imposed on the mill pricer and the uniform pricer, by definition, are given by Equations (3) and (4), respectively:

$$p_x = m + tx \tag{3}$$

$$p_x = p \tag{4}$$

where m stands for a unique FOB mill price, whereas p is a unique CIF price.

Subject to these constraints, the profit for the mill pricer Π_m and the uniform pricer Π_p can be respecified, via Equation (2), as

$$\Pi_m = (m - c)\int_0^{x_{0m}} (a - m - tx)(1/b)n(x)dx$$

$$\left(x_{0m} = \frac{a - m}{t} \right) \tag{5}$$

$$\Pi_p = \int_0^{x_{Op}} (p - tx - c)(a - p)(1/b)n(x)dx$$

$$\left(x_{Op} = \frac{p - c}{t} \right) \quad (6)$$

where x_{Om} is the mill pricer's market boundary whereas x_{Op} is the uniform pricer's boundary in terms of distance units. It should be noted that the mill pricer's demand vanishes at x_{Om}, that is, $m + tx_{Om} = a$, whereas additional profit for the uniform pricer vanishes at x_{Op}, that is, $p - tx_{Op} - c = 0$.

The spatial monopolist chooses mill price m or uniform price p to maximize profit. The first-order conditions for profit maximization for the mill pricer and the uniform pricer are

$$\frac{d\Pi_m}{dm} = \frac{\partial \Pi_m}{\partial x_{Om}} \frac{dx_{Om}}{dm} + \frac{\partial \Pi_m}{\partial m} = 0 \quad (7)$$

$$\frac{d\Pi_p}{dp} = \frac{\partial \Pi_p}{\partial x_{Op}} \frac{dx_{Op}}{dp} + \frac{\partial \Pi_p}{\partial p} = 0 \quad (8)$$

Since $\partial \Pi_m / \partial x_{Om}$ and $\partial \Pi_p / \partial x_{Op}$ both are required to be zero, Equations (7) and (8) can be reduced to

$$\frac{\partial \Pi_m}{\partial m} = \int_0^{x_{Om}} [a - m - tx - (m - c)](1/b)n(x)dx = 0 \quad (9)$$

$$\frac{\partial \Pi_p}{\partial p} = \int_0^{x_{Op}} [a - p - (p - c - tx)](1/b)n(x)dx = 0 \quad (10)$$

Equations (9) and (10) can be reduced further to a very simple form

$$2(m + t\bar{x}_m) - a = t\bar{x}_m + c$$

$$\left(\bar{x}_m = \int_0^{x_{Om}} xn(x)dx \div \int_0^{x_{Om}} n(x)dx \right) \quad (11)$$

$$2p - a = t\bar{x}_p + c \left(\bar{x}_p = \int_0^{x_{0p}} xn(x)dx \div \int_0^{x_{0p}} n(x)dx \right) \qquad (12)$$

where $\bar{x}$, to recall, is the average distance à la Hsu [7] and Beckmann [2]. Note that while the left-hand side of Equation (12) represents the marginal revenue derivable from *any* point of the firm's market radius given p, the left-hand side of Equation (11) represents the marginal revenue accruing from the *specific* buyer located at the average distance. Equations (11) and (12) require these apparently distinct marginal revenues to be equated with, respectively, the marginal costs of production and transportation to the consumer located at the average distance.

Recalling the constraints on price m or p and market radius x_{0m} or x_{0p}, namely, $m = a - tx_{0m}$ and $p = c + tx_{0p}$, and substituting these in Equations (11) and (12), we obtain

$$x_{0m} = [(a - c) + t\bar{x}_m]/2t \qquad (13)$$

$$x_{0p} = [(a - c) + t\bar{x}_p]/2t \qquad (14)$$

To be readily observed on Equations (13) and (14) in comparison with parenthesized parts of Equations (11) and (12), respectively, are the two functions ϕ and ψ in two variables, so that $\bar{x}_m = \phi(x_{0m})$ and $x_{0m} = \psi(\bar{x}_m)$, while $\bar{x}_p = \phi(x_{0p})$ and $x_{0p} = \psi(\bar{x}_p)$. Thus, it follows that[1]

$$\bar{x}_m^* = \bar{x}_p^* \qquad (15)$$

$$x_{0m}^* = x_{0p}^* \qquad (16)$$

These relations already were derived in Chapter 4 and are now in order as Proposition I.

Proposition I. The mill pricer's market area (average distance) and the uniform pricer's market area (average distance) are the same regardless of the form of consumer distribution $n(x)$.

---

[1]Cf. Beckmann [2, p. 621], which assumes in effect Equation (16) to derive (15), while both are derived as in Hsu's model.

Consider now differentiation of optimal mill (and uniform) price in (11), and (12), with respect t to obtain

$$\frac{dm}{dt} = -(1 + v_m)\bar{x}_m/2 \qquad \left(v_m = \frac{d\bar{x}_m}{dt}\frac{t}{\bar{x}_m} \right) \qquad (17)$$

$$\frac{dp}{dt} = (1 + v_p)\bar{x}_p/2 \qquad \left(v_p = \frac{d\bar{x}_m}{dt}\frac{t}{\bar{x}_p} \right) \qquad (18)$$

Therefore

$$\frac{dm}{dt} \lessgtr 0 \qquad \left(\frac{dp}{dt} \gtrless 0 \right) \qquad \text{iff} \quad v \gtrless -1 \qquad (19)$$

where v (equal to v_m, v_p) stands for the elasticity of the average distance. This establishes Hsu's other fundamental proposition as

Proposition II. A lower freight rate implies a higher mill (lower uniform) price if the elasticity of average distance v exceeds -1, and vice versa.

The v measures the sensitivity of market area expansion (or, possibly, reduction) as a result of a reduction in freight rate t. Since from (17) and (18) v is known to depend on $\bar{x}$, and $\bar{x}$ on $n(x)$ via (11) and (12), it follows that v depends, in principle, on $n(x)$. However, one finds no explicit relationship between the two, not knowing exactly what form of $n(x)$ yields the relation given in Proposition II.

Combining Propositions I and II, however, provides some clue to a deeper understanding of the meaning of v. For simplicity, assume zero marginal cost of production and let the marginal cost of transportation be represented by the line tx in Figure 5-1. Assume further that the uniform pricer's delivered price schedule, subject to a given $n(x)$, is given by $\bar{p}\bar{p}$. It then follows that $\bar{p} = tx$ at the market boundary x_0. The mill pricer's delivered price schedule, in turn, must be given uniquely by the line mp parallel to tx where the maximum delivered price p is required to be equal to the price intercept value of the assumed linear demand. Moreover, pursuant to Proposition I, this $p = a$ equality is required to occur at the same market boundary x_0 as Figure 5-1.

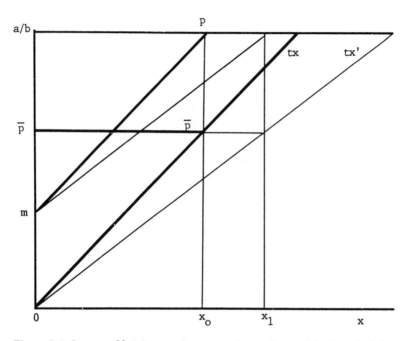

Figure 5.1. Impact of freight rate changes on alternative spatial price schedules.

Consider now a reduction in freight rate from t to t'. Let us assume our $n(x)$ is such that $\bar{x}$ remains the same. Then, given $t'x$ in Figure 5-1, the market boundary for the mill pricer as well as the uniform pricer is given uniquely as x_1, and the mill price also remains invariant. This result corresponds to the case of $v = -1$ under Proposition II. This result also can be derived from the uniform consumer density. However, we will see shortly that uniform density is not a required condition for the present invariant price result, invariant regardless of changes in freight rate.

What if $v \gtreqqless -1$? The case of $v < -1$ will be taken up alone, as the other case follows similar reasoning. The condition $v < -1$ implies that the market area expansion resulting from a reduction in t is greater than under $v = -1$ considered previously. Thus, it follows that the market boundary under t' subject to $v < -1$ is required to extend beyond (to the right of) x_1 in Figure 5-1. Therefore, there can be no ambiguity about the result. The uniform pricer's delivered price under t' will be strictly higher than $\bar{p}$ and the mill pricer's mill price lower than m, respectively, in Figure 5-1. (A geometric exercise to see this is straightforward in light of Proposition I.)

Conversely, when the consumer density $n(x)$ is such that the market area expansion induced by a reduction in freight rate is relatively small, in the sense of $v > -1$, the uniform price will be lower and the mill price higher than $\bar{p}$ and m, respectively, in Figure 5-1. Heffley's negative exponential consumer density over a plane (i.e., two-dimensional space) is just an example form of $n(x)$ that yields Hsu's condition $v > -1$ predicated on a one-dimensional space.

III. Preliminary Analysis for Monopoly Price Invariance: Neutrality of Freight Rate

Greenhut and Ohta [4; 5] have shown three alternative algebraic forms of consumer demand distributed uniformly along the linear market under which elasticity of the free spatial demand remains independent of freight rate. This independency can be shown to hold for any form f of consumer demand, thus relaxing Assumption B completely.

The proof is straightforward in light of Ohta [8]. The free spatial market demand, Q, defined there, may be redefined for the present purpose with explicit reference to freight rate t as follows:

$$Q = 2\int_0^{x_{0m}} f(m + tx)dx \qquad \left[x_{0m} = \frac{f^{-1}(0) - m}{t}\right]$$

$$= 2\int_m^{f^{-1}(0)} f(tx)\frac{1}{t}d(tx) \qquad \left[x_{0m} = \frac{f^{-1}(0) - m}{t}\right] \qquad (20)$$

Elasticity of free spatial demand e_F can accordingly be defined as

$$e_F = -\frac{dQ}{dm}\frac{m}{Q} = 2f(m)m/tQ = f(m)m/2\int_m^{f^{-1}(0)} f(tx)d(tx)$$

$$= F[f^{-1}(0), m] \qquad (21)$$

That is, e_F is independent of t—q.e.d.

Assuming constant marginal cost of production, we thus have established the following proposition:

Proposition III. Changes in freight rate provide no incentives for the spatial monopolist to change the mill (or uniform) price regardless of the form of consumer demand f insofar as it is uniformly distributed over the economic space.

When marginal cost of production, MC, slopes upward, a reduction in freight rate will cause the monopoly mill (uniform) price to rise, since the free spatial demand has been seen to shift upward along with the corresponding marginal revenue, equilibrium MC thus being higher after the freight reduction. Opposite relations clearly apply in the case of a downward-sloping MC. In any case, given production cost conditions, the impact of changes in freight rate upon monopoly pricing are well defined under a uniform consumer distribution, $n(x) = $ constant.

It is now possible to examine the form of $n(x)$ in relation to Hsu's elasticity of average distance v. The question is what form, if any, of $n(x)$, other than uniform density or Heffley's negative exponential density would yield the condition of $v = -1$ or $v > -1$, and what else would cause a substantial market area expansion due to reduction in freight rate.

To answer these questions, consider the definition of average distance $\bar{x}$ given in Equations (11) and (12):

$$\bar{x} = \int_0^{x_0} xn(x)dx \div \int_0^{x_0} n(x)dx \tag{22}$$

where the market boundary x_0 is to be determined by profit-maximizing calculus and given by[2]

$$x_0 = a/2t + \bar{x}/2 \tag{23}$$

As to the form of $n(x)$, let us consider the following algebraic form:

$$n(x) = \alpha x^\beta \quad (\alpha > 0) \tag{24}$$

---

[2] The formula in the text is only slightly different from Hsu's. In fact, marginal cost of production is assumed to be not only constant but zero, for visual simplicity.

where β is an arbitrary constant. The average distance $\bar{x}$ is then given by

$$\bar{x} = \frac{a(1 + \beta)}{(3 + \beta)t} \qquad (\beta > -1, \, t > 0) \tag{25}$$

It should be noted that the relevant range of $\bar{x}$ (i.e., $0 < \bar{x} < \alpha/t$) requires the domain for β to be constrained such that $\beta > -1$. Subject to this constraint on β, note further that a negative β represents a consumer density similar to Heffley's urban negative exponential density. When $\beta = 0$, $n(x) = $ constant may be interpreted to represent either a declining density over an urban plane or the uniform density along a line market. While a positive β (especially when $\beta > 1$) may also be considered to represent an urban population distribution, the assumed monopolist is required to be located at a suburban edge. Finally, note that in all these cases for β, the average distance $\bar{x}$ is homogeneous of degree -1 with respect to t; that is, Hsu's $v = -1$. Thus, Proposition III on invariant monopoly price may be generalized further as Proposition IV, subject to constant marginal production costs.

Proposition IV. Changes in freight rate provide no incentives for the spatial monopolist to change the mill (or uniform) price regardless of the form of consumer demand f and, moreover, regardless of consumer distributions, provided the form $n(x)$ is given by Equation (24).

IV. Conditions for Nonneutrality of Freight Rate

Before probing deeper into the form of consumer distribution $n(x)$, a preliminary observation is needed on the general conditions under which an improvement in the transportation technology or a freight rate reduction may cause mill (or uniform) price to rise, fall, or remain unchanged. Consider for this purpose the generalized form of free spatial demand, generalized over both Ohta [8], who assumed $n(x) = $ constant, and Hsu [7], who assumed linear demand

$$Q = 2 \int_0^{x_{0m}} f(m + tx) n(x) dx \qquad \left[x_{0m} = \frac{f^{-1}(0) - m}{t} \right]$$

$$Q = 2 \int_0^{f^{-1}(0) - m} f(m + u) n\left(\frac{u}{t}\right) \frac{1}{t} du \qquad (u = tx) \qquad (26)$$

where u stands for the unit cost of transportation as a proportionate function of distance units x. Thus, in general, the free spatial demand is seen to be a function of mill price m and freight rate t per unit of distance.

$$Q = F(m, t) \qquad (F_1 = \partial F/\partial m < 0; \; F_2 = \partial F/\partial t < 0) \qquad (27)$$

The elasticity of the free spatial demand e_F then is defined by

$$e_F = -F_1 m/F \qquad (28)$$

Partially differentiating e_F with respect to freight rate yields

$$\frac{\partial e_F}{\partial t} = e_F(e_t - e_s)/t \qquad (e_t = -F_2 t/F; \; e_s = -F_{12} t/F_1) \qquad (29)$$

where e_t (equal to $-F_2 t/F$) stands for the elasticity of free spatial demand with respect to the freight rate or, in short, the freight elasticity of demand, and e_s stands for the freight elasticity of demand *slope*. To appreciate the meaning of e_t and e_s more fully, note first that F_2 measures the responsiveness (expansion) of free spatial demand F to a change (reduction) in freight rate t. This F_2 is negative for an obvious reason, to obtain a positive freight elasticity e_t. The F_{12} in e_s, in turn, measures a change in the slope of free spatial demand F_1 in response to a change in freight rate t. While F_1 is negative, F_{12} is normally expected, although not required, to be positive. Thus e_s normally represents a positive measure of flattening out of demand as freight rate declines.

The relationship between e_t and e_s can be illustrated readily by Figure 5-2, where the two curves $f^{-1}(0)D_0$ and $f^{-1}(0)d_1$, respectively, represent the free spatial demand before and after a reduction in

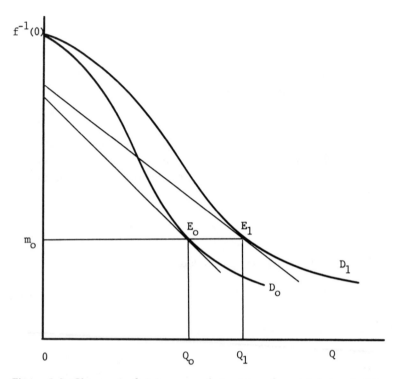

Figure 5.2. Changes in freight rate and elasticity of spatial demand. [Note: Figure illustrates a case for $e_f(E_1) < e_f(E_0)$.]

freight rate. Given an arbitrary level of mill price m_0 and the free spatial demand quantity being equal to Q_0 (equal to the length of $m_0 E_0$) and Q_1 (equal to the length of $m_0 E_1$), respectively, before and after the change in t, the gap $E_0 E_1$ clearly is larger when e_t is higher. Consider, in turn, the slope of the free spatial demand at E_0 and E_1, respectively. The slope gap is larger when e_s is higher. Thus, for example, suppose $e_t > e_s$. This condition requires that the gap $E_0 E_1$ be substantially large and/or the flattening-out effect of free spatial demand be negligible. More definitively, the required condition can be specified as the vertical intercept of the tangent line at E_1 exceeding that of the tangent at E_0, as in Figure 5-2. This condition readily follows from Equation (29). Under the present condition the elasticity of free spatial demand e_F is required to *decrease* as freight rate t declines. The opposite condition $e_t < e_s$ yields the opposite result. Adding the remaining case $e_t = e_s$ establishes Proposition V.

Proposition V. A reduction in freight rate causes the elasticity of free spatial demand to fall, rise, or remain unchanged accordingly as the freight elasticity of demand is greater, smaller than, or equal to the freight elasticity of demand slope, namely, $\partial e_F/ \partial t \gtreqless 0$ iff $e_t \gtreqless e_s$.

This proposition per se, however, seems to provide little information, if any at all, about the form of the consumer distribution $n(u)$ under which the mill price may rise or fall in response to freight rate reductions. However, at the same moment, the larger gap $E_0 E_1$ tends to yield a greater impact on the demand slope along D_1 vis-à-vis D_0 (thus rendering e_x greater) under the same conditions of population increase. Thus the net effect of freight rate changes upon monopoly pricing is hardly determinate, despite the common speculation that the optimal mill price is related inversely to freight rate under conditions of population decay. The final section explores further the question of freight neutrality.

V. Neutrality of Freight Rate: Generalized Conditions

Consider the consumer density function $n(u/t)$ in Equation (26). Assume that n is a separable function of u and t, such that $n(u/t) = \phi(t)\psi(u)$. Subject to this condition, Equation (26) can be rewritten as

$$Q = \int_0^{f^{-1}(0)-m} f(m + u)\phi(t)\psi(u)\frac{1}{t}du \qquad (u = tx)$$

$$= [\phi(t)/t]F(m)$$

$$\left[F(m) = 2\int_0^{f^{-1}(0)-m} f(m + u)\psi(u)du \qquad (u = tx) \right] \quad (30)$$

Thus, the free spatial demand is a separable function of mill price m and freight rate t. We thus have established Proposition VI.

Proposition VI. The elasticity of the free spatial demand e_F is independent of freight rate t regardless of the form of the basic demand f and, moreover, regardless of the form of consumer distributions provided that the density $n(u/t)$ is a separable multiplicative function of u and t.

An example form of the density function assumed in Proposition VI is given by Equation (24) repeated below as (31)

$$n(u/t) = n(x) = \alpha x^\beta = \alpha(u/t)^\beta = n(1/t)n(u)/\alpha \qquad (31)$$

Thus, a power function of u/t implies the separability condition of Proposition VI. Moreover, $n(u/t) = \alpha(u/t)^\beta$ if $n(u/t) = \phi(t)\psi(u)$.[3] This means that the form of $n(u/t)$ specified in Proposition VI is limited in effect to a power function and nothing else. In any case, the conditions under which changes in freight rate leave monopoly spatial prices unchanged appear fairly inclusive and perhaps also plausible, for a power function includes not only a constant function when $\beta = 0$ but also a decreasing as well as increasing function as $\beta < 0$ or $\beta > 0$. Moreover, the population density under a power function changes only at a decreasing percentage rate in absolute value, since $(dn/dx)/n = \beta/x$, a condition seemingly more plausible than an exponential population change with a constant percentage rate.

Exceptions to the class of density functions yielding the neutral price result include the exponential consumer density, be it negative or positive.[4] Heffley [6] has assumed a negative exponential density

---

[3] A proof for this result has been provided by H. Kataoka, Meisei University.

[4] Given an exponential population density, the free spatial demand (in one-space) is given by

$$Q = (1/b)\int_0^{x_0} (a - m - tx)e^{\delta x}dx$$

$$= t(e^{\delta x} - 1 - \delta x_0)/\delta^2 b \qquad (x_0 = (a - m)/t; \ \delta \neq 0)$$

The elasticity of free spatial demand e_F is then given by $e_F = \delta m(1 - e^{\delta x_0})/t(1 + \delta x_0 - e^{\delta x_0})$. Partially differentiate this with respect to t to obtain $(\partial e_F/\partial t)(t/e_F) = [(\delta x_0)^2 e^{\delta x_0} - (1 - e^{\delta x_0})^2]/(1 - e^{\delta x_0})(1 + \delta x_0 - e^{\delta x_0})$.

It can be shown that the sign of this partial is positive regardless of x_0 if $\delta < 0$. The sign is reversed for $\delta > 0$. Thus, the effect of freight reduction is to raise (lower) mill price if the consumer distribution is given by a negative (positive) exponential function. (The author is indebted to T. Wako, Waseda University, and David Greenstreet, Uni-

and conducted some simulation analysis to speculate, in effect, that a reduction in freight rate causes mill (uniform) price to rise (fall). In fact, Heffley's conclusion can be derived analytically by directly resorting to partial differentiation of his own demand elasticity formula with respect to freight rate (see Ohta and Okamura [10] for a proof).

A related note may be warranted. Although Heffley contemplates a negative exponential distribution of consumers over a plane, such a bivariate distribution, it should be recalled, can be transformed readily or simply reinterpreted as a distribution along a linear space with no change in analytical conclusions. Thus, for example, the negative exponential density distribution $n(x) = e^{-x}$ in a *two-dimensional* space is equivalent analytically to a density of the form $n(x) = xe^{-x}$ in a *one-dimensional* space. According to the latter specification, however, the consumer density does not decrease monotonically with an increasing x. In fact, the density increases up to a critical distance $x = 1/\delta$, although it decreases thereafter.[5]

In any case, the nonneutral price result seems to be related to an extraordinary change in the consumer density and, for that matter, the quantity of demand in response to an infinitesimal change in the market area. To better appreciate the unusual effect of an exponential function, consider the following example that Heffley used (with $\delta = 1$ and in the one-dimensional space):

$$n(x) = e^{-x} \tag{32}$$

The average distance $\bar{x}$ is then given by[6]

$$\bar{x} = \int_0^{x_0} xe^{-x}dx / \int_0^{x_0} e^{-x}dx$$

$$= [1 - (1 + x_0)e^{-x_0}]/(1 - e^{-x_0}) < 1$$

$$\text{(for all } x_0 > 0) \tag{33}$$

---

versity of Pennsylvania, who helped him spot a critical error in the original version of this note.)

[5] To see this simply requires differentiation of $n(x)$ with respect to x. The result is $n'(x) = (1 - \delta x)e^{-\delta x} < 0$ accordingly as $x < 1/\delta$.

[6] More generally, when $\delta \neq 1$ and $n(x) = e^{-\delta x}$, then $\bar{x} < 1/\delta$.

This means that regardless of the market size, x_0, however large it may be in terms of distance units, half the population is required to be located within the first distance unit from the center.[7] Moreover, the population density diminishes exponentially at a constant percentage rate; that is, it virtually disintegrates as the distance unit x increases. Recall and compare the case of power functions, under which the population diminishes only at a decreasing rate with increasing distances.

Under conditions of a positive exponential function, the consumer density is assumed to increase exponentially, that is, explosively, as the distance from the firm site increases. Aside from the question of why the monopolist firm willingly confined itself to such a peripheral location, the extraordinary nature of the assumed density should be manifest.

Except for these unusual cases, our basic conclusion of the neutrality of freight rate in regard to price applies to spatial monopoly pricing under conditions of constant marginal production costs, constant freight rate, and identical individual demands continuously distributed with a density given by a power function.

References

[1]   Beckmann, M. *Location Theory*. New York: Random House, 1968.

[2]   ———. "Spatial Price Policies Revisited." *Bell Journal of Economics* 7 (1976): 619–30.

[3]   Greenhut, M. L. *Plant Location in Theory and in Practice*. Chapel Hill: University of North Carolina Press, 1956.

[4]   Greenhut, M. L., and H. Ohta. *Theory of Spatial Pricing and Market Areas*. Durham, N.C.: Duke University Press, 1975a.

[5]   ———. "Discriminatory and Nondiscriminatory Prices and

---

[7] While $\bar{x}$ stands for the (statistical) mean, not median of x, the statement in the text applies also to the median, that is, med$(x) < 1$. Given $n(x) = xe^{-x}$, the result requires a slight modification, however. In this case, half the population is located within the first two units of distance from the center, that is, med$(x) < 2$.

Outputs under Varying Market Conditions." *Weltwirtschaftliches Archiv* 111 (1975b): 310–32.

[6] Heffley, D. "Pricing in an Urban Spatial Monopoly." *Journal of Regional Science* 20 (1980): 207–25.

[7] Hsu, S. K. "Pricing in an Urban Spatial Monopoly: A Generalized Analysis." *Journal of Regional Science* 23 (1983): 165–75.

[8] Ohta, H. "Spatial Competition, Concentration and Welfare." *Regional Science and Urban Economics* 10 (1980): 3–16.

[9] ———. "On the Neutrality of Freight in Monopoly Spatial Pricing." *Journal of Regional Science* 24 (1984): 359–71.

[10] Ohta, H., and M. Okamura. "A Note on Urban Monopoly Pricing." *Journal of Regional Science* 23 (1983): 287–90.

6.
The Output and Price Effects of Spatial Price Discrimination

In their classic analyses of regional price discrimination, Pigou [18] and Robinson [19] considered two—and only two—separate markets to be served, regardless of the price policy chosen by a monopolist. Greenhut and Ohta [5] extended the Pigou-Robinson analysis of price discrimination by introducing the variable of economic space, or market areas served under alternative pricing techniques, and related endogenous variables that depend on the price policy itself. Going beyond mere analytical generalization, Greenhut and Ohta have also arrived at a definitive conclusion that monopoly output tends to be strictly greater under discriminatory pricing between areas than under nondiscriminatory pricing.

The analysis of spatial price discrimination has been deepened further, and also widened in scope, by Greenhut and Ohta [7; 9], Holahan [11], Norman [14], and others. This analytical deepening has occurred as a generalizing of the form of functions, such as the individual demand function (as in [7]). The widening of scope has been carried out by these writers as they examined the impact of discrimination on outputs and other welfare conditions, as measured by consumer surplus under various conditions of spatial competition and monopoly.

The strength of the Greenhut-Ohta [7] findings is limited, however, by the algebraic form of the assumed individual demand, although this form is more general than the conventional linear demand. The form of the "basic" demand assumed by them belongs to the class of demands that are "relatively less convex" than a particular curve that is substantially convex.[1] Local demands (in terms of FOB mill prices), which derive from the basic demand of this particular form, are known to become increasingly elastic with increases in their distance from the firm (Ohta [16] and Chapter 10). It follows that the spatial aggregate demand becomes more elastic than the basic demand. Does it then follow that the output effects of spatial price discrimination remain positive only under these limited conditions? What happens to this output effect conclusion if the basic demand happens to be "relatively more convex"? The present chapter answers these questions, showing in particular that our basic conclusion remains unchanged even under a class of basic demands "relatively more convex."

Even if the aggregate output along with overall welfare levels were higher under conditions of spatial price discrimination compared with FOB mill pricing, some consumers may gain more than others whereas still others may lose. The present chapter also ponders the question of who gains and who loses under what conditions if the firm is permitted to freely switch its price policy from nondiscriminatory FOB mill to discriminatory pricing.

Section I states some basic assumptions for our analysis. Although not all of them are to be retained throughout the chapter, they are basic in the sense of constituting a point of reference. A basic model of spatial monopoly is set forth accordingly. Section II extends the analysis of the output effects of spatial price discrimination pursuant to the model set forth in Section I. Section III turns to the price effects of spatial price discrimination and attempts both a generalization and a terse summary of selected parts from Greenhut, Ohta, and Sailors [10]. Section IV concludes the chapter by summarizing the findings in the form of fundamental propositions.

---

[1] A local consumer demand (assumed to be identical) in terms of CIF price is called the *"basic" demand,* which is said to be "relatively more or less convex" than those local demands whose elasticity remains constant with respect to net mill price, net of freight rates, regardless of consumer location (Ohta [15; 16]).

I. The Basic Model of Spatial Monopoly

Assume the following:

Assumption A. A monopolistic firm is located at an arbitrary point of an unbounded linear market.

Assumption B. The basic demand (density) q is constantly elastic in terms of the CIF or delivered price, defined as the mill price m plus freight rate x, which is a monotonically increasing function of distance from the firm.

Assumption C. The basic demand is uniformly and continuously distributed along the linear market in terms of distance cost x to be defined more fully.

Pursuant to Assumption B, the basic demand q is given by

$$q = a(m + x)^{-\alpha} \qquad (a > 0, \alpha > 1) \tag{1}$$

where, for any given positive coefficient a, the parameter α stands for the elasticity e_B of the basic demand, that is, $e_B \equiv \alpha$, and x for the freight rate per quantity unit, which rate in turn is a monotonically increasing function of distance from the firm, and hence is a distance cost.

In the light of Assumptions A and C, Equation (1) can be integrated into the market demand Q_F for a spatial monopolist who practices FOB mill pricing.

$$Q_F = 2\int_0^\infty a(m + x)^{-\alpha}dx = \frac{2a}{\alpha - 1}m^{-(\alpha - 1)} \qquad (\alpha > 2) \tag{2}$$

Several notes on Equation (2) are in order.

First, for any given mill price, the firm's market area extends without bounds, approaching infinity as in (2) unless restricted technically or otherwise.[2]

Second, the elasticity e_F of spatial market demand, conventionally called the *free spatial demand,* is given by $e_F = \alpha - 1$. Thus, the

---

[2] The market area may be bounded, for example, if there is a threshold-sensitive level of the CIF price, above which the basic demand may vanish. Section III will reveal some implications of such threshold sensitivity in consumer behavior.

market demand is *less* elastic than the basic or individual demands. This means conversely that even if econometric estimates of the market demand happen to be inelastic, individual consumers may be more responsive to changes in price.

Third (and related to the others), insofar as a good is to be supplied by a local monopolist at a finite price, the consumers' basic demand is required to be sufficiently elastic. Specifically, since e_F (as equal to $\alpha - 1$) is required to be greater than unity, it follows that $e_B \equiv \alpha > 2$.

Fourth, the form of the basic demand (1) belongs to the class of demands that are "relatively more convex" in the sense that $e_F < e_B$. Under this condition, the basic demand in terms of mill price m becomes increasingly inelastic as the distance cost x increases and the net demand schedule for the monopolist, net of freight rate x, shrinks. It follows conversely that the elasticity of the spatial market demand, which derives from aggregating these shrinking net demands, tends to *increase* because of, say, spatial competition or entry à la August Lösch [13]. Indeed, the greater is spatial competition, the smaller is the market area, and the fewer the total number of these shrinking demands. If these shrinking demands yield monotonically decreasing elasticities, the greater competition, via smaller numbers of demands being aggregated, necessarily yields greater elasticity of aggregate demand (Ohta [16, p. 321]).

II. The Output Effects of Discrimination: The Constant Demand Elasticity Case

We are now in position to derive simple marginal revenue *SMR* and discriminatory marginal revenue *DMR*, à la Joan Robinson, from the basic assumptions and equations set forth previously in order to observe the output effects of spatial price discrimination. Chapter 7 will present in more detail the general *DMR-SMR* criterion in contrast with an alternative, "demand concavity," criterion (both proposed by Joan Robinson) for evaluating the output effect of discrimination.

SMR is readily derivable from the spatial market demand (2) by differentiating the total revenue *TR* with respect to *Q:*

$$TR = m(Q)Q = \left(\frac{\alpha - 1}{2a}\right)^{1/(1-\alpha)} Q^{1/(1-\alpha) + 1}$$

$$\therefore SMR = \frac{d(TR)}{dQ}$$

$$= \frac{2 - \alpha}{1 - \alpha}\left(\frac{\alpha - 1}{2a}\right)^{1/(1-\alpha)} Q^{1/(1-\alpha)} \quad (\alpha > 2) \tag{3}$$

Note that the spatial monopolist subject to the constraint of FOB mill pricing will equate this SMR with the marginal cost of production to obtain the optimal mix of a unique mill price and output (m^*, Q_F^*).

If the spatial monopolist is allowed to set different mill prices at different buying points (submarkets), the optimal policy for the firm is to separate each of the buying points along with its related marginal revenue curve, aggregate them horizontally, and equate the resultant curve with the marginal cost of production MC. The horizontal aggregate of local marginal revenues is called the *discriminatory marginal revenue*, DMR, because every local marginal revenue $MR(x)$, via the horizontal aggregation, can be equated with MC, thereby differentiating the optimal mix of mill price and quantity of output shipped to each buying point x; that is, $m^*(x)$, $q^*(x)$.

The $MR(x)$ is obtained via Equation (1) by differentiating the *local* total revenue $TR(x)$:

$$TR(x) = m(x)q(x) = a^{1/\alpha}q(x)^{1-(1/\alpha)} - xq(x)$$

$$\therefore MR(x) = \frac{\alpha - 1}{\alpha} a^{1/\alpha} q(x)^{-(1/\alpha)} - x \tag{4}$$

Equation (4) is then inverted to obtain DMR by holding all $MR(x)$ equal (equal to DMR) as we aggregate $q(x)$ over the entire market area:

$$q(x) = a\left(\frac{\alpha}{\alpha - 1}\right)^{-\alpha} (MR(x) + x)^{-\alpha}$$

$$\therefore Q = \int_0^\infty 2a \left(\frac{\alpha}{\alpha - 1} \right)^{-\alpha} (DMR + x)^{-\alpha} dx$$

$$= \frac{2a}{\alpha - 1} \left(\frac{\alpha}{\alpha - 1} \right)^{-\alpha} (DMR)^{1-\alpha}$$

$$\therefore DMR = \left(\frac{\alpha}{\alpha - 1} \right)^{\alpha/(1-\alpha)} \left(\frac{\alpha - 1}{2a} \right)^{1/(1-\alpha)} Q^{1/(1-\alpha)} \quad (5)$$

Equation (5) indicates the one-to-one correspondence of equal $MR(x)$'s (equal to DMR) and aggregate quantity of shipment Q. This relation holds if the firm regulates local shipments $q(x)$ in such a way as to equate each local $MR(x)$ with a common DMR, which, in turn, is to be equated with marginal cost of production for profit maximization.

Comparing Equations (3) and (5), it now is possible to demonstrate a strict relation $DMR > SMR$ insofar as $\alpha > 2$. For a proof, note that a sufficient condition for $DMR > SMR$ is $(-\alpha/1 - \alpha)^{\alpha/1-\alpha} > (2 - \alpha)/(1 - \alpha)$. The right-hand side of this inequality can be rewritten as $y = 1 - \Omega$ and the left-hand side as $g = (1 + \Omega)^{-(1+\Omega)}$, where $\Omega = 1/(\alpha - 1)$. Since α is assumed to be greater than two, the range for Ω is limited to $1 > \Omega > 0$. Over this domain, y and g have the following characteristics: $y(0) = g(0) = 1$, $y' = -1$, $g' < 0$, $g'(0) = -1$, and $g'' > 0$. Thus, it follows

$$g > y \qquad (1 > \Omega > 0) \qquad (6)$$

This establishes a sufficient condition for $DMR > SMR$. Thus, it follows that regardless of the shape of the marginal cost-of-production function $MC(Q)$, the level of output produced under spatial discriminatory pricing Q_D, in equilibrium, is greater than that under simple FOB mill pricing Q_S, even if the form of the basic demand happens to be relatively more convex.[3] Combined with the previous knowledge, the present result leads to Proposition I.

---

[3] The profit-maximizing market areas for the two alternative pricing policies under the present demand convexity conditions, that is, $e_F > e_B$, turn out to be unbounded.

Proposition I. Spatial price discrimination tends to yield greater output than FOB mill pricing under fairly comprehensive cost and demand conditions, that is, regardless of the forms of the basic demand and cost functions.

III. The Price Effects of Spatial Price Discrimination: Who Gains and Under What Conditions?

The CIF prices are presumed to depend on pricing policies chosen by the firm. Typically, discriminatory prices are known to be higher for nearby customers and lower for distant customers than nondiscriminatory CIF prices under FOB mill pricing (see Beckmann [1], Greenhut and Ohta [5; 6; 7], etc.). An interesting implication of this is that whereas the nearby (distant) customers are better (worse) off under FOB mill pricing, the distant (nearby) buyers are better (worse) off under discriminatory pricing. This asymmetric relation derives from particular demand and cost conditions. The required conditions include the basic demand, which is "relatively less convex," and negligible economies of scale. Contrasting results can be derived, however, if either of these conditions is reversed. This section presents some results or implications of the changing condition.

Consider initially the standard case of constant marginal cost of production and a "relatively less convex" basic demand. Since, in this case, the local demand in terms of FOB mill price shrinks and becomes increasingly elastic as distance from the firm increases, the aggregate demand is unambiguously more elastic than the local demand at a location nearest the firm's mill. In light of constant MC, it then follows that the price at the firm's mill under FOB mill pricing stays strictly below the comparable price under discriminatory pricing, the former being related to the more elastic aggregate demand and the latter to the less elastic local demand at the mill (the basic demand). Moreover, while the lower mill price remains constant under FOB mill pricing, the initially higher mill price under dis-

This means that the positive output effect of price discrimination is in no way related to the market area "expansion" effect of discrimination observed under different demand convexity conditions. Cf. Greenhut and Ohta [5; 6].

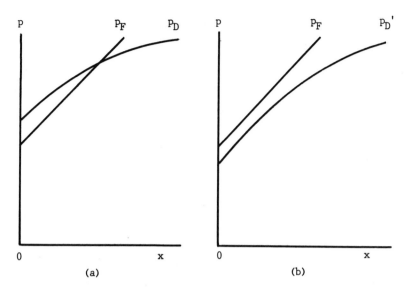

Figure 6.1. Alternative spatial price schedules under alternative cost conditions. (a) *MC* sloping upward, (b) *MC* sloping downward.

criminatory pricing starts declining as the elasticity of local demand increases with distance. The same freight rates being added to these mill prices under the two alternative pricing techniques, the CIF prices as a schedule, in terms of distance (costs) from the firm, thus turn out to be flatter under discriminatory pricing than they are under FOB mill pricing (see Figure 6-1).

In Figure 6-1(a) the straight line p_F depicts a nondiscriminatory CIF price schedule over economic space and p_D, which is always flatter than p_F, represents a discriminatory CIF price schedule. The p_F-p_D intersection in Figure 6-1(a) is no coincidence. Related to it are the facts that whereas the p_D is always flatter than p_F and $p_D > p_F$ at the firm site, the p_D becomes strictly lower than p_F at the market boundary point applicable to FOB mill pricing; this is because, under the assumed basic demand convexity, the local demand, in terms of mill price, is more elastic than the aggregate demand. In passing, although p_F must be a straight line, the flatter line p_D need not.

A welfare loss for nearby customers due to a price policy change from FOB to discriminatory pricing will be greater if the marginal cost of production increases with output and p_D in Figure 6-1(a) is shifted upward accordingly. Distant buyers still benefit from price discrimination in this case of increasing MC insofar as p_D intersects, as it does, with p_F from above.

What if MC goes down as output is increased when pricing policy is changed? The price schedule p_D will then be shifted downward instead of upward. It is thus possible for everybody to benefit from spatial price discrimination under conditions of substantial scale economy. This result requires that the MC curve slope downward and intersect with DMR at a level substantially lower than with SMR. A substantial reduction in equilibrium MC along with a drastic expansion in output upon adoption of discriminatory pricing is not only a theoretical possibility but also implies a downward shift in the discriminatory price schedule $p_D{}'$ below the nondiscriminatory counterpart p_F, as in Figure 6-1(b).[4]

The foregoing findings are based on Assumptions A and C, but not Assumption B, of Section I. They are summarized as follows:

Proposition II. Provided that the local demand becomes increasingly elastic as distance (from the firm) increases, at least the most remote customers benefit from discriminatory pricing regardless of the assumed cost conditions; moreover, everybody benefits from discrimination under conditions of substantial economies of scale.

The analysis of the present section so far has deviated from the assumed form of the basic demand (1) set forth in Section I. This form of basic demand is often avoided in the spatial pricing literature for two reasons. First, although it theoretically predicts discriminatory CIF prices will increase with distance more rapidly than will freight rates, the empirical verification is alleged, by writers such as Hoover [12] and Smithies [20], to be unlikely on grounds of resale possibilities by nearer buyers to more distant buyers. Second, the demand specification (1) that lacks a finite price intercept value may be considered empirically irrelevant, especially to the space economy. However, the first point has been rebutted by Dewey [3] and Olson [17]

---

[4] As a straightforward example of this result, consider a linear basic demand with the price intercept value of a. Assume that MC in equilibrium under FOB mill pricing happened to be $a/2$ whereas equilibrium MC under discriminatory pricing went down radically to approach nil. In this event, discriminatory price starts with $a/2$ at the mill whereas FOB mill price clearly exceeds this level and slopes everywhere steeper than the former schedule.

on grounds of monopolistic power and/or extra repackaging costs. Regarding the second point, a finite price intercept can be imposed on (1), whose constraint would simply involve the concept of consumer thresholds à la Devletoglou [2]. The a priori basis for rejecting the form of demand (1) thus would be eliminated. The need, therefore, arises to reevaluate the basic assumptions of Section I in the particular context of spatial price discrimination and its price effects.

The basic demand (1) as revised may now be defined as

$$q = ap^{-\alpha} \qquad (p_0 \geqslant p \geqslant 0, \; p = m + x)$$

$$= 0 \qquad \text{(elsewhere)} \tag{7}$$

The market demand Q_F under FOB mill pricing is accordingly given by

$$Q_F = 2\int_0^{x_0} a(m + x)^{-\alpha}dx \qquad (x_0 = p_0 - m)$$

$$= \frac{2a}{\alpha - 1}(m^{1-\alpha} - p_0^{1-\alpha}) \tag{8}$$

Note that the average revenue curve, or the inverse of (8), now has a finite price intercept value p_0. Correspondingly, the simple marginal revenue $SMR \equiv d(mQ_F)/dQ_F$ derivable from (8) as

$$SMR = m - \frac{Q_F}{2a}m^{\alpha},$$

$$m = \left(\frac{\alpha - 1}{2a}Q_F + p_0^{1-\alpha}\right)^{1/(1-\alpha)} \tag{9}$$

has the same vertical intercept value p_0. Moreover, $\partial(SMR)/\partial p_0 > 0$ can be observed for any $Q_F < 2ap_0^{1-\alpha}$. Thus, in the event of substantial threshold-sensitive consumer reactions, the SMR is shifted downward; the lower the p_0, the lower the SMR.

To evaluate the impact, if any, of the consumer thresholds upon equilibrium FOB mill price, initially assume the marginal cost of production to be constant. Then, the first order condition for profit maximization for the mill pricer is given by

$$m - \frac{Q_F}{2a} m^\alpha = c \tag{10}$$

where c stands for the marginal cost of production MC, and Q_F is defined via Equation (8) as a function of mill price m. It then follows from Equations (8) and (10) that

$$(\alpha - 1)c - (\alpha - 2)m = p_0^{1-\alpha} m^\alpha \tag{11}$$

where, for purposes of analytical continuity, the assumption of $\alpha > 2$ is preserved, though it is no longer needed here. The optimal solution

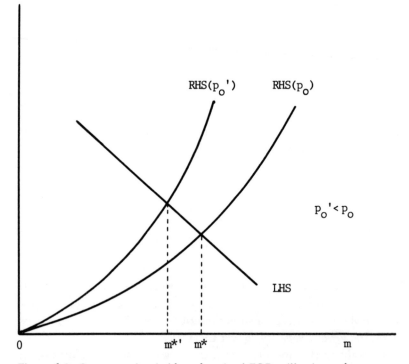

Figure 6.2. Consumer thresholds and optimal FOB mill price under constant MC conditions.

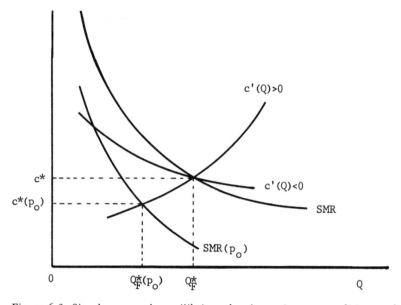

Figure 6.3. Simple monopoly equilibria under alternative cost conditions and consumer thresholds.

for m^* is now obtainable diagrammatically by depicting the right-hand side (RHS) and left-hand side (LHS) of (11), as in Figure 6-2. Moreover, the RHS curve alone will be shifted upward as p_0 decreases. The result is a decline in the equilibrium (optimal) mill price of the firm, from m^* to $m^{*\prime}$.

The price-lowering effects of the consumer threshold reactions will be reinforced even further when the marginal cost curve slopes upward. This follows because, upon a downward shift in the SMR with the imposition of p_0, the equilibrium MC declines with the equilibrium output along the upward sloping MC curve labeled as $c'(Q) > 0$ in Figure 6-3. In the figure, the initial reference point of equilibrium without consumer thresholds is given at (Q_F^*, c^*) and the new equilibrium, after the imposition of p_0, is given at $[Q_F^*(p_0), c^*(p_0)]$.

Thus, we have established the following:

Proposition III. When the basic demand is of constant elasticity and the marginal cost of production c stays constant, the level of optimal FOB mill price m^* depends upon the level of consumer threshold p_0: m^* will be higher or lower depending on whether p_0 is higher or lower, unless there exist substantial economies of scale.

If, however, there exists a substantial economy of scale in the sense that not only the average cost curve but also the marginal cost curve slope downward, then it is possible, though not necessary, that the equilibrium mill price will rise because of an increase in equilibrium MC as equilibrium output is reduced along the negatively sloping MC curve $c'(Q) < 0$ in Figure 6-3.

It now is possible to consider discriminatory pricing under conditions of consumer threshold sensitivity. The marginal revenue from location x may be defined via (7) as

$$MR(x) = a^{1/\alpha}\left(\frac{\alpha - 1}{\alpha}\right)q^{-1/\alpha}, \qquad q \geqslant ap_0^{-\alpha}$$

$$= p_0, \qquad ap_0^{-\alpha} > q > 0 \qquad (12)$$

The discriminatory monopolist will then try to maximize profits by equating each local marginal revenue $MR(x)$ to the marginal costs of production c and transportation x. However, since Equation (12) has a discontinuity at $q = ap_0^{-\alpha}$, the true optimality conditions include inequality terms:

$$MR(x) \geqslant c + x \qquad (13)$$

where c, as before, is a function of the total output Q.

From Equations (7), (12), and (13), the spatial price schedule under discriminatory pricing will be given by

$$p_D = \frac{\alpha}{\alpha - 1}(c + x), \qquad \frac{(\alpha - 1)p_0}{\alpha} - c \geqslant x \geqslant 0$$

$$= p_0, \qquad p_0 - c \geqslant x \geqslant \frac{(\alpha - 1)p_0}{\alpha} - c \qquad (14)$$

The slope of this price schedule $\alpha/(\alpha - 1)$ is strictly greater than unity and is steeper than the nondiscriminatory price schedule with

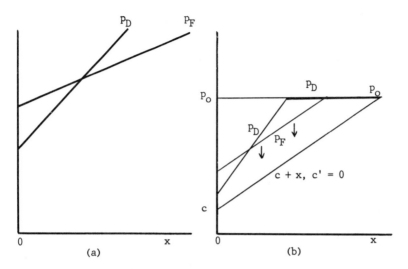

Figure 6.4. Impact of threshold-sensitive consumer reactions on alternative spatial price schedules under constant MC conditions. (a) Before consumer reaction, (b) after consumer reaction.

a unitary slope. Starting with conditions of no threshold sensitivity and the positive output effect of price discrimination established in Section II, the two alternative spatial price schedules may be initially compared in Figure 6-4(a), where the discriminatory price schedule p_D cuts the nondiscriminatory counterpart p_F *from below*. We have thus established the following proposition.

Proposition IV. When the basic demand is of constant elasticity, customers at locations relatively proximate to the firm tend to benefit from discriminatory pricing rather than FOB mill pricing, in the absence of threshold-sensitive reactions.

Following Hoover [12] and Smithies [20], Proposition IV may be rejected on grounds of resale possibilities by nearer buyers to more distant ones. However, Dewey [3], on the grounds of monopolistic power over buyers, and Olson [17], on the grounds of the extra cost of packaging, accept, as we do, the feasibility of phantom freight extras being added to delivered prices in demand situations characterized by Equation (7).

As a price ceiling is imposed on the delivered price schedules p_F and p_D in Figure 6-4(a) as a result of threshold-sensitive reactions by consumers, the p_F will be shifted downward as already demonstrated, unless the MC curve slopes downward rapidly. The remaining question asks what happens to the p_D. The answer depends partly on the form of MC.

As can be readily seen, if the marginal cost of production stays constant, the price schedule p_D remains basically unaltered. However, as the p_D reaches the price ceiling p_0, this p_0 will turn out to be the CIF price thereafter, until the firm's marginal costs of production c and transportation x approach this threshold level. The impact of the threshold sensitivity upon p_D and p_F are illustrated by Figure 6-4(b).

When the marginal cost of production increases as output increases, the equilibrium MC will also rise as the firm switches its FOB mill policy to discriminatory pricing, provided that the DMR undergoes no substantial downward shift in the event of the threshold-sensitive reactions by consumers. Recall in this connection that the imposition of the price ceiling p_0 was shown to cause a downward shift in the SMR. In contrast, the DMR can be shown to remain unchanged, being completely independent of the price ceiling p_0.

This asymmetric and seemingly puzzling result is derived from solving Equations (12) and (13) for the local sales quantities $q(x)$ and summating (i.e., integrating) them over the relevant spatial market domain given by Equation (14) to obtain

$$Q_D = \int_0^{x_1} a\left(\frac{\alpha}{\alpha - 1}\right)^{-\alpha} (c + x)^{-\alpha}dx + \int_{x_1}^{x_2} ap_0^{-\alpha}dx$$

$$\left(x_1 = \frac{(\alpha - 1)p_0}{\alpha} - c, \qquad x_2 = p_0 - c\right)$$

$$= \frac{a}{\alpha - 1}\left(\frac{\alpha}{\alpha - 1}\right)^{-\alpha} c^{1-\alpha} \tag{15}$$

Equation (15) relates the output produced by the discriminating monopolist Q_D and the *equalized* net marginal revenue from each and every relevant local market point that, in turn, is to be equated with the marginal cost of production c in equilibrium.

Two related notes on Equation (15) are needed. First, while Q_D is defined as a function of c *in equilibrium*, the c itself is a function of

total output. The equilibrium c is to be determined at the intersection
of Equation (15) and the MC or c curve. Second, the Q_D in Equation
(15) is a function of the equilibrium c alone; the DMR thus is completely independent of the price ceiling p_0.

All these findings and implications are summarily illustrated by
Figure 6-5. Thus, compared with the reference point E of the equilibrium under the FOB mill pricing system, the mill pricer's equilibrium MC is shown to be lower or higher in the event of threshold-
sensitive reactions by consumers, according to whether MC is sloping
upward or downward. (Compare the intersection points generated by
curves $SMR(p_0)$, $c'(Q) > 0$ and $c'(Q) < 0$.) The discriminator's
equilibrium MC, in contrast, will be shifted conversely under the
same circumstances. (See the intersecting points generated by DMR,
$c'(Q) > 0$ and $c'(Q) < 0$.) The related price and output effects of
discrimination vis-à-vis nondiscrimination under threshold-sensitive

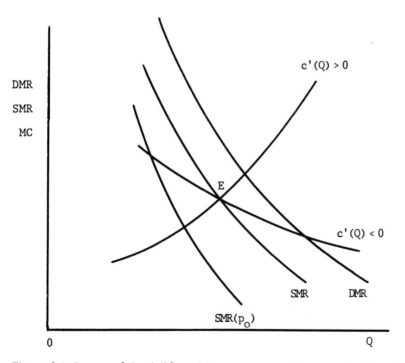

Figure 6.5. Impact of threshold-sensitive consumer reactions on simple and
discriminatory monopoly equilibria under alternative MC conditions.

Table 6-1. Price and output effects of threshold-sensitive consumer
reactions under alternative pricing policies

	p_F	p_D	Q_F	Q_D
$c'(Q) > 0$	Down	Up	Down	Up
$c'(Q) = 0$	Down	No change	Down	Up
$c'(Q) < 0$	Depends	Down	Down	Up

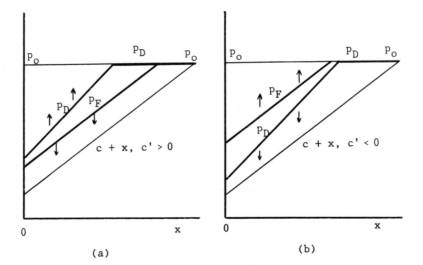

Figure 6.6. Impact of consumer threshold-sensitive reactions on alternative
spatial price schedules under alternative *MC* conditions. (a) *MC* sloping upward, (b) *MC* sloping downward.

consumer reactions should be easily observed as they are summarized
by Table 6-1 and illustrated by Figure 6-6, as well as by Figures 6-4
and 6-5.

Of particular interest is the relation exhibited by Figure 6-6(a),
which can be stated in the form of Proposition V.

Proposition V. When both constant elasticity of the basic demand
and threshold-sensitivity exist, the number of nearer buyers
who benefit from discrimination will decrease unless *MC* slopes
downward substantially. If, indeed, *MC* slopes upward substantially and/or the consumer threshold level p_0 is sufficiently low,

then it is possible that virtually all consumers are better off under FOB mill pricing than under discriminatory pricing.

This is not to say, however, that the last result in Proposition V invalidates the latter part of Proposition II. According to the earlier result, everybody was shown to be better off under discriminatory pricing, whereas the present result contends strict superiority of FOB mill pricing over discriminatory pricing. Underlying these conflicting results are opposite technological conditions: substantial economies of scale versus diseconomies of scale. In fact, the superior result of discriminatory pricing proposed by Proposition II is reinforced even if scale economy is combined with consumer threshold reactions. This follows because, under conditions of scale economy, imposition of threshold sensitivity upon consumer demands will lower the equilibrium MC for the discriminatory pricer on one hand, shifting the p_D downward accordingly, and on the other hand, shift the p_F *upward*, which will not occur without the imposition of p_0.[5]

IV. Summary and Conclusion

This chapter has considered the overall welfare effects of spatial price discrimination. Spotlighted were local CIF prices as well as the aggregate outputs produced under discriminatory pricing vis-à-vis FOB mill pricing, to allow determination of who gains under what conditions. Conditions for evaluation, including alternative production technologies and consumer tastes, were represented by contrasting forms of the cost and revenue curves. The impact of threshold-sensitive reactions by consumers upon their own welfare was also examined. Selected findings were summarized in Propositions I–V

[5] It can be readily shown that the elasticity of spatial market demand is increased by the imposition of a threshold price ceiling regardless of the form of the basic demand. Since a concomitant downward shift in SMR will yield a constant or lower equilibrium MC in the absence of a scale economy, it follows that the equilibrium FOB mill price will be lower and so will the nondiscriminatory spatial price schedule p_F. However, when economies of scale exist, the equilibrium MC will rise due to a downward shift in $SMR!$ Thus, while the net effect of consumer threshold sensitivity upon equilibrium mill price is unknown when economies of scale exist, the more substantial the degree of scale economy is, the more likely that effect is to be positive: The mill price tends to rise as a result of threshold consumer reactions.

of the text. Further summarizing these propositions, it was possible to conclude that although the output effect of spatial price discrimination is generally positive, some consumers may gain and others lose from discrimination, depending on where they are located under a given combination of these conditions. Moreover, these relations may be reversed under a different combination of the environmental conditions. It also is possible that every consumer can benefit from discrimination (Proposition II) or, on the contrary, from FOB mill pricing (Proposition V) depending on well-defined demand and cost conditions. These findings seem to indicate the need for special care in the evaluation and application of industrial policies and regulations.

References

[1]   Beckmann, J. "Spatial Price Policies Revisited." *Bell Journal of Economics* 7 (1976): 619–30.
[2]   Devletoglou, N. E. *Consumer Behavior*. London: Harper and Row, 1971.
[3]   Dewey, D. "A Reappraisal of F.O.B. Pricing and Freight Absorption." *Southern Economic Journal* 22 (1955): 48–54.
[4]   Greenhut, M. L., J. Greenhut, and S. Y. Li. "Spatial Pricing in the United States." *Quarterly Journal of Economics* 94 (1980): 329–50.
[5]   Greenhut, M. L., and H. Ohta. "Monopoly Output under Alternative Spatial Pricing Techniques." *American Economic Review* 62 (1972): 705–13.
[6]   ———. "Discriminatory and Nondiscriminatory Spatial Prices and Outputs under Varying Market Conditions." *Weltwirtschaftliches Archiv.* 111 (1975a): 310–32.
[7]   ———. *Theory of Spatial Pricing and Market Areas*. Durham, N.C.: Duke University Press, 1975b.
[8]   ———. "Joan Robinson's Criterion for Deciding Whether Market Discrimination Reduces Output." *Economic Journal* 86 (1976): 96–97.
[9]   ———. "Output Effects of Spatial Price Discrimination un-

der Conditions of Monopoly and Competition." *Southern Economic Journal* 46 (1979): 71–84.

[10] ———, and J. Sailors. "Reverse Dumping: A Form of Spatial Price Discrimination." *Journal of Industrial Economics* 34 (1985): 167–81.

[11] Holahan, W. L. "The Welfare Effects of Spatial Price Discrimination." *American Economic Review* 65 (1975): 498–503.

[12] Hoover, E. M. "Spatial Price Discrimination." *Review of Economic Studies* 4 (1937): 182–91.

[13] Lösch, A. *Economics of Location.* New Haven, Conn.: Yale University Press, 1954.

[14] Norman, G. "Spatial Competition and Spatial Price Discrimination." *Review of Economic Studies* 48 (1981): 97–111.

[15] Ohta, H. "Spatial Competition, Concentration and Welfare." *Regional Science and Urban Economics* 10 (1980): 3–16.

[16] ———. "The Price Effects of Spatial Competition." *Review of Economic Studies* 48 (1981): 97–111.

[17] Olson, J. E. "Price Discrimination by Regulated Motor Carriers." *American Economic Review* 62 (1972):395–402.

[18] Pigou, C. C. *The Economics of Welfare.* 3d ed. London: Macmillan, 1929.

[19] Robinson, J. *The Economics of Imperfect Competition.* London: Macmillan, 1933.

[20] Smithies, A. "Monopolistic Price Policy in a Spatial Market." *Econometrica* 9 (1941): 63–73.

7.
Notes on the Literature
of Spatial Price Discrimination

This chapter reviews selected earlier writings on spatial price discrimination in order to deepen our understanding of the subject.

Joan Robinson [10, chapter 15] sets forth the proposition that discriminatory pricing yields more or less output than simple monopoly pricing, depending on whether the more elastic demand curve in one market is more or less concave than the less elastic demand curve in another market. Robinson speculated that her adjusted concavity criterion provides the output effect of price discrimination *if* the elasticities of the separate market demands are "not very different." But this *if* is unacceptable methodologically simply because discrimination itself requires "different" market demand elasticities. Moreover, even if one accepted this unacceptable *if* for the sake of argument, her conclusion would not follow. The present chapter deals with this point more fully than did Greenhut and Ohta's [5] brief critique on that proposition. Section I demonstrates that the conditions under which the concavity criterion would hold true have limited relevance. Section II reviews in detail an alternative, more general criterion proposed in the preceding chapter as *DMR-SMR* comparisons, which in fact originated with Robinson but essentially was overlooked. Finally, in Section III, earlier findings on the output effects of market discrimination will be presented summarily along the lines of [3; 4] as discrimination over spatially continuous, dispersed market areas is evaluated.[1]

---

[1] A recent contribution by G. Norman [8] takes a slightly different approach to the theory of spatial price discrimination. Specifically, Norman shows that in a generalized Greenhut-Ohta (GO) model, (a) the form of the delivered price schedule or the degree of

I. The Adjusted Concavity Criterion

Assume first for counterexample that Robinson's separate but *nonspatially* conceived markets are characterized by demand curves of the form

$$p = \alpha q^{-1/e_1} \tag{1}$$

$$p = \beta q^{-1/e_2} \qquad (\alpha, \beta > 0, \ e_1 > e_2 > 1) \tag{2}$$

where p and q stand, respectively, for the price and quantity demanded, α and β are arbitrarily positive constants, and e_1 and e_2 are assumed to be constant elasticities of demand with $e_1 > e_2$ applying to markets 1 and 2, respectively. This section initially demonstrates that throughout the entire nonnegative range of p ($0 < p \leq \infty$), the more elastic demand curve, that is, the graph of Equation (1), remains less concave than the less elastic demand curve of Equation (2).

Recall that Robinson's adjusted concavity is defined by $eq^2 (d^2p/dq^2)$, which simply involves adjusting the demand concavity (or convexity in the contemporary usage) d^2p/dq^2 by the multiplier eq^2. Applying this to Equations (1) and (2) yields adjusted concavities for each curve:

$$\left(eq^2 \frac{d^2p}{dq^2} \right)_1 = \left(1 - \frac{1}{e_1} \right) p \tag{3}$$

---

price discrimination itself depends upon the degree of spatial competition, and (b) the firm always opts to practice spatial price discrimination unless otherwise constrained: no switching point à la GO [4]. Moreover, he has also proposed (c) that the degree of price discrimination is increased with the degree of spatial competition, a conclusion contra Greenhut-Ohta!

To demonstrate these results Norman begins with the following delivered price schedule as a linear function of distance x from the firm: $p(x) = \alpha + \beta x$. He then seeks to find α^* and β^* that provide the firm with the greatest profit. This procedure proves to be more practical than GO's when optimization is constrained by a price ceiling type of spatial competition, more practical in the sense that this solution set (α^*, β^*) actually provides the firm with greater profit than the GO solution. Theoretical purism, however, requires finding $p(x)$ that maximizes $\Pi = 2\int_0^{x_0} [p(x) - x][a - p(x)]dx$, subject to $p_0 \geq p(x) \geq 0$, $p_0 = p(x_0)$, $p(x) \geq x$, and $p_0 \leq a$, where p_0 stands for the exogenously determined price ceiling.

$$\left(eq^2\frac{d^2p}{dq^2}\right)_2 = \left(1 - \frac{1}{e_2}\right)p \tag{4}$$

Since $e_1 > e_2$, it follows that $(1 - 1/e_1)p < (1 - 1/e_2)p$ for any $p > 0$ regardless of how small the difference may be between e_1 and e_2. This example thus indicates that the more elastic demand curve, given by Equation (1), is consistently *less* concave than the less elastic demand curve, Equation (2).

This result, however, is unacceptable to Robinson in view of her concavity criterion, as she asserted that the more elastic demand curve cannot be "consistently less concave" [10, note 1, p. 198]. She particularized her argument further by observing that "if at any price the more elastic curve is less concave, there must be some higher price where it becomes more concave" [10, note 1, p. 200]. But this argument is specious, since it is based on the premise that the more elastic (and only temporarily less concave) demand curve approaches the vertical intercept "more rapidly than the less elastic curve" [10, note 1, p. 200]. She then concluded that there can be no two ways about it: The more elastic curve must become more concave either by having a vertical intercept point or by approaching such a point. If it has a vertical intercept value, it would be "infinitely concave at the point of impact"; and even if it does not cross the vertical price intercept "it must eventually become more concave" [10, note 1, p. 200].

Robinson's argument is untenable in two respects. First, the present counterexample sets forth a more elastic demand curve, which never has a vertical intercept but remains consistently less concave than the less elastic curve. Second, the concavity of a demand curve at a point approaching a vertical intercept is indeterminate, not infinite. In fact, although the elasticity of demand at the price intercept *does approach* infinity, the quantity demanded approaches zero, so that the value of the adjusting multipliers eq^2 is indeterminate.[2] The "adjusted concavity" therefore also is indeterminate. In sum, a more

---

[2] To be more precise, the value of eq^2 at the price intercept typically is not an indefinite value, *much less infinite*. In fact, its value approaches zero in so far as dq/dp remains finite in the neighborhood of (or at) the price intercept. If dq/dp approaches infinity, $pq(dq/dp)$ becomes indefinite at the price intercept point, as stated in the text.

elastic demand curve can be consistently less concave than a less elastic demand curve.

The error in Robinson's concavity criterion also is revealed by noting a contradiction intrinsic to it as well as stemming from her interpretation. Under her criterion, a monopolist subject to market conditions (1) and (2) would necessarily sell a smaller discriminatory output than nondiscriminatory output regardless of cost. But, this result applies only if the discriminatory marginal revenue curve lies consistently below the simple marginal revenue curve, the condition of which was correctly shown by Robinson to be impossible, since the total revenue under discrimination (as represented by the area under the discriminatory marginal revenue curve DMR) *cannot be less* than that under nondiscriminatory monopoly (as represented by the area under the simple marginal revenue curve SMR). There must be some quantity range over which $DMR > SMR$; otherwise, total revenue under discrimination would be less than under simple monopoly pricing. Robinson's concavity criterion, in other words, leads to the logical contradiction of A and not-A existing at the same moment.

In order for Robinson's adjusted concavity concept to hold completely with respect to the output effects of price discrimination, further specifications (i.e., constraints) are required. In particular,

1. The demand elasticities in the two (separate) markets cannot be sharply different.
2. The separate demand curves cannot be so sharply concave (convex) that the slopes of the corresponding marginal revenue curves change rapidly as sales quantities are changed, especially when both curves are of the same concavity.

The need for proviso 1 was established by Robinson herself. The necessity for proviso 2 is also readily apparent since Robinson's concavity criterion underestimates the positive output effect of price discrimination when the more elastic demand curve is concave *and* the marginal revenue slope related to it changes very rapidly. At the same time, her criterion overestimates the negative output effect of price discrimination in the other market, if its demand curve is *also* concave and its corresponding MR slope changes rapidly. The net effect of Robinson's criterion therefore entails considerable underestimation of the total output produced under discrimination. In fact, as previously shown by another counterexample [5], her criterion actually may yield the opposite net output effect to what in fact is the case. The converse proposition also holds: Convexity (not concavity), when combined with rapid changes in slope along the MR curve(s), tends to cause a Robinsonian overestimate of the output effects of price discrimination. Corresponding error in net output conclusions, therefore, is quite possible.

A further caveat is in order. The two constraints just set forth are not only unacceptably rigid but also theoretically invalid. To begin with, the Robinson proviso (constraint 1), which specifies very small differences in demand elasticities, is unacceptable because it contradicts the essential basis for discrimination; namely, substantially different demand elasticities in the separable markets. Constraint 2 is also subject to the corresponding critique because the less concave (convex) the MR curves, and hence the less concave (convex) the corresponding demand curves, the smaller the net output effect resulting from price discrimination.[3] Real interest in the effects of price discrimination tends naturally to center on instances of sharply distinctive concavities.[4] Robinson's concavity criterion for evaluating output effects therefore can be criticized as being both too restrictive and subject to error.

II. The *DMR-SMR* Criterion

A modified output effect criterion can be proposed that does not involve constraints 1 or 2 and that simply requires that the form of the separate market demand functions be known over the relevant ranges of price and quantity. It follows, of course, that the functional form of the marginal revenue curves also must be known over the corresponding ranges. The consequence is that the amount of output

[3] When $(d^2p)/(dq^2) = 0$, the output effect of discrimination is zero. See Pigou [9] and Robinson [10].

[4] This statement, however, does not hold when discriminatory price policy is extended over spatially separated markets. Spatial price discrimination can be shown to yield greater outputs than does an FOB mill price policy, regardless of Robinson's concavity criterion, or for that matter regardless of proviso 2 and most significantly regardless of the market condition, be it monopolistic or oligopolistic. See [1] and [3].

sold in each separate market under discrimination is determinable. Consider

$$MR_i \equiv \phi_i(q_i) = MC \tag{5}$$

where MR_i stands for the marginal revenue obtainable from the ith market, q_i, for the quantity of output sold in the market, and MC for the marginal cost of production as a function of aggregate output Σq_i.[5] Since the functional form ϕ_i is assumed to be known, Equation (5) may be solved readily for the q_i quantity of output sold in market i under conditions of discriminatory monopoly. But, how can discriminatory output Σq_i be determined and accordingly yield a unique MC in Equation (5) along with the individual market q_i's? To answer this question, it should be recognized that the horizontal sum of the MR_i's, that is, $\Sigma \phi_i^{-1}$, basically generalizes Robinson's DMR for the case of n separate markets. This generalized DMR equates readily with MC in establishing the total output Σq_i.

$$DMR(\Sigma q_i) = MC(\Sigma q_i) \tag{6}$$

Manifestly, total output is increased or decreased by discrimination depending on whether Σq_i given by Equation (6) is greater or less than the total output currently produced under conditions of simple monopoly.

This method of comparing outputs, which was implicitly set forth by Robinson in her comparisons of DMR and SMR, avoids the rigid constraints otherwise required (see Section I).[6] Moreover, it applies

[5]MC is not required to be constant in Equation (5). However, a constant MC is a simplifying, nondistortive device for comparing outputs under the alternative pricing techniques evaluated here.

[6]One might contend that from an operational standpoint this particular method for comparing outputs produced under alternative pricing techniques is inferior to Robinson's concavity criterion because knowledge of the exact shape of each separate demand curve is required, at least in the neighborhood of the equilibrium simple monopoly price. In this way, it contrasts with her criterion, which is based on price, elasticity, and concavity evaluated only at the equilibrium point. But, clearly, the magnitude of the concavity can be known only from the second derivative of the demand curve, which in turn may never be known unless the exact shape of the demand curve is provided, at least in the neighborhood of the relevant point under evaluation. We contend, accordingly, that the operational value of (6) is essentially the same as Robinson's concavity proposition, while being superior with respect to generality and accuracy.

directly to the general case involving more than two markets, the sizes of which depend on whether the seller is a monopolist or a competitor who practices discriminatory pricing. The advantages of this alternative to Robinson's concavity criterion include not only greater precision but also application to what may well be the most prevalent form of price discrimination in the world—geographic price discrimination [2]. In this context, note that Robinson's concavity criterion is directly and readily applicable only to the case where two separate markets are served by the monopolist. In the real world, firms typically sell over costly distances and the market areas served by such firms change as their price policies are changed. To include output effects, any analysis along spatial lines requires the alternative method just proposed, as can be seen readily in [3; 4], too. It was indeed along the same path—one step too few in generalization and one step too many in specification—that a general theorem on the output effects of *spatial* price· discrimination was initially set forth [3]. In that paper, the method proposed for comparing alternative outputs established the thesis that discriminatory pricing *always* yields greater outputs than FOB pricing in economies characterized by successively shrinking net linear demand curves (as viewed by a supplier who sells over varying distances). In particular, the increased output from discrimination was shown to relate to a corresponding "enlargement" of the monopolist's market area and to apply generally to any combination of shapes of *MC* and local demand curves. That method also was used to analyze output effects under conditions of spatial competition, with the same basic conclusions being obtained [4; 6]. The analysis was further extended to examine the effect of discrimination on *industry* output [6].

III. The Output Effects of Spatial Price Discrimination: Earlier Findings

The earlier findings on the output effects of spatial price discrimination [3] can now be reviewed by replacing Assumption B of Chapter 6 by Assumption B′:

Assumption B′. The basic demand q is an algebraic function of CIF price p.

With the other assumptions of Chapter 6 remaining intact, this assumption yields the following *spatial* individual demand q_x and market demand Q, respectively, in terms of FOB mill price m.

$$q_x = \left(\frac{a - m - x}{b} \right)^{\alpha} \qquad (a, b, \alpha > 0) \tag{7}$$

$$Q = 2 \int_0^{a-m} \left(\frac{a - m - x}{b} \right)^{\alpha} dx$$

$$= \frac{2b}{a(1 + \alpha)} \left(\frac{a - m}{b} \right)^{1+\alpha} \qquad (a \geqslant m \geqslant 0) \tag{8}$$

The form of the basic demand equation [Equation (7)] depends on the value of α; if $\alpha > 1$, then the demand curve is convex, whereas if $\alpha < 1$, then the curve is concave. The special case is when $\alpha = 1$ and yields a linear demand.

The inverse function of simple marginal revenue (SMR) and the output of the simple monopolist may be obtained directly from Equation (8). This provides

$$Q_F = \frac{2b}{a(1 + \alpha)} \left(\frac{1 + \alpha}{2 + \alpha} \right)^{1+\alpha} \left(\frac{a - R}{b} \right)^{1+\alpha}$$

$$(a \geqslant R \geqslant 0) \quad (9)$$

where Q_F refers to output produced under simple FOB mill monopoly and where for notational simplicity R is used in place of MR to represent the value of marginal revenue equal to marginal cost.

Consider next the individual marginal revenue functions. The individual marginal revenue MR_x from market point x can be derived from Equation (7), which provides

$$MR_x = a - x - b(1 + 1/\alpha)q_x^{1/\alpha} \qquad (a \geqslant x \geqslant 0) \tag{10}$$

or, equivalently, by rearranging terms,

$$q_x = \left(\frac{a - x - MR_x}{b(1 + 1/\alpha)} \right)^{\alpha} \qquad (a \geqslant x \geqslant 0) \tag{11}$$

The discriminatory marginal revenue DMR, or its inverse function, involves summation of Equation (11) over x for a uniform level of MR_xs; that is, $MR_x = R$. Thus,

$$Q = \int_0^{a-R} \left(\frac{a - x - R}{b(1 + 1/\alpha)} \right)^{\alpha} dx \tag{12}$$

Evaluating this integral gives

$$Q_D = \frac{b}{2\alpha} \left(\frac{\alpha}{1 + \alpha} \right)^{1+\alpha} \left(\frac{a - R}{b} \right)^{1+\alpha} \qquad (a \geqslant R \geqslant 0) \tag{13}$$

where Q_D refers to output produced under discrimination.

The final steps of comparing outputs produced under alternative pricing techniques, which is equivalent to comparing Q_D with Q_F, are at hand. For this purpose, divide Equation (13) by Equation (9), and record the result as

$$\frac{Q_D}{Q_F} = y^{\alpha} \qquad \left[y = \frac{\alpha}{1 + \alpha} \left(1 + \frac{1}{1 + \alpha} \right)^{1 + 1/\alpha} \right] \tag{14}$$

To prove that y in Equation (14) is strictly greater than unity if $\alpha > 0$, consider the following real function:

$$g(x) = x^{1 + 1/\alpha} \qquad (x > 0) \tag{15}$$

This function implies the inequality of (16), as depicted in Figure 7-1:

$$g(1 + h) > g(1) + g'(1)h \qquad \left(g' = \frac{dg}{dx}, h > 0 \right) \tag{16}$$

The relation of Equation (16) is equivalently specifiable via Equation (15) as

$$(1 + h)^{1 + 1/\alpha} > 1 + (1 + 1/\alpha)h \quad (h > 0 \text{ and } \alpha > 0) \tag{17}$$

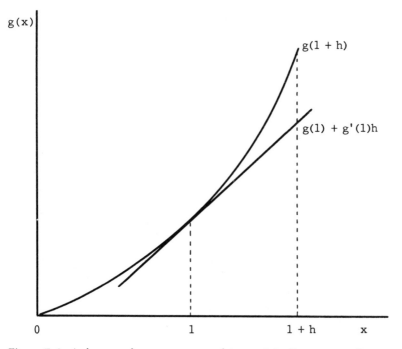

Figure 7.1. A downward convex curve and its straight-line tangent (Source: Greenhut and Ohta [8, chapter 4]).

Substituting $h = 1/(1 + \alpha)$ into Equation (17) yields

$$\left(1 + \frac{1}{1 + \alpha}\right)^{1 + 1/\alpha} > 1 + 1/\alpha,$$

$$\text{that is,} \quad \frac{\alpha}{1 + \alpha}\left(1 + \frac{1}{1 + \alpha}\right)^{1 + 1/\alpha} > 1 \qquad (\alpha > 0) \quad (18)$$

Thus, the relation (18) proves that y in Equation (14) is strictly greater than unity. Furthermore, since $\alpha > 0$ and $y > 1$, y^α must also be greater than unity.

Proof exists that Q_D/Q_F is greater than unity; that is, $Q_D > Q_F$, irrespective of the value of α, provided $\alpha > 0$. In other words, output produced under spatial price discrimination is necessarily greater than that produced under simple spatial monopoly, regardless of the shape or concavity (convexity) of the demand function.

IV. Conclusion

The present chapter has shown that measures of outputs attributable to discriminatory and nondiscriminatory pricing should be based on *DMR* and *SMR*. Comparisons between these functions avoid the contradictions stemming from elementary comparisons of demand curve shapes and elasticities. They reveal that greater outputs generally obtain from price discrimination. This and several other related conclusions drawn earlier were based on the assumptions that buyers are evenly distributed along a line, with each having identical tastes or identical gross demand curves. These assumptions, however, are neither intrinsic nor crucial to the basic conclusions. As long as successively shrinking net demand curves characterize the demands of more distant buyers, the conclusions hold, regardless of other facets of buyer distribution or tastes.

As stressed in Greenhut and Ohta [3, pp. 712–13]:

> This conclusion justifies Pigou's anticipation that total output is likely to be greater under discriminatory monopoly than simple monopoly as the number of separate markets increases [9, p. 287]. But Pigou based his expectation on the claim that third degree discrimination blends into first degree discrimination as the number of separate markets increases, an identity requiring a perfectly inelastic demand curve in each submarket and, in turn, complete appropriation of consumer surplus. Pigou's expectation of greater outputs was, therefore, circumscribed unnecessarily. From a somewhat different perspective, Robinson also stressed output effects. She pointed, in general, to the indeterminacy of total output quantities under simple monopoly and discriminatory pricing. Our own basically general formulation applies to economic space, and relates to the inevitable separation of DMR and SMR.

The proposed analysis applies both to the cases of spatial monopoly and spatial competition [4; 6; 8]. Moreover, besides measuring output effects, the *DMR-SMR* technique facilitates other welfare comparisons, including those relating to a unit of distance [6; 7].

References

[1] Dewey, D. "A Reappraisal of F.O.B. Pricing and Freight Absorption." *Southern Economic Journal* 22 (1955): 48–54.

[2] Greenhut, M. L., J. Greenhut, and S. Y. Li. "Spatial Pricing in the United States." *Quarterly Journal of Economics* 94 (1980): 329–50.

[3] Greenhut, M. L., and H. Ohta. "Monopoly Output under Alternative Spatial Pricing Techniques." *American Economic Review* 62 (1972): 705–13.

[4] ———. *Theory of Spatial Pricing and Market Areas.* Durham, N.C.: Duke University Press, 1975.

[5] ———. "Joan Robinson's Criterion for Deciding Whether Market Discrimination Reduces Output." *Economic Journal* 86 (1976): 96–97.

[6] ———. "Output Effects of Spatial Price Discrimination under Conditions of Monopoly and Competition." *Southern Economic Journal* 46 (1979): 71–84.

[7] ———. "A General Method for Determining Output and Welfare Effects of Discriminatory Pricing" (unpublished manuscript).

[8] Norman, G. "Spatial Competition and Spatial Price Discrimination." *Review of Economic Studies* 48 (1981): 97–111.

[9] Pigou, A. C. *The Economics of Welfare.* 3d ed. London: Macmillan, 1929.

[10] Robinson, J. *The Economics of Imperfect Competition.* London: Macmillan, 1933.

PART III

Spatial Competition and Market Areas

8.
The Nonoverlapping Market Areas Approach

I. Introduction

A monopolist may enjoy a monopoly profit that, however, eventually tends to induce new entry. As long as consumers' basic demands are price elastic, a subsequent entry will take place at a location apart from any existing firm. After completion of optimal location or relocation of all firms, each firm must decide *to whom* to sell its product and *at what price*. There are two alternative approaches to these interrelated problems. The solution considered in this chapter is predicated upon one of the two approaches and postulates several alternative pricing techniques that will enable each firm to strictly monopolize its own market area with no part shared with rivals. Thus, any buying point in a nonoverlapping market area is served by one and only one firm.

The chapter demonstrates some contrasting impacts of alternative types of spatial competition upon the spatial price schedule and related market area of the former spatial monopolist. Section II presents a model of Hooverian spatial competition. Models covered in the subsequent sections include the so-called Löschian competition, Hotelling-Smithies competition, and Greenhut-Ohta competition. While each of these models is based on its own distinctive behavioral assumption, considered later, the following simplifying assumptions are requisite throughout the present chapter.

Assumption A. The basic identical demand is distributed continuously and uniformly along a linear circular market developed, say, around a mountainside.

Assumption B. The market is dotted and equally spaced (in all directions) by two homogeneous sellers:[1] one is the former monopolist and the other a new entrant who challenges and is countered by the incumbent.

Assumption C. The freight rate per unit of distance is constant.

Assumption D. The marginal cost of production is constant.

Pursuant to these simplifying assumptions, it now is feasible to consider contrasting behavioral assumptions regarding spatial competition.

II. The Hooverian Model of Spatial Competition

E. M. Hoover [6] proposed that a competitive firm trying to make sales to any market point expects its rival to behave as a perfect competitor who practices marginal cost pricing at that point. In order to secure and monopolize that market point, it is necessary to undercut the rival's expected price, which is expected to be equal to the firm's marginal costs of production and transportation. In other words, the Hooverian competitor endeavors to maximize profits subject to the constraint that the firm's CIF prices cannot exceed its rival's marginal-cost prices, which are parametrically fixed at any given point.

The optimization problem for the firm is therefore stated formally as

$$\underset{p(x)}{\text{Max }} \Pi = 2\int_0^{x_0} [p(x) - c - tx]f\{p(x)\}dx$$

$$\text{subject to } p(x) \le c + t(X - x) \quad (1)$$

---

[1] The famous Hotelling solution [7] for the duopolists' location problem, that is, the back-to-back location at the same central point, does not apply here, because the crucial Hotelling assumption regarding consumer demand elasticity has not been employed. The Hotelling assumption that the basic demand is perfectly inelastic is not rejected because it is unrealistic per se, but because it is irrelevant to the space economy, where the distance cost matters. In the Hotelling model of spatial pricing, the distance cost is irrelevant to consumers, who remain willing to pay an exorbitant price for a product; otherwise, their demands are required to be elastic. The startling Hotelling conclusion collapses, being replaced by the Smithies finding that duopolists tend to seek separate locations [11].

where Π stands for profit, $p(x)$ for CIF price as a function of distance x from the firm site, x_0 for the distance from the firm site to the market boundary point, which is circumscribed by the rival firm located at a given distance X from the firm site, and c and t are the marginal costs of production and transportation, respectively, and constant pursuant to Assumptions B and C.

Clearly, the optimal price schedule $p(x)$ for the spatial monopolist developed in Chapter 3 remains the optimal price schedule for the duopolist(s) $p_D(x)$ as well, unless it violates the constraint of (1). Remember in this connection that $p(x)$ is a monotonically increasing function of x, whereas the rival's CIF price, perceived as $c + t(X - x)$, is a decreasing function of x. It is thus possible that these two price schedules have a positive point of intersection, say, at $x = x_{-1}$, on Figure 8-1. It then follows that the solution for (1)

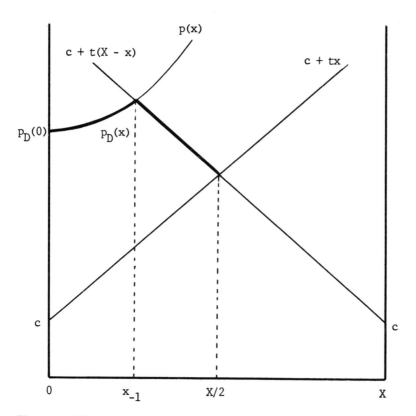

Figure 8.1. The Hooverian spatial price schedule.

includes this unconstrained $p(x)$ only for the limited domain of $x_{-1} > x > 0$. Beyond this domain, the firm's optimal price must start *declining* along the perceived rival's price schedule, that is, $p_D(x) = c + t(X - x)$, until $p_D(x)$ reaches its own marginal costs of production and of transportation, that is, $p_D(x) = c + t(X - x) = c + tx$. This critical point is where the firm's market area ends and is given by $x_0 = X/2$. Thus, the optimal solution for (1) is stated formally as

$$p_D(x) = p(x) \qquad (x_{-1} > x > 0)$$
$$= c + t(X - x) \qquad (X/2 \geqslant x \geqslant x_{-1}) \qquad (2)$$

Equation (2) is illustrated by the heavy lined $p_D(x)$ in Figure 8-1, where one duopolist is assumed to be located at 0 while the other is at X. The price schedule applicable to the duopolist at 0 is depicted by $p_D(x)$; but the other one that is to start from X leftward, being strictly symmetric about the point $X/2$, is omitted from the figure for simplicity (cf., however, M. Greenhut and H. Ohta [5, chapter 8]).

The Hooverian price schedule $p_D(x)$ leads to fantastic aspects of the fundamental nature of spatial pricing. It combines an extreme case of monopoly pricing with an extreme case of competition. There is optimal spatial price discrimination over the spatially protected domain $x_{-1} > x > 0$. Outside this domain, the price schedule reflects the firm's hyperreactions to pricing by the rival seller, *perceived* as a perfect competitor, that is, a strict marginal cost pricer. It is the perfectly competitive reaction, *not the monopolistic behavior,* of firms in economic space that prompts the apparent dumping of goods in areas most remote from the firms' locations. Thus, the Hooverian price schedule, which is optimal for a firm under purely noncollusive spatial competition, involves seeming paradoxes of economic space: *coexistence of pure monopoly and hypercompetition and growth of dumping provoked by competition.*

Because of this feature of dumping (even if apparently caused by hypercompetition), Hooverian competitors may be subjected to antitrust prosecution. Because of this fear, the firms may be forced to adopt the familiar FOB mill pricing. The subsequent sections will

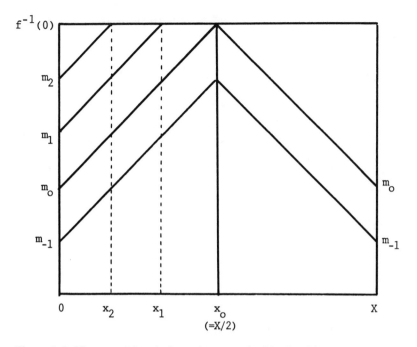

Figure 8.2. Hypersensitive rival reactions perceived by Löschian competitors.

deal with alternative types of spatial competition subject to the basic constraint of mill pricing.[2]

III. The Löschian Model of Spatial Competition

By definition, Löschian competition takes place when all (two) firms, behaving as FOB mill pricers, treat their market areas as given exogenously. This condition stems from the hypersensitive reactions of rival prices to the (representative) firm's price change [3, p. 672]. To appreciate this relation, consider the firm located at the point of the line market in Figure 8-2 and confronted by the rival firm located at point

---

[2]Selected portions of this section are taken from Ohta [9] and reorganized for the purposes of the subsequent sections.

X. Thus, for example, if the mill price of the firm located at point 0 in Figure 8-2 is as high as m_1, the delivered price schedule over the line market may be represented by the line m_1m_1, the slope of which is given by the fixed freight rate t, per Assumption C. Given the basic demand of the form $f(p)$, the delivered price reaches its maximum $f^{-1}(0)$ at distance x_1, where demand vanishes. Accordingly, $0x_1$ constitutes the firm's market area when mill price is set at m_1. A lowering of mill price from m_1 to m_0 (or a rise from m_1 to m_2) causes the delivered price schedule to shift down (up) to the line m_0m_0 (m_2m_2). This change increases (reduces) the firm's market limit from x_1 to $x_0 = X/2$ (or from x_1 to x_2). In either event, the firm's market area is so small over this range of prices that rivals' hypersensitive reactions in price at point X hardly interfere with the firm's change in price and market area.

The same relation would not hold, however, if the firm's mill price were lowered below the critical level m_0. Any reduction in mill price, say from m_0 to m_{-1}, could be expected to induce immediate and identical change in price by the rival firm located at point X. The market boundary point therefore would be left unchanged at $X/2$. The exogenous treatment of the firm's market area thus constitutes the characteristic feature of Löschian competition, as Gannon [2] noted.[3]

The spatial market demand Q_L that a Löschian competitor may face is given formally by

$$Q_L = 2 \int_0^{x_0} f(m + tx)dx \qquad (3)$$

where x_0 (equal to $X/2$) stands for the distance from the firm's location to its market boundary point, which is a fixed parameter.

Two notes are in order on the present model in comparison with

[3] Cf. M. Beckmann [1], and B. Stevens and C. Rydell [12], where the market area of the firm is treated as an exogenous variable notwithstanding the spatial monopoly assumption of their models. These writers demonstrated that the mill price of the firm falls (or rises) as the exogenous market area is enlarged (or reduced). Stevens and Rydell were apparently surprised by the result and called it a "paradox of spatial monopoly" [12]. However, the market area of the firm can hardly be treated as a constant unless the firm is subjected to spatial competition, not spatial monopoly. Thus, the "paradox of space" applies more appropriately to spatial competition than it does to spatial monopoly (Ohta [10]).

the previous one. First, the aggregate market demand of (3) applies only to FOB mill pricing; the aggregate demand in terms of common mill price is simply nonexistent in the previous model of discriminatory pricing. Second, while the Hooverian competitor takes his rival's marginal costs and CIF prices as parameters under marginal cost pricing, the Löschian competitor considers market area to be the fixed parameter.

The optimization problem for the Löschian competitor can now be written, using Equation (3), as

$$\text{Max}_{m} \ \Pi = (m - c)Q_L = 2(m - c) \int_0^{x_0} f(m + tx)dx \qquad (4)$$

where c, to recall, is the marginal cost of production (per Assumption D). The solution of (4) is

$$m\left(1 - \frac{1}{e_L}\right) = c \qquad \left\{ \begin{aligned} e_L &= -\frac{dQ_L}{dm}\frac{m}{Q_L} \\ &= \frac{m[f(m) - f(m + tx_0)]}{\int_0^{x_0} f(m + tx)dx} \end{aligned} \right\} \qquad (5)$$

where e_L stands for the elasticity of Löschian demand.

Equation (5) represents the familiar $MR = MC$ optimization condition for the firm, except that the MR part involves e_L, which is a function of not only mill price m but also the market area parameter x_0.

It follows from Equation (5) that equilibrium mill price under Löschian competition depends not only on marginal cost of production c but also on the exogenously given market area x_0. It is not readily known, however, whether e_L may increase, and equilibrium mill price m decrease, as a direct consequence of a new entry and the consequent decrease in x_0. The results depend presumably on the form of the basic demand f. (This question will be examined in more detail in Chapter 10. For the time being, it suffices to note that, given x_0, a unique equilibrium mill price can be derived from (5), since e_L is a monotonic function of m.)

IV. The Hotelling-Smithies Model
of Spatial Competition

In his famous model of spatial duopoly, Hotelling [7] assumed that each firm considers its rival's mill price to be fixed. Smithies [11] adopted this assumption but rejected another assumption of Hotelling—perfectly inelastic individual (basic) demands. Smithies instead assumed elastic demands. Combining Hotelling's assumption of parametric treatment of rival's mill price with Smithies' assumption of elastic basic demands yields a model of spatial pricing distinct from the previous models. This model we call the Hotelling-Smithies (HS) model of.spatial competition.

While Löschian competitors consider their own market areas as fixed, HS competitors do not. Nevertheless, under conditions of fixed firm locations and uniform interfirm behavior, the market area of each firm will turn out to be invariant ex post regardless of the *conjectural variations* assumed. For if one firm conjectures its rival's reaction to be insensitive and attempts to enlarge its own 'market area by lowering its mill price, the other firm will follow suit. Thus, although alternative firm behaviors may yield different equilibrium mill prices, all the equilibria must lie on the same Löschian demand curve defined as the sum or integrand of all individual (local) demands over a fixed market area.

The HS model of spatial competition may be illustrated diagrammatically and then formulated mathematically. Suppose in Figure 8-3 that firms located at points 0 and X initially set forth an optimal Löschian mill price m_L^*, which will bisect the market area OX at the market boundary point x_0.

We will now show that the equilibrium mill price m_L^* under Löschian competition, obtainable from Equation (5), no longer is applicable to HS competition. Given m_L^* as his rival's mill price, the HS competitor at 0 can expect his own market area to be enlarged beyond x_0 (rightward) by a lowering of his own mill price below m_L^*, say, to m'. The resultant expected market area increment would be $x_0 x_0'$ or $(m_L^* - m')/2$ in terms of distance costs. Related to this extra market area *perceived* by each HS seller is an additional market demand quantity *perceived* beyond Löschian demand. Thus, an HS firm conjecturing "insensitive" rival reactions would visualize a more

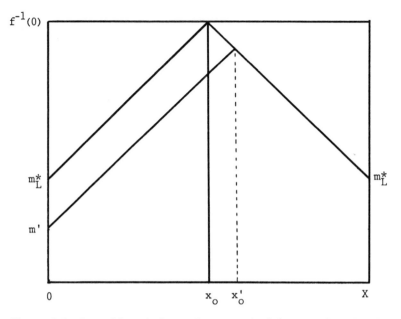

Figure 8.3. Insensitive rival reactions perceived by Hotelling-Smithies competitors.

elastic demand such as $HS(m_L^*)$ in Figure 8-4, as compared with the Löschian demand $L(x_0)$.

The HS demand can be represented by

$$Q_{HS} = 2\int_0^{x_0} f(m + tx)dx + 2\Phi(m^* - m) \tag{6}$$

where m^* is the rival's perceived mill price, Φ a function such that $\Phi' > 0$ and $\Phi(0) = 0$. Thus, at $m^* = m_L^*$, the elasticity of the HS demand e_{HS} becomes higher than the elasticity of the Löschian demand e_L; that is, $e_{HS}(m_L^*) > e_L(m_L^*)$. Under HS competition with perceived insensitive rival reactions the equilibrium price m_{HS}^* must accordingly be lower than m_L^*. However, once equilibrium m_{HS}^* is established, every firm will end with the same market area as before. Moreover, since HS equilibrium yields $m^* = m_{HS}^* = m$, the quantity of HS demand at the equilibrium price m_{HS}^* is seen via Equation

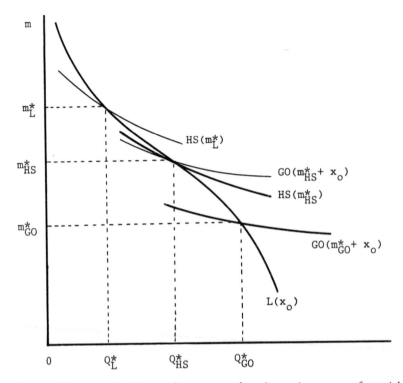

Figure 8.4. Perceived demand curves under alternative types of spatial competition.

(6) to be exactly equal to the Löschian demand quantity evaluated at the same price; that is, $Q_{HS}(m_{HS}^*) = Q_L(m_{HS}^*)$. In other words, the ex post quantity of HS (or any other) demand must always lie on the Löschian demand curve.

In sum, given the Löschian demand curve illustrated by curve $L(x_0)$ in Figure 8-4, the HS demand depends temporarily on the rival's mill price such as m_L^*, which, however, requires further adjustment until the equilibrium mill price m_{HS}^* is finally attained. In any case, every HS demand curve is flatter than the $L(x_0)$ curve (i.e., $e_{HS} > e_L$) at each intersection point because of market expansion (reduction) anticipated when the firm varies its own mill price below (above) its rivals' mill prices. However, the firm's market area remains unchanged regardless of the alternative types of spatial competition examined so far or the one that will be introduced.

The optimization problem for the HS competitor may be stated formally, using Equation (6), as

$$\text{Max}_m \; \Pi = (m - c)Q_{HS}$$

$$= 2(m - c)\left[\int_0^{x_0} f(m + tx)dx + \Phi(m^* - m)\right] \quad (7)$$

The solution for Equation (7) is given by

$$m\left(1 - \frac{1}{e_{HS}}\right) = c \quad \left(e_{HS} = -\frac{dQ_{HS}}{dm}\frac{m}{Q_{HS}}\right) \quad (8)$$

where e_{HS} is the elasticity of demand under HS competition.

Since $e_{HS} > e_L$, it follows that $m_{HS}{}^* < m_L{}^*$ in equilibrium. The related market areas for the firm, however, remain the same and invariant: $x_{HS}{}^* = x_L{}^* = X/2$.

V. The Greenhut-Ohta Model of Spatial Competition

Basically, the same flattening characteristics apply to the demand curve under the Greenhut-Ohta (henceforth GO) type of spatial competition [4]. It is assumed in this model that the firm regards neither its own market area nor its rival's mill price as fixed, treating them both as variable. The only datum is the firm's delivered price at a market boundary, as yet an undetermined market boundary. The firm does not even take into consideration its rival's exact location. Alternatively, only the perceived delivered price ceiling is given parametrically in the GO model of spatial competition. Consider this price ceiling p_0 at the point of market boundary x_0 under the HS type of spatial competition. Assuming that $m_{HS}{}^* + tx_0$ happens to be equal to this price ceiling p_0, consider in turn a price reduction below $m_{HS}{}^*$ subject to no constraints but the fixed delivered price ceiling p_0. Then, the market area expansion and related demand expansion *perceived* by the GO competitor would be even greater than that

expected under conditions of the HS type of spatial competition
discussed earlier.

That the GO demand becomes even flatter than the HS demand is
illustrated by Figure 8-4, being more generally defined by

$$Q_{GO} = 2\int_0^{x_0} f(m + tx)dx + 2\psi(m^* - m) \qquad (9)$$

where $\psi' > 0$, $\psi(0) = 0$ and $|\psi(x)| \geq |\Phi(x)|$ with the equality sign
being applicable when $x = 0$; that is, $\psi(0) = \Phi(0) = 0$. Elasticity
of the GO demand is therefore even higher than that of the HS
demand, with both elasticities evaluated at $m = m^* = m_{HS}^*$. The
equilibrium price subject to the GO type of competition accordingly
must be even lower than the equilibrium HS mill price, that is,
$m_{GO}^* < m_{HS}^*$, as illustrated in Figure 8-4.

The optimization problem for the GO competitor subject to Equation (9) is given by

$$\operatorname*{Max}_{m} \Pi = (m - c)Q_{GO}$$

$$= 2(m - c)\left[\int_0^{x_0} f(m + tx)dx + \psi(m^* - m)\right] \qquad (10)$$

The solution for (10) is

$$m\left(1 - \frac{1}{e_{GO}}\right) = c \qquad \left(e_{GO} = -\frac{dQ_{GO}}{dm}\frac{m}{Q_{GO}}\right) \qquad (11)$$

where e_{GO} is the elasticity of demand under GO competition, and
as we have seen earlier, $e_{GO} > e_{HS}$. It follows, ceteris paribus, that
$m_{GO}^* < m_{HS}^*$. Nevertheless, the equilibrium market areas under
the alternative types of competition remain the same: $x_{GO}^* = x_{HS}^* = X/2$.

VI. Concluding Remarks

Although the Hooverian problem of pricing given by Equation (1) seeks to optimize the entire spatial price schedule $p(x)$, three alternative models formulated respectively as Equations (4), (7), and (10) seek only to derive a unique FOB mill price m. The direct comparison of mill prices in equilibrium is therefore applicable to the latter three models. Our findings can be summarized as $m_{GO}{}^* < m_{HS}{}^* < m_L{}^*$.

Directly related to these price results in the short-run (i.e., fixed-location) equilibrium is the finding that the quantity of output produced (industry output as well as individual firm output) under Löschian competition is less than that under HS competition, which in turn is less than that under GO competition, as can be readily observed in Figure 8-4. This is an important result. Imposition of the price-ceiling type of spatial competition, which can be legislatively imposed if not voluntarily developed, brings about greater industry output than other types of spatial competition, *at least in the short run*.

It still is not possible to know, however, whether the same result applies to the long-run equilibrium state. This problem will be probed more deeply in Chapter 10. For the time being, it suffices to note that the Löschian type of competition yields a higher short-run profit than the HS type, whereas GO competition provides the lowest profit for the firm. This result readily follows from the fact that the short-run equilibrium average revenue for each of the three alternative types of competition is represented along the Löschian demand curve; that is, $L(x_0)$ in Figure 8-4. The profit-maximizing point on $L(x_0)$ can be identified, via equalization of its marginal curve with the marginal cost, as $(Q_L{}^*, m_L{}^*)$. Departure from this point along the curve $L(x_0)$, therefore, simply diminishes profit.

While GO competition poses the highest degree of spatial competition among the three models considered in terms of equilibrium mill price, the Hooverian competition, as we have seen, involves even more severe competition; the Hooverian spatial price schedule reveals a sharp kink beyond which point the CIF price starts declining in spite of the transport cost, which increases with distance! Moreover, the apparent dumping is provoked by rival sellers, who are perceived as perfect competitors.

Independent of these contrasting price and output effects of alternative types of spatial competition, the related equilibrium market areas for individual firms remain identical, that is, $x_H^* = x_L^* = x_{HS}^* = x_{GO}^* = X/2$. Behavioral variants lead to the constant–market-area result because the present model is predicated on short-run conditions of fixed location with neither entry nor exit and with a conjectural symmetry or "copy-cat" assumption in firm behavior (Assumption B).

References

[1]   Beckmann, M. *Location Theory*. New York: Random House, 1968.

[2]   Gannon, C. A. "Fundamental Properties of Löschian Spatial Demand." *Environment and Planning* 3 (1971): 283–306.

[3]   Greenhut, M. L., M. J. Hwang, and H. Ohta. "Observations on the Shape and Relevance of the Spatial Demand Function." *Econometrica* 43 (1975): 669–82.

[4]   Greenhut, M. L., and H. Ohta. "A Model of Market Areas under Discriminatory Pricing." *Western Economic Journal* 10 (1972): 402–13.

[5]   ———. *Theory of Spatial Pricing and Market Areas*. Durham, N.C.: Duke University Press, 1975.

[6]   Hoover, E. M. "Spatial Price Discrimination." *Review of Economic Studies* 4 (1937): 182–91.

[7]   Hotelling, H. "Stability in Competition." *Economic Journal* 39 (1929): 41–57.

[8]   Lösch, A. *The Economics of Location*. New Haven, Conn.: Yale University Press, 1954.

[9]   Ohta, H. "Spatial Competition, Concentration and Welfare." *Regional Science and Urban Economics* 10 (1980): 3–16.

[10] ———. "The Price Effects of Spatial Competition." *Review of Economic Studies* 48 (1981): 317–25.

[11] Smithies, A. "Optimum Location in Spatial Competition." *Journal of Political Economy* 49 (1941): 423–39.

[12] Stevens, B. H., and C. P. Rydell. "Spatial Demand Theory and Monopoly Policy." *Papers of the Regional Science Association* 17 (1966): 195–204.

9.

The Overlapping Market Areas Approach

I. Introduction

The foregoing models of pricing predict that spatially separated firms producing homogeneous goods tend to create local monopolies, so that each enjoys an exclusive market area. However, such prediction seems inconsistent with casual empiricism. In fact, we often observe overlapping market areas, shared by more than one firm. One possible interpretation of this may be made by apparent product differentiation: Lemon Motors and Friday Automobiles may be selling different cars. Even if they are effectively making sales to the same market point or area, we should certainly not consider this a case of overlapping markets. If not, can there be any genuine form of overlapping markets with spatially separated firms producing strictly homogeneous products?

The answer is yes. The familiar Cournot oligopoly model provides the basis for this phenomenon. The present chapter shows, in particular, how readily the Cournot model can be converted to acquire a spatial dimension. Section II presents the fundamental Cournot model of spatial competition along the lines of Greenhut and Ohta [3, chapter 8] and also Greenhut and Greenhut [2].[1] Section III in

---

[1]Greenhut and Greenhut [2] consider their model to be independent of or more general than others based on some restrictive assumptions such as the crucial Cournot assumption regarding conjectural variations. As a matter of fact, however, their model, too, requires the firms to behave as Cournot oligopolists, who conjecture other firm(s), that is, rival(s), to be perfectly inelastic in their supplies. Also, a recent paper by Brander and Krugman [1] on reciprocal dumping theory can be seen as a straightforward application of the Cournot model of spatial competition.

turn shows how the general spatial model of Cournot competition may be simplified to preserve an analytical continuity cum contrast with the previous chapter, by recapitulating the basic assumptions set forth at the beginning of Chapter 8. Section IV concludes the chapter by presenting some comparative static analysis of Cournot competition in economic space as a prelude to the Part IV applications.

II. The Cournot Model of Spatial Competition

Prior to the introduction of a simplified Cournot model of spatial competition for direct comparison with the models examined so far, the fullest generality of the version should be constructed. The general model of Cournot competition in economic space is based on the following assumptions:

> Assumption A. Producers of some homogeneous good, say, mineral water, are scattered over a landscape; henceforth a firm located at point i ($= 1, 2, \ldots m$) will be called *firm i*.
>
> Assumption B. Local markets or buying points are also scattered over the plane and indexed as j ($= 1, 2, \ldots n$).
>
> Assumption C. Firm i considers its rival firms' supplies to point j to be fixed, being perfectly inelastic: The firm is a Cournot competitor.
>
> Assumption D. The local market demand depends on the product price (CIF) alone.
>
> Assumption E. The freight rate per unit quantity applicable to the distance from the firm's site i to buying site j is given constant.

Pursuant to these assumptions the local demand at market point j may be defined as

$$q_j = f_j(p_j) \qquad (j = 1, 2, \ldots n) \tag{1}$$

where q_j is the quantity demanded at market point j as a function f_j of price p_j to prevail in market j. This quantity q_j is to be distinguished from q_i, which represents the quantity produced by firm i.

The quantity demanded q_j at market point j must in equilibrium equal the aggregate of all nonnegative quantities supplied to that point by m firms. Thus, we have

$$q_j = \sum_{i=1}^{m} q_{ij} \qquad (j = 1, 2, \ldots n) \qquad (2)$$

where q_{ij} is the quantity supplied by firm i to market point j.

It goes without saying that the quantity supplied q_{ij} by firm i to market point j is only part of the total quantity q_i produced and supplied by that firm. It follows that the q_{ij} must be aggregated over all market points $j = 1, 2, \ldots n$ to obtain the total supply quantity by firm i. Thus,

$$q_i = \sum_{j=1}^{n} q_{ij} \qquad (i = 1, 2, \ldots m) \qquad (3)$$

The firm's cost of production is given by

$$C_i = C_i(q_i) \qquad (i = 1, 2, \ldots m) \qquad (4)$$

where C_i stands for the total cost of production for firm i as a (monotonic) function of its output q_i. Together with costs of transportation the firm's total cost TC_i is accordingly defined as

$$TC_i = C_i(q_i) + \sum_{j=1}^{n} t_{ij} q_{ij} \qquad (i = 1, 2, \ldots m) \qquad (5)$$

where t_{ij} stands for the freight rate per unit of quantity.

Subject to these demand and cost conditions the firm's optimization problem is to find its quantity of shipment to each buying point j in order to maximize its profit Π_i. Thus,

$$\max_{q_{ij}} \Pi_i = \sum_{j=1}^{n} p_j q_{ij} - TC_i \qquad (i = 1, 2, \ldots m) \qquad (6)$$

where the first terms on the right-hand side represent the total revenue for firm i. The first order conditions for (6) are

$$\frac{\partial \Pi_i}{\partial q_{ij}} = p_j + q_{ij} \times \partial f^{-1}(q_j)/\partial q_j - c_i - t_{ij}$$

$$= p_j\left(1 - \frac{s_{ij}}{e_j}\right) - c_i - t_{ij} = 0$$

$$(i = 1, 2, \ldots m_j \geq m, j = 1, 2, \ldots n) \quad (7)$$

where e_j is the elasticity of demand at buying point j; s_{ij} is firm i's market share at buying point j defined as $s_{ij} = q_{ij}/q_j$; c_i is firm i's marginal cost of production defined as $c_i = dC_i/dq_i$, not $c_i = dC_i/dq_{ij}$; t_{ij}, the freight rate per unit quantity, is assumed as constant pursuant to Assumption E; and m_j is the number of firms making sales to market point j.

In Equation (7), only m_j firms may be able to make sales to market point j because of prohibitive transportation and/or production costs keeping $(m - m_j)$ firms out of that market point. If indeed the marginal cost applicable to market point j for a given firm exceeds the equilibrium price at that point, that is, $c_i + T_{ij} > p_j$, no sales will be made there by that firm.

The system of Equations (1) to (7) may be solved in Walrasian style for all relevant variables. There are n equations in (1), n in (2), m in (3), m in (4), m in (5), m in (6) and $\Sigma_{j=1}^{n}m_j$ in (7); that is, $2n + 4m + \Sigma_{j=1}^{n}m_j$ in total. We have n variables, respectively, for q_j and p_j; m variables, respectively, for C_i, q_i, Π_i, and TC_i; and $\Sigma_{j=1}^{n}m_j$ variables for q_{ij}, that is, the same total number as the number of equations.

Going beyond counting the number of equations and unknown variables, we can derive some operationally meaningful results by summing the equations of (7) over all m_j to obtain

$$m_j p_j + q_j \times \partial f^{-1}(q_j)/\partial q_j - \sum_{i=1}^{m_j} c_i - \sum_{i=1}^{m_j} t_{ij} = 0$$

$$(j = 1, 2, \ldots n) \quad (8)$$

Dividing both sides of (8) by m_j yields

$$p_j\left(1 - \frac{1}{m_j e_j}\right) - c - t_j = 0$$

$$p_j = \frac{c + t_j}{1 - (1/m_j e_j)} \qquad (j = 1, 2, \ldots n) \qquad (9)$$

where c and t_j stand, respectively, for the "average" marginal costs of production and transportation, that is, $c = (1/m_j)\Sigma_i\, c_i$ and $t_j = (1/m_j)\Sigma_i\, t_{ij}$.

It is important to note here that the unknown market share variable, s_{ij} in (7), cancels out in the process of aggregating costs and sales over the markets in obtaining (8) and (9).

Of greater importance perhaps is the revelation that although the individual Cournot firm's behavior is based on its own marginal costs, the market price p_j is determined ex post as it is via (9), on the basis of the "average magnitude" of mutually competing firms' "marginal costs." Cournot pricing, however, should not be confused with average cost pricing. The Cournot price in economic space depends only on individual competitors' marginal costs of both production and transportation *on the average*. It also depends on the number of firms competing in the market and the market elasticity of demand.

The magnitudes on the right-hand side of Equation (9), however, are not strictly constant, being instead endogenous variables to be determined simultaneously with p_j.[2] Operational practicality nevertheless may require them to be assumed or estimated as constant parameters.[3] Equation (9) may be considered in this limited sense as a testable formula for the regional market price p_j under the Cournot type of spatial competition. Equation (9) is testable in the sense that empirically observable regional prices p_j's can in principle be compared with the theoretical counterparts estimated or computed via (9).

[2] Although t_j's (or t_{ij}'s) are assumed to be constants in the present chapter, e_j's and c (or c_i's) are not. Even the number m_j of firms capable of making sales to market point j cannot be strictly independent of such variables as p_j and c *in equilibrium* beside exogenous variables such as t_j. However, being strictly independent from purely endogenous variables *before equilibrium*, the number m_j may nevertheless be classified as a parameter exogenous to the firm at least.

[3] Although e_j may readily be estimated as a function of p_j, estimation of c_i as a function of q_i, not q_j, will not help determine p_j. The determination of p_j directly by Equation (9) requires the marginal cost of production c_i to be assumed as a constant, which in turn requires the production function to be of constant returns to scale with respect to variable inputs.

Verifiable relationships uncovered by (9) include the following: The greater the number of firms selling to any market point j and/or the higher the elasticity of demand at that market point, the lower the equilibrium price p_j. (This relationship is only a spatially generalized version of Cournot's theorem on nonspatial prices and number of sellers.) More interesting is that the higher the individual firm's marginal costs of production and/or transportation *on the average* applicable to market point j, the higher will be the equilibrium price p_j at that point. It follows in particular that the more distant the firms' locations are from market point j, the higher the prices at that point.

The p_j being determined, the relationship between them and the firm's transportation costs t_{ij} is readily specified. Call this relationship the individual seller's *delivered price schedule* (*DPS*). For any given firm, its *DPS* may be evaluated by plotting the transportation costs t_{ij} from the plant site of the subject firm i to market point j against the relevant delivered prices p_j, as determined by (9). It is manifest that the *DPS* may not be in simple relationship to the firm's transportation costs t_{ij} because the delivered price p_j is a function of t_j, not directly of t_{ij}. For example, even if the firm's transportation cost increases, say from t_{ij} to $t_{i(j+1)}$, the delivered price p_j may remain constant or even decline, depending on the change (possibly zero or negative) taking place in average transportation cost t_j. FOB pricing is, therefore, in principle inapplicable to a spatially *competitive* equilibrium in our generalized Cournot model. Competition over economic space is a sufficient condition for price discrimination, and the delivered price at any one location may be said to be unaffected by the delivered price at any other location.

III. A Simplified Cournot Model
of Spatial Competition

The spatial version of Cournot competition uncovers the possibility of any given market point being served by more than one firm. The general Cournot model introduced earlier points to this particular relation by the number m_j (≥ 1) of firms capable of making sales to market point j. Whereas this number m_j is not a purely endogenous variable like p_j and q_j, it nevertheless is a variable to be determined simultaneously with *equilibrium* price p_j (cf. footnote 2). But how? The present section answers this question by a simple illustrative description of how Cournot competition can create overlapping market areas; that is, how m_j is determined. For purposes of direct comparison with the spatial models of Chapter 8, the general Cournot model can be simplified radically by recapitulating the basic assumptions of that chapter.

Assumptions of the present section are

Assumption A. The basic demand is identical and distributed uniformly along a linear (circular) market; that is, $f_j = f$ for all market points j's distributed discretely or $f_x = f$ for all x continuously along the line market.

Assumption B. The market is duopolized by two spatially separated but otherwise homogeneous sellers; that is, m_x or $m_j \leqslant 2$ and $c_i = c$ ($i = 1, 2$).

Assumption C. The marginal cost of transportation is a monotonic, say linear, function of distance; that is, $t_{1x} = tx$ and $t_{2x} = t(X - x)$, where x (in place of j) represents the distance variable from the site of firm 1 whereas X stands for the fixed distance between firm 1 and firm 2.

With these simplifying assumptions Equation (9) reappears as

$$p_x = \frac{c + (1/m_x)\sum_{i=1}^{m_x} t_{ix}}{1 - 1/m_x e_x} \qquad (m_x = 1 \text{ or } 2, \ X \geqslant x \geqslant 0) \qquad (10)$$

where p_x is the equilibrium price that would prevail at market point x, c is marginal cost of production; t_{ix} is marginal cost of transportation (from firm i to market point x), e_x is market elasticity of demand at x, and, most important, m_x is the number of firms making sales at market point x.

It can be seen readily from (10) that the market price p_x is determined uniquely in terms of the given constants c, t_{ix}, and X, provided that m_x is known either as 1 or 2. (Although e_x in (10) may not be a given parameter, it causes no problem in determination of p_x by (10) since e_x is a function of p_x.) The question then is how the firm number m_x is to be determined. To answer this question, suppose for a moment that $m_x = 2$ at all market points. Then Equation (10) can be reduced to

$$p_x = \frac{c + t[x + (X - x)]/2}{1 - 1/2e_x}$$

$$= \frac{c + tX/2}{1 - 1/2e_x} \tag{11}$$

while each duopolist can make sales to any market point x at a uniform price p_x determined by (11), it is possible that the marginal costs of production *plus* transportation exceed this price, if the firm intends to make sales beyond a certain market boundary point, x_1 for firm 1 and x_2 for firm 2. Insofar as each firm refrains from making sales beyond these market boundary points x_1 and x_2, Equation (11) must be constrained to the domain such that $x_1 > x > x_2$. Thus,

$$p_x = \frac{c + tX/2}{1 - 1/2e_x} \qquad (x_1 > x > x_2) \tag{12}$$

where x_1 and x_2 are given, respectively, by

$$\frac{c + tX/2}{1 - 1/2e_x} = c + tx_1 \tag{13}$$

$$\frac{c + tX/2}{1 - 1/2e_x} = c + t(X - x_2) \tag{14}$$

where e_x is given by (11) in terms of fixed parameters such as c, t, and x.

Equation (12) defines a flat market equilibrium price under conditions of Cournot duopoly over the market domain $x_1 > x > x_2$ shared by the two firms and illustrated by the flat part $p_{x_2}p_{x_1}$ of the Cournot *DPS* of Figure 9-1, based on Equation (15). The market boundary point for firm 1 located at 0 is given at x_1 on the line market *OX*, while the market boundary point for firm 2 located at X is given by x_2. At these boundary points, each single firm's marginal costs of production c and of transportation tx (or $t(X - x)$) cross from below

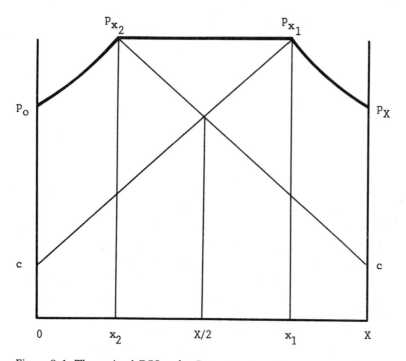

Figure 9.1. The optimal *DPS* under Cournot competition.

the constant *DPS* generated by the two firms.[4] It follows that the
market area beyond firm 1's boundary point x_1, that is, x_1X, and the
market area beyond firm 2's boundary x_2, that is, $0x_2$, are to be
served, respectively, by firm 2 alone and firm 1 alone.

The *DPS* over these virtually monopolized market areas, along
with the overlapping market area of (12), accordingly must be
given by[5]

[4]The market boundary points x_1 and x_2 defined by Equations (13) and (14) may
therefore be defined alternatively:

$$\frac{c + t(X - x_1)}{1 - 1/e_x} = c + tx_1$$

$$\frac{c + tx_2}{1 - 1/e_x} = c + t(X - x_2)$$

[5]The (optimal) *DPS* over a monopolized market area has already been derived in Part
I of the book and is also readily obtainable in this chapter from Equation (9) by letting
$m_j = 1$ (or in the present context $m_x = 1$ for the relevant x.)

$$p_x = \frac{c + tx}{1 - 1/e_x} \qquad (x_2 \geqslant x \geqslant 0)$$

$$= \frac{c + tX/2}{1 - 1/2e_x} \qquad (x_1 > x > x_2)$$

$$= \frac{c + t(X - x)}{1 - 1/e_x} \qquad (X \geqslant x \geqslant x_1) \tag{15}$$

where x_1 and x_2 are defined, respectively, by Equations (13) and (14).

The first line of (15) defines the optimal price schedule $p_0 p_{x_2}$ by firm 1 located at 0, while the third (last) line defines firm 2's optimal price schedule $p_x p_{x_1}$ under symmetric conditions of virtual monopoly. These two schedules must be monotonically increasing functions of distance from the firm site, as illustrated by Figure 9-1. Moreover, the maximum price levels p_{x_1} and p_{x_2} on these price schedules can both be shown to be equal to $(c + tX/2)/(1 - 1/2e_x)$, that is, the constant duopoly price given by $p_{x_2} p_{x_1}$, which in turn is exactly equal to the rival's marginal costs of production plus transportation evaluated at x_1 and x_2, respectively. This means that the monopoly and duopoly prices are equal at the boundary points x_1 and x_2. This should cause no interpretative confusion since Cournot duopoly approaches virtual monopoly as firm 1's (or firm 2's) market share approaches zero at market point x_1 (or x_2) because of prohibitive transportation costs. The Cournot *DPS* as simplified and illustrated most appropriately may be compared with the Hooverian *DPS* introduced at the beginning of Chapter 8. Unlike other models of spatial competition, these two models are not subject to FOB mill pricing. Firms in these models instead are allowed to practice price discrimination freely if desired. However, the two models are distinct from each other in their behavioral assumptions. While Hooverian competitors accept their rivals' marginal costs of production and transportation as their own market prices, Cournot firms consider the quantity of rivals' supply as constant at any given market point. The resultant *DPS*s may be compared readily in Figure 9-2 as Cournot's $p_0 p_{x_2} p_{x_1} p_x$ versus Hoover's $p_0 p_{x_2} p_{x/2} p_{x_1} p_x$. Clearly, Hooverian competitors perceive increasingly intense competition in price, price cuts in effect, over

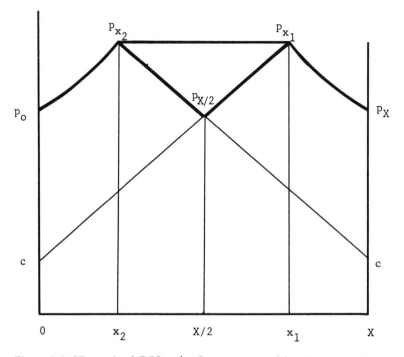

Figure 9.2. The optimal DPS under Cournot competition ($p_0 p_{x_2} p_{x_1} p_X$) versus Hooverian competition ($p_0 p_{x_2} p_{X/2} p_{x_1} p_X$).

the market domain $x_2 x_1$ where Cournot duopolists end up with a milder form of uniform pricing.

A flat DPS derivable from Cournot competition does not require that competing firms be homogeneous in terms of production costs. Even if marginal production costs, c_i's, are unequal, their *average* magnitude remains constant as long as c_i's are assumed as constants. Recall that what counts in Cournot pricing are the *average* marginal costs. However, this does not imply that the Cournot DPS is always flat over an overlapped market area. For, even if the *average* of marginal production costs remains constant, being independent of market points x regardless of the number or efficiency of firms, the *average* marginal costs of transportation cannot remain constant unless equal numbers of firms from competing locations are selling in the area of overlap. Thus, for example, if a third firm enters the duopolized industry and locates its plant at market point X alongside firm 2, the *DPS* formula (15) must be replaced by

$$p_x = \frac{c + tx}{1 - 1/e_x} \qquad (x_2 \geq x \geq 0)$$

$$= \frac{c + [tx + 2t(X - x)]/3}{1 - 1/2e_x} \qquad (x_1 > x > x_2)$$

$$= \frac{c + t(X - x)}{1 - 1/2e_x} \qquad (X \geq x \geq x_1) \tag{16}$$

where x_1 and x_2 are defined by

$$\frac{c + [tx + 2t(X - x)]/3}{1 - 1/3e_x} = c + tx_1 \tag{17}$$

$$\frac{c + [tx + 2t(X - x)]/3}{1 - 1/3e_x} = c + t(X - x_2) \tag{18}$$

or alternatively by

$$\frac{c + t(X - x_1)}{1 - 1/2e_x} = c + tx_1 \tag{17'}$$

$$\frac{c + tx_2}{1 - 1/e_x} = c + tx_2 \tag{18'}$$

The Cournot *DPS* after a new entry can be illustrated by Figure 9-3. Several related observations are in order.

First, an immediate impact of a new entry at market point x upon the monopoly price line $p_X p_{x_1}$ is to pull it down. Its slope, however, may or may not get steeper after entry.[6]

---

[6]Cf. McBride [4] and also Greenhut and Greenhut [2]. Their result requires a specific form of the basic demand that they, in effect, assume. To better appreciate this, differentiate the third line of (16) with respect to x to obtain

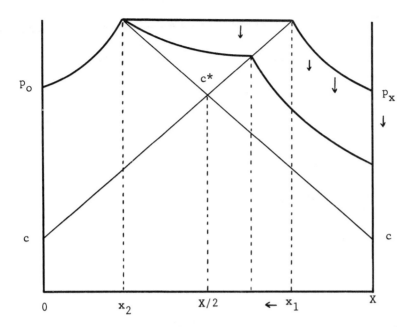

Figure 9.3. Impact of Cournot entry on *DPS* and the market overlap.

Second, a related impact is to reduce the market overlap x_2x_1 because the market boundary point x_1 moves left while boundary point x_2 remains unaltered. [Cf. (13)' and (14)' in footnote 4 with (17)' and (18)'.] The market overlap is now shared by three firms, one from 0 and two from X. Although the market area Xx_1 is also served now by two firms, it should not properly be called a market overlap since the two firms are located at the same site.

Third, the *DPS* over the overlap x_2x_1 is a curve declining mono-

$$\frac{dp_x}{dx} = -\frac{t}{1 - [(1 - \varepsilon)/2e_x]} , \qquad \varepsilon = \frac{de_x}{dp_x} \frac{p_x}{e_x}$$

where numeral 2 in front of e_x stands for the number of firms located at X. As this numeral increases with entry, the slope $|dp_x/dx|$ also increases *only* if $\varepsilon > 1$; otherwise, if $\varepsilon < 1$, the slope declines. In any case, the Cournot *DPS* approaches FOB mill pricing under conditions of unlimited entry at the same point as $\lim_{m \to \infty} (1 - \varepsilon)/me_x = 0$ and dp_x/dx approaches $-t$ accordingly.

tonically to the right. However, it may *not* necessarily be a straight line as commonly believed.[7] Thus, for example, while an algebraic form of the basic demand defined by (19) certainly yields a straight *DPS* line over the overlap x_2x_1, a seemingly equivalent class of demands specified by (20) yields a nonlinear one.

$$p_x = a - bq_x^\alpha \qquad (a, b, \alpha > 0) \tag{19}$$

$$q_x = a - bp_x^\alpha \qquad (a, b, \alpha > 0) \tag{20}$$

For a proof, differentiate (16) over the domain x_2x_1 with respect to x to obtain

$$\frac{dp_x}{dx} = -\frac{t}{3 - [(1 - \varepsilon)/e_x]} \qquad \left(\varepsilon = \frac{de_x}{dp_x} \frac{p_x}{e_x} \right) \tag{21}$$

In light of Equation (21) the slope of the Cournot *DPS* in the overlap x_2x_1 is seen to be negative.[8] The slope is also constant, however, only if $(1 - \varepsilon)/e_x$ is constant. The required constancy obtains if $\varepsilon = 1$.[9] It also obtains when the basic demand takes the form of (19) not (20).

To prove the last sentence initially derive e_x and ε from (19) to compute $(1 - \varepsilon)/e_x$ in (21). Thus,

$$e_x = \frac{p_x}{\alpha(a - p_x)}$$

$$\varepsilon = 1 + \alpha e_x$$

$$\therefore (1 - \varepsilon)/e_x = -\alpha \tag{22}$$

---

[7] E.g., McBride [4, p. 1016] states that "due to the assumption of Cournot behavior, the price line in the overlap is linear." In fact, however, the linearity of the Cournot *DPS* derives only when the number of competitors at two separate plant sites are equal. Otherwise, the Cournot *DPS* need not be linear as shown in the text.

[8] Note that $dp_x/dx < 0$ insofar as $\varepsilon > 1 - e_x$, which, to recall Chapter 3, is the condition required for market stability.

[9] The basic demand in this case takes the form of neither Equation (19) nor (20). Instead, it takes a negative exponential form in price: $q_x = \exp(\lambda p_x)$, λ = negative constant.

Substituting (22) in (21) yields $dq_x/dx = -t/(3 + \alpha)$, which is constant. However, from (20) we obtain

$$e_x = \frac{p_x^\alpha}{(a/b - p_x^\alpha)/\alpha}$$

$$\varepsilon = \frac{a/b}{(a/b - p_x^\alpha)/\alpha}$$

$$\therefore (1 - \varepsilon)/e_x = \frac{(a/b)(1 - \alpha)/p_x^\alpha - 1}{\alpha} \tag{23}$$

Substituting (23) in (21) yields

$$\frac{dp_x}{dx} = -\frac{t}{3 + 1/\alpha - (a/b)(1 - \alpha)/\alpha p_x^\alpha} \tag{24}$$

Equation (24) is a function of p_x, which in turn is a negative function of x. It therefore follows that

$$\frac{d^2 p_x}{dx^2} \geqq 0 \qquad \text{according as } \alpha \geqq 1 \tag{25}$$

In light of (25), it can be concluded that the form of the Cournot DPS in the market overlap tends to be convex (concave) if the basic demand is concave (convex) in the form of (20). Exceptions to this general rule include cases in which the basic demand is linear, that is, $\alpha = 1$, or defined by (19), or when firms from competing locations (0 and X) are equal in number. In all these exceptional cases the Cournot DPS becomes strictly linear.

IV. Concluding Remarks

The present chapter presented the fundamental formulas for spatial pricing under competitive conditions of the Cournot type. The most general formula is Equation (9), which defines local market prices in terms of marginal costs of production and transportation applicable to all relevant firms, the number of the firms, and the elasticity of demand at the local market in which they compete. We have proposed that Equation (9), along with the underlying Cournot hypothesis, is empirically testable, at least in principle. One way to do this would involve collecting actual or estimated data on transportation and production costs of similar products, such as compact cars, produced by a given number of competing firms and the elasticity of demand for the product estimated at a specified local market area. Formula (9) then can be used to compute the predicted Cournot price as against the actual price to prevail in that locality. An observed discrepancy, if any, between the two estimates would serve as one test of the Cournot theory of spatial competition.

Another test might be based on a comparative static analysis of Equation (9). The test would involve checking the sign of partial derivatives such as $\partial p_j / \partial m_j$ with the estimated coefficients based on an econometric model.

For a visual interpretation of Equation (9), a particular simplification of the assumption set is needed. For the sake of comparison with the previous models examined in Chapter 8, the same set of assumptions also have been readopted to convert Equation (9) to Equation (15). Equation (15) illustrates how the spatial delivered price schedule DPS would appear under locational and other technical conditions similar to those assumed in Chapter 8. While detailed welfare analyses are reserved for later chapters, we have shown that spatial competition tends to be more severe under the Hooverian rule of the game than it is under the Cournot model, as illustrated by Figure 9-2.

Finally, we also have seen that the Cournot DPS is required to be neither flat nor linear in the market overlap. As shown by Equation (16) and illustrated by Figure 9-3, asymmetric entry at firm sites 0 and/or X helps create a downward-shifted DPS, which may be concave or convex according to whether the basic demand is assumed to be convex or concave in the form of (20). As entry increases, the market overlap decreases and the Cournot DPS approaches FOB mill pricing and the MC line; that is, cc^*c in Figure 9-3.

References

[1] Brander, J., and P. Krugman. "A 'Reciprocal Dumping' Model of International Trade." *Journal of International Economics* 15 (1983): 313–21.

[2] Greenhut, J., and M. L. Greenhut. "Spatial Price Discrimination, Competition and Locational Effects." *Economica* 42 (1975): 401–409.

[3] Greenhut, M. L., and H. Ohta. *Theory of Spatial Pricing and Market Areas.* Durham, N.C.: Duke University Press, 1975.

[4] McBride, M. E. "Spatial Competition and Vertical Integration: Cement and Concrete Revisited." *American Economic Review* 73 (1983): 1011–22.

10.

The Price and Market Area Effects of Spatial Competition

I. Introduction

Chapter 8 presented alternative models of spatial competition in their crudest possible forms. This chapter extends selected elements of Chapter 8 and poses questions of what happens to mill prices, outputs, market areas, consumer surpluses, and so on, under well-defined alternative conditions. More exactly, the objective of this chapter is to examine the short-run and long-run welfare implications of alternative types of spatial competition and related spatial concentration vis-à-vis dispersion along the lines of previous works by Ohta [19; 20]. In particular, this chapter, in a sense, aims at a disproving of the popular "number-size" myth, which maintains that a greater number of smaller-sized firms would yield lower prices and approximate more ideally the conditions of perfect competition and accordingly yield greater consumer welfare to the society. [1]

Related to this is the question of evaluating the welfare implications of localization vis-à-vis dispersion of firms subject to alternative types of spatial competition. This chapter shows in particular that certain forms of spatial competition, which require localization of

---

[1] T. R. Saving [21] has shown that the parametric treatment of market price, that is, the basic conditions for perfect competition, does not require innumerable atomistic firms. Moreover, as correctly stressed by C. E. Ferguson [6], one might observe an even greater competitive nature under imperfect competition compared with virtually no competition among firms under perfect competition. Also see Greenhut [9; 10], where he explores the "isomorphic nature" of perfect competition and imperfect competition. See also Dewey [5], Demsetz [4], Ohta [17; 18], and Greenhut and Ohta [13; 14] for attacks on the so-called excess capacity theorem and the myth of atomism.

fewer firms, each occupying greater market areas, could be considered
more desirable than other forms of competition, which require dispersion of more firms with smaller market areas that they control
individually.

Section II will posit the departure point assumptions to set forth
some fundamental theorems on the spatial demand functions. These
fundamental theorems are then used in Section III to refine and
generalize the Chapter 8 analysis of spatial competition. The focal
point of the analysis is the exact meaning and implications of alternative types of competition under conditions of short-run fixed location. Section IV briefly summarizes conditions under which spatial
competition raises or lowers the firm's equilibrium mill price. Section
V finally relaxes the assumed conditions of fixed firm locations to
compare the states of alternative long-run zero-profit competitive
equilibrium with an emphasis on their welfare implications. Section
VI concludes the chapter.

II. Fundamental Theorems on Spatial
Demand Function

The departure point for our investigations is based on the following
fundamental assumptions.

Assumption A. A representative firm is located at the center of a
line (or plane) market.

Assumption B. The firm is separated spatially from rival firms.[2]

Assumption C. Buyers (or local markets) are distributed evenly
along the line (or over the plane) market.

Assumption D. The local (basic) demand functions are identical.

Assumption E. The freight rate per unit of distance is constant.

A. The Fundamental Theorem on Spatial Monopoly

Pursuant to Assumptions A and B, consider a linearly extended
spatial market. Distributed along the line market pursuant to As-

---

[2] Depending on how far the firms are separated from one another, the representative
firm may be defined as either spatial monopolist or spatial competitor [11].

sumptions C and D, in turn, are the demand density functions of the general form:

$$q = f(m + tx) \qquad f' < 0 \tag{1}$$

where q stands for the demand density,[3] m for mill price of a firm located at an arbitrary point of the line market, and tx for the unit freight cost applicable to buyers who are x distance units from the firm site, where the freight rate is t dollars *per unit of distance.*

Integrating q with respect to x yields the free (monopoly) spatial demand Q_M:

$$Q = 2 \int_0^{x_{0m}} f(m + tx)dx$$

$$= 2 \int_m^{f^{-1}(0)} f(tx)d(tx) \qquad \left(x_{0m} = \frac{f^{-1}(0) - m}{t} \right) \tag{2}$$

where the multiplier 2 relates to the number of the market areas linearly extended in opposite directions from the firm site:[4] The adjective *free* refers to the absence of spatial competition; x_{0m} is the boundary distance from the firm given m.

Elasticity of the free spatial demand e_F is now generally specifiable via (2) as

$$e_F = -\frac{dQ}{dm}\frac{m}{Q} = \frac{f(m)m}{\displaystyle\int_m^{f^{-1}(0)} f(tx)d(tx)} \tag{3}$$

---

[3] The demand "density" q, defined earlier as a function of x, is distinct from "demand" as an integrated q with respect to x. However, following the usual convention, the term *demand* will be used interchangeably to represent the demand "density" as well.

[4] Without loss of generality, the present multiplier can be replaced by a more general integer number n as in [11]. Note, however, that a large number n does not imply uniform distribution of buyers over a plane, nor does it require linear dispersion of buyers. However, a uniform distribution of buyers over a plane can be treated analytically as a nonuniform (monotonically increasing) distribution of buyers along a linear market space.

In contrast, elasticity of the basic (nonspatial) demand function e_B is given via (1) as

$$e_B = -\frac{dq}{dm}\frac{m}{q} = \frac{f(m)m}{\alpha f(m)} \qquad [\alpha = f(m)/f'(m)] \qquad (4)$$

where elasticity is measured at the mill price m with no freight cost added.

A fully general and yet simple diagrammatic representation and comparison of the elasticity formulas (3) and (4) is available in Figure 10-1. Thus, for any given mill price m, the numerator of (3) can be represented by the rectangular area S in Figure 10-1(a), whereas the denominator of (3) is equal to the area under the basic demand curve $f(tx)$ over the domain m to the price intercept $f^{-1}(0)$, whose area is represented by the S' of Figure 10-1(a).

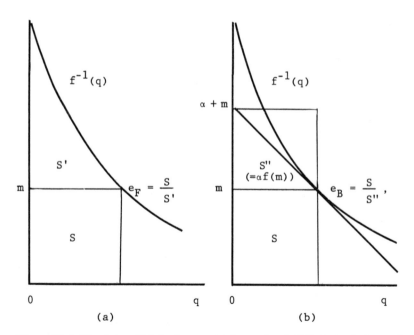

Figure 10.1. Elasticity of (a) the free spatial demand and of (b) the basic demand (Source: Adapted from Ohta [19, p. 5]).

For a diagrammatic representation of e_F in (4), note initially that the numerator of this formula is exactly the same as that in (3). Observe in turn the straight auxiliary line tangent to the basic demand curve at the point where elasticity is measured. This straight line determines the vertical length of $\alpha + m$ in Figure 10-1(b), which in turn determines the rectangular area $S'' = \alpha f(m)$, that is, the denominator of (4). It can be observed from the previous mathematical (as well as diagrammatic) specifications that an elasticity of spatial demand tends to be greater than the elasticity of the basic nonspatial demand when the demand curve $f^{-1}(q)$ is relatively less convex to the origin. Indeed, as the basic demand function becomes less convex, linear, or concave to the origin, the area S' becomes increasingly smaller relative to the area S'' with the result $e_F > e_B$.

If, on the other hand, the basic demand function is relatively more convex, it follows that $S' > S''$ and $e_F < e_B$.

It is to be carefully noted that the term *convex* in the present context is much broader and less restrictive than that in conventional usage. In particular, the demand curve is designated here as relatively more convex if (and only if) $S' > S''$ or $S'/S'' > 1$; conversely, it is relatively less convex if $S'/S'' < 1$. The basic demand curve is thus not even required to be consistently convex (in the ordinary sense) in order for it to be "relatively more convex" at the point of elasticity measurement; it could be partly linear or even concave, if the remaining part is sufficiently convex.[5] Thus, the following theorem is established, along with Definition I.

Definition I. The basic demand curve is relatively more (or less) convex if $S' > S''$ (or $S' < S''$), where $S' = \int_m^{f^{-1}(0)} f(tx)d(tx)$, $S'' = f(m)^2/f'(m)$.

Theorem I. The elasticity of free spatial demand e_F is lesser (or greater) than the elasticity of the basic demand e_B if and only if the basic demand curve is relatively more (or less) convex.

In light of Theorem I, the basic demand curve used by Greenhut, Hwang, and Ohta [11] can be seen as *a* member of the class of functions that are relatively less convex and therefore with the prop-

---

[5] Our present concept of "relative convexity" thus is more general or less restrictive than similar concepts proposed by Benson [2], Greenhut et al. [10], and so on; in particular, the present definition of relative convexity does not even require a particular benchmark form of the function, that is, "a negative exponential function" proposed by those other writers.

erty $e_F > e_B$. It is under this class of demand curves that a well-known "paradox of space" can be derived.[6] Otherwise, the free spatial demand is required to be less elastic than the basic demand; that is, $e_F < e_B$, thus involving no paradox of space.

B. The Fundamental Theorem on Spatial Competition

The fundamental theorem on the spatial demand function is based upon conditions of spatial monopoly. Theorem I, however, is of crucial importance to the analysis of spatial competition. In fact, it serves as the basis for the fundamental theorem that will be set forth regarding spatial competition of a particular type, à la Lösch. Recall from Chapter 6 that the Löschian demand is defined as taking place when all firms treat their market areas as exogenously given, and this condition in turn stems from the hypersensitive reactions of rival prices to the (representative) firm's price change.

Inasmuch as the exogenous treatment of the firm's market areas constitutes the characteristic feature of Löschian competition, the spatial market demand Q_L for the firm under Löschian competition may be given by

$$Q_L = \frac{2}{t} \int_0^{x_{0L}} f(m + tx)d(tx) \tag{5}$$

where x_{0L} is an exogenously fixed distance from the firm. The elasticity of Löschian market demand accordingly is

$$e_L = -\frac{dQ_L}{dm}\frac{m}{Q_L} = \frac{m[f(m) - f(m + tx_0)]}{\int_0^{x_{0L}} f(m + tx)d(tx)} = \frac{A}{B} \tag{6}$$

---

[6]When $e_F > e_B$, spatial separation of firms, which supposedly creates spatial monopoly, nevertheless adds, at the same moment, to the degree of competition as measured by the elasticity of demand. Such a condition is referred to as a *paradox of spatial monopoly* by Stevens and Rydell [23]. It warrants emphasis that a Siamese twin paradox is readily derivable from this condition, that is, what may be called a *paradox of spatial competition*, provided that the type of competition is of Löschian order requiring deprivation of the most elastic part of spatial demands. This will be discussed more fully in the text in connection with Theorem II.

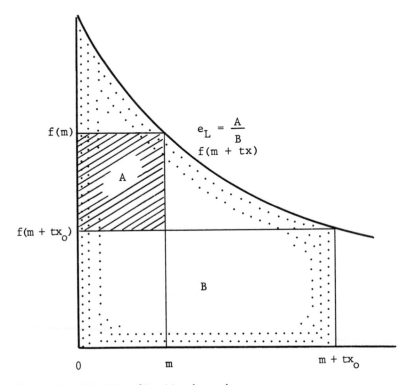

Figure 10.2. Elasticity of Löschian demand e_L.

where A and B represent, respectively, the shaded rectangular area and the dotted area below $f(m + tx)$ in Figure 10-2. The formula clearly indicates that e_L tends to increase as x_{0L} decreases, only if the basic demand f is sufficiently convex to the origin. A sufficiently convex demand is illustrated in Figure 10-2, where area B tends to be reduced more substantially than rectangular area A when x_{0L} is diminished.

   It is important to note, however, that a greater (or lesser) elasticity of free spatial demand compared with the basic demand does not require ipso facto those shrinking local demands $f(m + tx)$ to become monotonically more (or less) elastic as x increases. However, this requirement does hold if the basic demand curve is *well behaved* according to Definition II.

Definition II. The basic demand is well behaved if the elasticity of the individual or local demand e_x (as equal to $-f'(m + tx)m/q$) is a monotone function of x.

It now is feasible to establish the following theorem with the aid of Definition II and two lemmas.

Theorem II. If the well-behaved basic demand is relatively less (more) convex, then Löschian competition results in the FOB mill price of the firm being higher (lower) than the spatial monopoly price.

Lemma 1. If the basic demand is relatively less (more) convex, and if in addition it is well behaved, then the elasticity of the spatial individual or local demand is a monotonically increasing (decreasing) function of x, namely, $\partial e_x/\partial x > 0$ ($\partial e_x/\partial x < 0$).

Lemma 2. If $f(m + tx)$ becomes more (less) elastic as x increases, then the spatial market demand under Löschian competition is less (more) elastic than the spatial market demand under monopoly but more (less) elastic than the basic demand: $\partial e_x/\partial x \gtrless 0$ implies $e_F \gtrless e_L \gtrless e_B$.

Lemma 1 readily follows from Theorem I. Recall in this connection that if the basic demand is relatively less convex ($S' < S''$), for example, then Q is more elastic than the basic demand f. Also recall that Q derives from aggregating the spatial individual demands, which shrink successively as x increases. Thus, if the aggregate of these shrinking demands is more elastic than f and if, pursuant to the assumed well-behavedness of f, e_x is a monotone function of x, then furthermore it additionally is required to be a monotonically *increasing* function of x.

Proof of Lemma 2 requires the observation that the Löschian demand derives from aggregating successively shrinking spatial demands, the least of which represents the demand at an exogenously given market boundary. The greater the competition, the smaller the market area, and the fewer the total number of these shrinking demands. It follows, therefore, that if these shrinking demands yield monotonically increasing elasticities, the greater competition, via a lesser number of them being aggregated, necessarily yields lesser elasticity of aggregate demand. However, if shrinking demands yield monotonically decreasing elasticities, greater competition must yield greater elasticity of aggregate demand. By the same argument, it follows that the lesser competition yields either greater or lesser elasticity of aggregate demand accordingly as the shrinking demands yield monotonically increasing or decreasing elasticities. In any case, the resultant elasticity value must remain between the two extreme elasticity values related to the basic demand and the aggregate of *all* shrinking demands.[7]

III. The Nature of Alternative Types of Spatial Competition

While Löschian competition requires the firm to consider its market area x_{OL} as an exogenous variable, an alternative type of competition à la Hotelling-Smithies (HS) requires the firm to consider its rivals' mill price to be an exogenous variable. An HS competitor accordingly visualizes a more elastic demand than the Löschian demand. Associated with this condition is an expected enlargement of the firm's market area beyond x_{OL} as a result of any arbitrary price cut below the rivals' mill price m^*. Recall from Chapter 8, the HS demand as perceived by the firm is given by

$$Q_{HS} = 2 \int_0^{x_{OL}} f(m + tx)dx + 2\phi(m^* - m) \qquad (7)$$

where ϕ is a function such that $\phi' > 0$ and $\phi(0) = 0$. The perceived elasticity of demand under HS competition is therefore given by

$$e_{HS} = e_L + \frac{2m\phi'}{Q} > e_L \qquad (Q = Q_L = Q_{HS}) \qquad (8)$$

Thus, the expected enlargement of the firm's market area beyond x_{OL} results in the perceived elasticity e_{HS} exceeding e_L. However, when

[7] This relationship requires the elasticity of the aggregate demand e derivable from two separate markets with elasticities of demand e_1 and e_2 to be characterized such that $e_1 \leqq e \leqq e_2$. This in fact is the case, since it can be easily shown that e is a weighted average of e_1 and e_2.

firm locations are fixed as they are in the short run, the ex post market area for an HS competitor is no larger than x_{0L}, the realized HS elasticity of demand correspondingly being no larger than e_L.

The market area under HS competition is the same as that under Löschian competition ex post, which does not, however, imply that equilibrium prices under the two alternative competitive conditions (subject to fixed locations) also are equal. They, in fact, are not! Since an HS firm is more optimistic in demand expectation than a Löschian firm [as in (7) an additional demand 2ϕ is always expected for any $m < m^*$] it follows that the equilibrium price is *always* lower under HS competition than under Löschian, even if the market areas under the alternative types of spatial competition end up the same.

While in Section I it was shown that Löschian demand is strictly more (or less) elastic than the free spatial demand, when the basic demand is relatively more (or less) convex, the same relations cannot be expected to hold between HS demand and the free spatial demand, even though the two alternative types of competition yield the same market areas ex post. The problem arises since elasticity tends to rise under HS competition even when the basic demand is relatively less convex. Theorem II may be used to conclude $e_L < e_F$ under the present conditions. Why is the same theorem inapplicable to the HS demand, which, like Löschian demand, is composed of only part, not all, of the shrinking spatial demands that are increasingly elastic? The fundamental reason is that HS demand, unlike Löschian demand, is subjected to a *change in the (perceived or actual) number of spatial markets served* as a result of price change. This extra change in demand (quantity) associated with a change in the market size makes e_{HS} more elastic than e_L and even more elastic than e_F. The result is the possibility that $e_{HS} > e_F$ even when $e_L < e_F$. However, the elasticity result is more likely to be "down" the less convex the basic demand is, and vice versa.

While the impact of spatial competition upon the elasticity of demand and equilibrium mill price is thus diverse and depends crucially on the form of the basic demand function, the price effects of GO (Greenhut-Ohta) competition are definitive. To see this, let us go back to Equation (3) or Figure 10-1(a), where e_F is defined. Remember that the GO type of competition imposes the price ceiling upon the basic demand curve $f^{-1}(q)$ and reduces the area under S' in the figure accordingly.[8] The immediate straightforward implication of GO competition, therefore, is to increase the elasticity of GO demand. In other words, $e_F < e_{GO}$ *regardless* of the shape of the basic demand curve.

IV. Impact of Alternative Types of Spatial Competition upon Mill Prices in the Short Run

Depending on the form of the basic demand and/or the type of spatial competition, it has been shown that the equilibrium mill price may be lowered, raised, or unchanged, albeit the GO competition always lowers mill price regardless of the form of demand. The results may be summarized by Table 10-1.

Thus, for example, if the form of the assumed basic demand function is relatively less convex, then the Löschian type of spatial competition would necessarily lower the elasticity of the spatial individual or regional demand function, and accordingly raise the equilibrium mill price of the firm, provided that the marginal cost of production remains constant as assumed. In contrast, under the same demand conditions, the GO type of spatial competition lowers the equilibrium mill price of the firm, the elasticity of spatial demand being unambiguously raised.

A note is warranted, however: the HS type of competition yields

---

[8] More accurately phrased, the GO entry raises the elasticity of demand e_{GO} regardless of the form of the basic demand function f. To see this, consider the definition of e_{GO}:

$$e_{GO} = -\frac{\partial Q_{GO}}{\partial m}\frac{m}{Q_{GO}}$$

$$Q_{GO} = \frac{2}{t}\int_0^{tx_0''=p_0-m} f(m+tx)d(tx) = \frac{2}{t}\int_m^{p_0} f(tx)d(tx)$$

where x_0'' is the GO market radius and p_0 is the firm's delivered price under GO competition. Since $\partial Q_{GO}/\partial m$ is $-(2/t)f(m)$, it follows: $e_{GO} = [2f(m)m]/(tQ_{GO})$. Any decline in p_0 as a result of additional entry with smaller x_0'' necessarily reduces Q_{GO} (upper part of S' in Figure 10-1 being taken away increasingly with lower p_0); the upshot is a rise in e_{GO}, namely, $\partial e_{GO}/\partial p_0 < 0$, regardless of the form of f.

Table 10-1. Impact of alternative types of spatial competition and forms of basic demand on mill price

Types of Competition	Forms of Basic Demand		
	$S' > S''$	$S' = S''$	$S' < S''$
Lösch	Down	No change	Up
HS	Down	Down	Depends
GO	Down	Down	Down

somewhat indefinite results under the same demand conditions. In particular, the price result has a greater tendency to be "up," the less convex the basic demand is, and vice versa. However, the elasticity of the HS demand tends to increase and price to decrease regardless of the demand convexity *if fixed costs are sufficiently low.*

To better appreciate this last proposition, consider an alternative specification of the HS demand that is equivalent to Equation (7):

$$Q_{HS} = 2 \int_0^{x'_{OL}} f(m + tx)dx \qquad (7)'$$

where x'_{OL} stands for the *variable* market boundary visualized (conjectured) by the HS competitors. Recall that under the present type of competition a one-dollar change (reduction) in mill price is considered to yield a half-dollar change (enlargement) in market area distance; that is, $\partial x'_{OL}/\partial m = -1/2$. Elasticity of demand is then given by

$$e_{HS} = \frac{-\left[\int_0^{x_{OL}} f_m(m + tx)dx - f(m + tx'_{OL})/2\right]m}{\int_0^{x_{OL}} f(m + tx)dx} \qquad (9)$$

where $x'_{OL} = x_{OL}$ in equilibrium, and therefore Equation (9) is rewritten as

$$e_{HS} = \frac{-m \int_0^{x_{OL}} f_m(m + tx)dx}{\int_0^{x_{OL}} f(m + tx)dx} + \frac{mf(m + tx'_{OL})/2}{\int_0^{x_{OL}} f(m + tx)dx}$$

$$= e_L + \frac{mf(m + tx'_{OL})}{2\int_0^{x_{OL}} f(m + tx)dx} \tag{9)'}$$

Observe now that as x_{OL} approaches 0, the denominator of the second term of the right-hand side vanishes, whereas the numerator does not. Thus, since e_L is nonnegative, e_{HS} must approach infinity as x_{OL} approaches zero as entry continues subject to HS competition. Thus, while slight entry may raise mill price as exemplified in the case of linear demand [2], further entry sooner or later will lower the mill price if fixed costs are sufficiently low to warrant sufficient entry.

V. The Welfare Effects of Spatial Competition in the Long Run

A. The Price and the "Number-Size" Effects of Spatial Competition

We may now relax our basic assumption of fixed firm locations to examine zero-profit equilibrium conditions brought about by entry of new firms and corresponding relocation of established firms. Relocation is required for homogeneous firms to be dispersed symmetrically over a homogeneous spatial market area at any stage of entry under any type of spatial competition.

Consider as a departure point short-run fixed location equilibrium under alternative competitive conditions illustrated in Figure 8-4, repeated here as Figure 10-3. For purposes of contrast, consider the Löschian and GO types of spatial competition. Associated with Löschian competition are the highest mill price, the lowest output, and the largest profit in the short-run equilibrium, whereas the opposite results apply to GO competition. Consequently, the former type of competition calls for greater entry than the latter. The long-run Löschian equilibrium therefore requires a greater number of firms

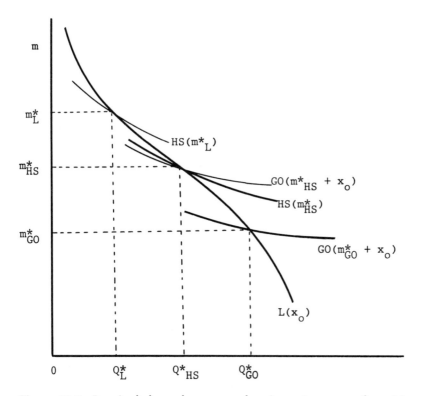

Figure 10.3. Perceived demand curves under alternative types of spatial competition.

each controlling a smaller market area, that is, a smaller market share, than the GO equilibrium. In other words, Löschian competition tends to yield the lowest industry concentration.[9]

Should we accordingly conclude that Löschian competition is the more desirable on account of this number-size (concentration) criterion for optimal social welfare? To answer this question, recall the

[9]Gannon [7] shows that firms selling *differentiated* products tend to cluster at the center of a bounded market. The clustering result, however, is unrelated to this model, which focuses its attention on optimal pricing for spatially separated firms selling homogeneous goods. The term *concentration* referred to earlier in the text therefore should not be confused with clustering in Gannon's sense. The concept in the text simply refers to the state of a market controlled by a limited number of firms with greater individual market shares (areas).

short-run price gap between m_L and m_{GO}, as in Figure 10-3. Consider now an additional entry subject to Löschian competition. The mill price will then be *raised* pursuant to Theorem II, if the basic demand is relatively less convex, as typically assumed in the literature (Capozza and Van Order [3]; Gannon [7], Takayama and Judge [24], etc.). On the contrary, GO entry always lowers mill price. The short-run price gap ($m_L > m_{GO}$) therefore will be enlarged, not diminished, in the long run. Löschian competition, which creates the least spatial concentration with smallest individual market areas could at the same instance yield the long-run price result that is not unconditionally desirable.

B. The Output Effects of Spatial Competition

The price increase associated with Löschian competition does not imply ipso facto a resultant decline in industry output because the former stems from reduced market areas for individual firms, with the highest part of their short-run delivered price schedules being chopped off by the delivered price schedule(s) of new entrant(s), such as a firm at point C in Figure 10-4. Assumed in this figure are two representative firms located at points A and B on a line market AB with two alternative delivered price schedules $m_L m_L$ and $m_{GO} m_{GO}$ under Löschian and GO competition. The long-run Löschian equilibrium with the new firm C is assumed to yield the third alternative delivered price schedule $m_L' m_L'$. It is also assumed that no other firm can enter the market under GO competition.

Note that initially price schedule $m_{GO} m_{GO}$ definitely creates greater market demand than does price schedule $m_L m_L$. It is not certain, however, whether the $m_{GO} m_{GO}$ schedule also creates greater market demand than does the long-run price schedule $m_L' m_L'$. However, some general propositions can be set forth.

Consider the basic demand function that is "lesser" convex. Then, it follows that the delivered price schedule over the entire market area would be pushed up more distinctively than otherwise, subject to Löschian competition, while the GO delivered price would be pushed down at each additional entry. For generally distinctive price gaps over the entire market to be created by the two alternative types of spatial competition, a sufficient number of firms are required to enter the market before the zero-profit equilibrium obtains.

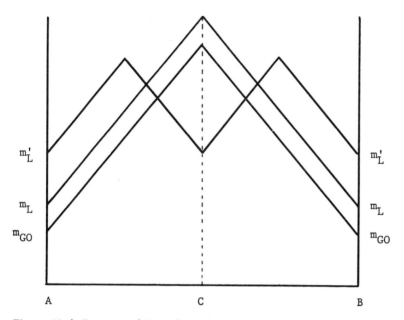

m'_L

m_L

m_{GO}

m'_L

m_L

m_{GO}

A   C   B

Figure 10.4. Long-run delivered price schedules under alternative types of competition.

Sufficient entry in turn requires the firms' production costs to be sufficiently low. In an extreme case, in which all production costs are zero, individual firms will end up with virtually zero market areas under the zero-profit equilibrium condition: [10]

$$mQ = m \int_0^{x_0} f(m + tx)dx = 0 \tag{10}$$

where x_0 is required to vanish unless m vanishes. Thus, insofar as mill price m monotonically decreases as entry increases under GO competition, whereas just the opposite relation applies to Löschian competition, the GO prices must be lower than Löschian prices throughout the entire market. This establishes the following theorem.

[10] Zero market areas with zero profit equilibrium do not always require all production costs to be zero. It is well known that the necessary conditions for spaceless equilibrium with nonnegative profit are that the unit cost of production be strictly a nondecreasing function of output and that it be covered by the product price at the mill.

Theorem III. There exists a (sufficiently low) level of production costs combined with the basic demand curve of the lesser convexity under which GO competition provides invariably lower prices (delivered as well as mill) than does Löschian competition in the long-run zero-profit equilibrium.

Directly related to this theorem is the definite output effect of GO competition. This is because the generally lower prices under GO competition would create greater demand than would generally higher prices under Löschian competition subject to the lesser convex demand conditions.

VI. Concluding Remarks

The conventional notion that the effect of greater competition is to lower industrial prices appears to have scarcely been challenged by economic theorists. The introduction of spatial elements into economic theory, however, led August Lösch to the innovative idea of "chain oligopoly," in which an increase in the number of spatially dispersed sellers, that is, greater competition for the product, could entail an increase, not decrease, in FOB mill prices. Models presented by Greenhut, Stevens and Rydell, and others have confirmed the Löschian perversity.

Generalizing the analysis along the lines of those spatial microeconomists, the present chapter has spelled out conditions under which greater competition may yield lower or higher prices. Alternative types of spatial competition in combination with alternative types of consumer preference patterns have been shown to yield divergent price results, including seemingly paradoxical, or somewhat puzzling, results, summarized in Table 10-1.

To appreciate the nature of the whole problem one may consider, say, a local steak house confronted by a nearby entrant threatening to take away some of its original customers. The question then is whether the restaurant should lower the price of steak. The answer provided in this chapter is positive only if the demand elasticities of loyal customers, those close to the old steak house, exceed the elasticities of converters now preferring the new one. For this reason the answer to the question depends not only on the form of consumer demand but also on the factors related to spatial competition. This follows because a change in the elasticity of demand after entry depends upon the number of loyal customers, which in turn depends on the rival reactions to the firm's own price policy. Under this framework of thought, this chapter has demonstrated ways and conditions under which a particular type of spatial competition among local firms may raise equilibrium price in the short run to be followed eventually, however, by a decline, as further entry increases competition.

Short-run welfare comparisons set forth in Section IV combined with the examination of the impact of spatial entry upon mill prices provided the setting for the long-run welfare comparisons in Section V. Related to the short-run welfare implications of spatial competition is the fact that the price ceiling GO type of competition creates the least profit for individual firms. It therefore restricts new entry and in effect requires the greatest concentration in terms of the number and size of the firms in the long run. However, pursuant to Theorem III, it should not be discouraged, insofar as it generates lowest prices and greatest industry output compared with other types of competition; the consumer surplus is maximized accordingly.

Being primarily concerned with consumer welfare, the question of social welfare has been disregarded, along with that of productive efficiency. However, insofar as the long-run alternative equilibria in the spatial models are found on a conventional U-shaped average cost curve, they constitute alternative Chamberlinean tangency points. And, insofar as Chamberlinean tangency equilibria are claimed to yield the so-called excess capacity, the price ceiling type of spatial competition may then be interpreted to create the least excess capacity and the greatest efficiency in production.

References

[1] Beckmann, M. *Location Theory*. New York: Random House, 1968.

[2] Benson, B. "Löschian Competition under Alternative Demand Conditions." *American Economic Review* 70 (1980): 1098–1105.

[3]   Capozza, D. R., and R. Van Order. "Pricing under Spatial Monopoly and Spatial Competition." *Econometrica* 45 (1977): 1329–38.

[4]   Demsetz, H. "The Nature of Equilibrium in Monopolistic Competition." *Journal of Political Economy* 67 (1959): 21–30.

[5]   Dewey, D. *The Theory of Imperfect Competition: A Radical Reconstruction.* New York: Columbia University Press, 1969.

[6]   Ferguson, C. E. *Microeconomic Theory.* 3d ed. Homewood, Ill.: Richard D. Irwin, Inc., 1972.

[7]   Gannon, C. A. "Fundamental Properties of Löschian Spatial Demand." *Environment and Planning* 3 (1971): 283–306.

[8]   ———. "Product Differentiation and Locational Competition in Spatial Markets." *International Economic Review* 18 (1977): 293–322.

[9]   Greenhut, M. L. *A Theory of the Firm in Economic Space.* Reprint. Austin, Tex.: Lone Star Publishers, 1974.

[10] Greenhut, M. L., C. S. Hung, G. Norman, and C. W. Smithson. "An Anomaly in the Service Industry: The Effect of Entry on Fees." *Economic Journal* 95 (1985): 169–77.

[11] Greenhut, M. L., M. J. Hwang, and H. Ohta. "Observations on the Shape and Relevance of the Spatial Demand Function." *Econometrica* 43 (1975): 669–82.

[12] Greenhut, M. L., and H. Ohta. *Theory of Spatial Pricing and Market Areas.* Durham, N.C.: Duke University Press, 1975.

[13] ———. "Related Market Conditions and Interindustrial Mergers." *American Economic Review* 66 (1976): 267–77.

[14] ———. "Vertical Integration of Successive Oligopolists." *American Economic Review* 69 (1979): 137–41.

[15] Hotelling, H. "Stability in Competition." *Economic Journal* 39 (1929): 41–57.

[16] Lösch, A. *The Economics of Location.* New Haven, Conn.: Yale University Press, 1954.

[17] Ohta, H. "On Efficiency of Production under Conditions of Imperfect Competition." *Southern Economic Journal* 43 (1976): 1124–35.

[18] ———. "On the Excess Capacity Controversy." *Economic Inquiry* 15 (1977): 153–65.

[19] ———. "Spatial Competition, Concentration and Welfare." *Regional Science and Urban Economics* 10 (1980): 3–16.

[20] ———. "The Price Effects of Spatial Competition." *Review of Economic Studies* 48 (1981): 317–25.

[21] Saving, T. R. "Concentration Ratios and the Degree of Monopoly." *International Economic Review* 11 (1970): 139–46.

[22] Smithies, A. "Optimum Location in Spatial Competition." *Journal of Political Economy* 49 (1941): 423–39.

[23] Stevens, B. H., and C. P. Rydell. "Spatial Demand Theory and Monopoly Policy." *Papers of the Regional Science Association* 17 (1966): 195–204.

[24] Takayama, T., and G. G. Judge. *Spatial and Temporal Price and Allocation Models.* Amsterdam: North-Holland Publishing, 1971.

11.

Agglomeration and Competition

I. Introduction

Spatial agglomeration is characterized by the concentration of firms and/or households in a relatively small area on a given landscape. Why they do as they do in this regard, and in general, may be best explained by the optimizing behavior of these economic agents. To the extent that they consider distance a cost rather than a benefit, their rational behavior is to minimize it by flocking together rather than "living in separation."

One knows, however, that the cost of distance has become increasingly negligible in the world of modern technology. In fact, the drastically reduced time and cost of commuting by automobiles and airplanes, along with instant telecommunication seems to make the entire globe a "small world." However, the very development of modern technology along these lines simply reflects the quest for minimizing or overcoming the significant cost of distances; it does not prove the *insignificance* of economic space.

One example would suffice to show how the cost of economic distance is rampant. As of summer 1981, a bank in Oregon quoted the exchange rate of a U.S. dollar into ¥400 (Japanese yen), whereas in New York as well as in Tokyo the rate was less than ¥230. The same liquid commodity—as liquid as "money" indeed—can hardly fetch different prices unless prospective buyers and sellers of the commodity are effectively separated from one another by regulations, ignorance, and most important, the "tyranny" of economic distances.

This chapter considers some related aspects of agglomeration in light of developments in location theory along the lines established by Moses [9] and Sakashita [12], which culminated in papers by Eswaran, Kanemoto, and Ryan [2] and Higano [6]. In this chapter, of particular interest and a point of departure is what Louveaux, Thisse, and Beguin [7] call the Hakimi Theorem or Higano's Exclusion Theorem [6]. The theorem refers to the locational problem in one dimension and claims that the cost-minimizing (or profit-maximizing) firms tend to locate at the market site or one of the input locations, an intermediate location thus being excluded.

Section II presents a very simple model of location under conditions of imperfect competition to reveal the nature of the Exclusion Theorem. However, this chapter goes beyond the locational problem of the single representative firm. Perhaps more important, its model is also designed to take into consideration a specific structure of production, namely successive monopoly and oligopoly à la Greenhut and Ohta [4; 5], for later analysis (in Section V) of related aspects of agglomeration.

The model set forth in Section II leads to a preliminary analysis in Section III of conditions under which a representative firm may move toward the market site or toward an input site. In particular, it is shown that although production at relatively small or large levels promotes location at an input site, an intermediate output level requires location at the market site. This result is shown to be related to the conventional hill-shaped "average" product curve with respect to variable input. As a more general dual statement, the same result derives from a U-shaped average cost curve.

Based on the preliminary analysis in Section III, Section IV probes deeper into the firm behavior under conditions of imperfect competition. The dynamic adjustment process toward three alternative equilibria will be sketched with the aid of a simple phase diagram. It is also suggested that the market site concentration of firms in related industries, as well as in a given industry, is the most likely result of market competition.

Section V considers two related factors of agglomeration, related in particular to aspects of industrial organization: division of labor and vertical merger or collusion of divided labor and firms. In fact, these seemingly polar industrial organizations can be shown to be not in conflict with each other but mutually advantageous in terms of productive efficiency. Moreover, they can be shown to interdependently promote spatial agglomeration of increased economic activities. Section VI concludes the chapter with a brief reference to the problem of externality related to agglomeration and the effect of property tax.

A final introductory note: For purposes of the present chapter we abstract from the "areal" market demand factors of location stressed by Greenhut [3], instead focusing our attention basically on "point" market demands.

II. The Basic Model

Assume the following:

Assumption A. A representative firm, firm i, is located at a site alongside a linearly extended route of transportation. The firm site is x_i miles away from an arbitrarily fixed point on the line.

Assumption B. Firm i located at x_i purchases its input from firm $i + 1$ located at x_{i+1}, produces its output at x_i, and sells it at the market site x_{i-1}, with initial conditions, without loss of generality, being such that $x_{i+1} > x_i > x_{i-1}$, and with all transactions being effected on the bases of FOB mill pricing. Assumption B suggests that firm i bears the transportation cost from x_{i+1} to x_i, and by sequence firm i in turn charges to firm $i - 1$ the transportation from x_i to x_{i-1}. In general, not only firm i at site x_i is thus related to firm $i + 1$ at t_{i+1} and firm $i - 1$ at x_{i-1} but also this sequence applies to all i's ($i = 1, 2, \ldots n$) *under conditions of n vertically related industries* or stages of production.

Assumption C. The firm is subject to a well-behaved production function with a hill-shaped average product curve.

Assumption D. Freight rates per unit per mile are constant for all inputs and outputs.

Assumption E. Firms as sellers are subject to Cournot competition. An alternative assumption of oligopolistic competition along with explicit behavioral assumption alters our model only slightly, but yields basically the same conclusions.

Assumption F. Firms as buyers of inputs, however, are perfect competitors possessing no monopsony power.

Assumption G. At each x_i there exist n_i homogeneous firms with homogeneous behavior.

Pursuant to these assumptions our basic model can be presented in terms of the system of equations as follows:

$$q_i = f_i(p_{i-1}), \qquad p_{i-1} = m_i + t_i|x_{i-1} - x_i| \tag{1}$$

$$q_{i+1} = \phi_i(q_i) \tag{2}$$

$$C_i = p_i q_{i+1}, \qquad p_i = m_{i+1} + t_{i+1}|x_i - x_{i+1}| \tag{3}$$

$$\Pi_i = m_i q_i - C_i = (f_i^{-1} - t_i|x_{i-1} - x_i|)q_i - p_i \phi_i \tag{4}$$

$$\frac{\partial \Pi_i}{\partial q_i} = f_i^{-1'} q_i + f_i^{-1} - p_i \phi_i' - t_i|x_{i-1} - x_i| \tag{5}$$

$$\frac{\partial \Pi_i}{\partial x_i} = t_{i+1} \phi_i(q_i) - t_i q_i, \qquad x_{i+1} > x_i > x_{i-1} \tag{6}$$

Explanation of each equation is in order.

Equation (1) stands for the "perceived" demand function f_i that firm i faces for its output q_i produced at site x_i; this f_i is given in terms of the CIF price p_{i-1} at market site x_{i-1} subject to Assumption E. While the function f_i can be derived directly from the market demand prevailing at x_{i-1} pursuant to Assumption E, the latter in turn is related to the final market demand at x_0 in our model of successive oligopolies. Thus, the "perceived" demand f_i itself can be derived from the final market demand at x_0.

For example, if we assume for simplicity a linear final market demand, $q = f(p)$, $f' = $ constant < 0, and normalized fixed coefficients of production (contra Assumption C) at all n stages of production, $q_{i+1}/q_i = 1$, $i = 1, 2, \ldots n$, then f_i or its inverse f_i^{-1} in our model can be specified as follows:

$$f_i^{-1} \equiv f^{-1}(q) + f^{-1\prime}q\left(\sum_{j=1}^{c_1}\frac{1}{n_j} + \sum_{j\neq k}^{c_2}\frac{1}{n_j n_k} + \ldots\right.$$

$$\left. + \sum_{j\neq k\neq l\ldots}^{c_{i-1}}\frac{1}{n_j n_k n_l \ldots n_{i-1}}\right) - \sum_{j=1}^{i-1} t_j|x_{j-1} - x_j| \quad (1)'$$

where $C_y = [y|(i-1)]$ stands for the number of combinations that y different n's can take out of $i-1$ different n's. It goes without saying that the price intercept value $f^{-1}(0)$ is required to be large enough for f_i to be nonnegative, namely, $f^{-1}(0) \geq \sum_{j=1}^{i-1} t_j|x_{j-1} - x_j|$.

Equation (2) specifies the input requirement function ϕ_i for firm i in terms of output q_i pursuant to Assumption B. Since Assumption C requires the "average" product curve to be strictly concave, the form of ϕ_i is neither concave nor convex; instead, it is a cubic nonnegative function with $\phi_i(0) = 0$ and $\phi_i' > 0$.

Equations (3) and (4) define respectively the cost of production and profit of firm i. Under the framework of Assumption B, the cost of production C_i is defined as $p_i q_{i+1}$, as equal to $p_i\phi_i(q_i)$, where p_i stands for the CIF input price for firm i, which is the FOB mill price m_{i+1} at input site x_{i+1} plus the unit transportation cost of input over distance $|x_i - x_{i+1}|$ with freight rate t_{i+1}. The production cost thus defined as subtracted from the total revenue in terms of mill price accruing from sales at market site x_{i-1}, in turn, defines the profit of firm i. This profit function thus reveals that only the transportation costs of the input are charged to the firm, the impact of freight on output being integrated into demand.

We are now in position to show the meaning of Equations (5) and (6). Equation (5) indicates the impact of a marginal change in output q_i upon profit Π_i. The first-order condition for profit maximization requires the result to be zero, which thus represents the familiar $MR = MC$ principle to yield the optimal output q_i^*. Note, however, that the subject solution depends on the firm's location x_i among other parameters underlying f_i besides x_{i-1}, x_{i+1}, m_{i+1}, t_i, and t_{i+1}. While these other parameters are exogenously given to firm i (pursuant to Assumptions B, D, and F), its own locational decision need not be equally fixed. Given optimal output q_i^*, optimal location x_i^* can be obtained via the marginal adjustment under Equation (6). That equation shows the impact of a change in x_i upon profit Π_i, given the arbitrary amount of output q_i. Customarily, this equation is equated to zero to obtain x_i^* for the first-order condition; then, taking zeroes of Equations (5) and (6), one would expect to obtain the simultaneous solution for the optimal output and location for firm i, provided the second-order conditions were also satisfied. However, this procedure does not hold for Equation (6), since the sign of the partial derivative $\partial \Pi_i / \partial x_i$ can be positive, negative, or zero; in fact, it is independent of x_i, depending instead only on the quantity of output q_i, given the constant freight rates t_i and t_{i+1}. Thus, pursuant to Assumption C the sign tends to be positive for smaller q_i, negative for larger q_i, and positive again for still larger q_i, *regardless of x_i*. This means that for any given q_i, profit for the firm is either increased or decreased monotonically or else fixed trivially as x_i is moved in one and the same direction. This is the result known in location theory as the Exclusion Theorem, which proposes that the firm should locate either at one of the input sites or at the market site, excluding an intermediate location.

The Exclusion Theorem itself can be established straightforwardly from the profit equation [Equation (4)] as follows. Given an optimal solution (m_i^*, x_i^*), (q_i^*, x_i^*) is obtained; given q_i^*, maximizing Π_i can be seen to minimize the "total cost" TC with respect to x_i, where TC is defined as[1]

$$TC = t_i |x_{i-1} - x_i| q_i^*$$
$$+ (m_{i+1} + t_{i+1} |x_{i+1} - x_i|) \phi_i(q_i^*) \quad (7)$$

Since t_i, t_{i+1}, x_{i-1}, x_{i+1}, and m_{i+1} in (7) all are given parameters, it then follows that $x_i^* \in \{x_{i-1}, x_{i+1}\}$. This result, known as the Hakimi Theorem, generally applies to the case of n input sites and one market site.

III. Preliminary Analysis

Conditions under which firm i at x_i may move toward x_{i-1} or x_{i+1} may now be determined. Given the conventional form of the input

---

[1] Even if the transportation of output is charged to the customers, it still is a relevant cost to the firm and is included in TC accordingly.

requirement function ϕ_i or its inverse, the production function ϕ_i^{-1}, the relations in Equations (5) and (6) may be presented diagrammatically, as in Figure 11-1. Note that the two terms on the right-hand side of (6) are depicted in Figure 11-1(a), whereas the total marginal cost in Equation (5) is given by TMC in Figure 11-1(b). The curve *TMC* and the corresponding *ATC* and *AC* are all well defined and strictly determined by ϕ_i and hence its linear transform $t_{i+1}\phi_i$.

It is elementary to observe that both *AC* and *ATC* are required to be U-shaped subject to Assumption C. Moreover, the form of these curves remains invariant, to be U-shaped even when production requires multiple inputs, provided that the production function is homothetic and under increasing returns to scale over smaller outputs followed by decreasing returns to scale with larger outputs.[2] This result readily derives from the facts that the CIF prices of inputs remain constant when the producer's location is fixed *and* that freight rates on inputs are also constant.

Several related comments are warranted for Figure 11-1 and the related Figure 11-2.

First, because the form of ϕ_i is cubic, as in Figure 11-1(a), it follows that for any quantity of output q_i below a certain critical level q_{i0}, the relation $t_{i+1}\phi(q_i) > t_i q_i$ holds so that $\partial\Pi_i/\partial x_i > 0$ via Equation (6). Note,

$$q_{i0} = \text{min.} \ [q_i \mid t_{i+1}\phi(q_i) = t_i q_i] \qquad (8)$$

Thus, if the size of the market demand at site x_{i-1} and/or the extent of competitive entry is such that the firm produces a small amount of output, it should locate at the input site x_{i+1}.[3] The scale of production assumed herein yields output in Region I in Figure 11-1.

Second, for a greater quantity of output such that $q_{i1} > q_i > q_{i0}$, this relation is reversed, so that $\partial\Pi_i/\partial x_i$ becomes negative. The

---

[2] Figure 11-1(a) also can readily be shown to remain unchanged under these generalized conditions. It should be stressed in this connection that each term $t_i q_i$ on the right-hand side ($\Sigma \pm t_i q_i$) of Equation (6) under the generalized conditions represents either additional cost or additional benefit of transporting q_i ($i = 1, 2, \ldots$) by relocating the firm's plant toward a neighboring input or market site, the sign of the total sum indicating the net effect of relocation.

[3] This proposition, however, clearly requires freight rate t_i of output to be sufficiently small relative to t_{i+1} so that the subject inequality may not be reversed for any $q_i > 0$.

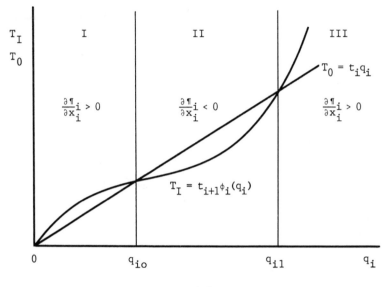

(a)

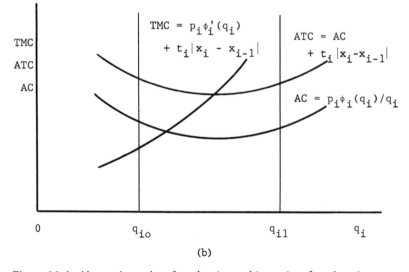

(b)

Figure 11.1. Alternative scales of production and incentives for relocation.

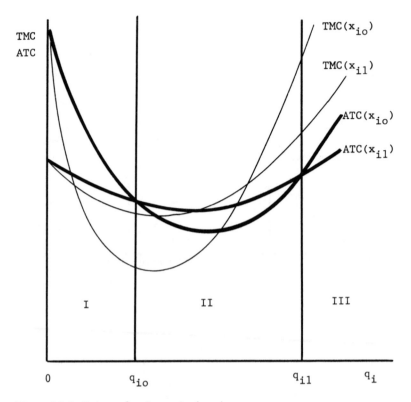

Figure 11.2. Costs under alternative locations.

firm should move to the market site accordingly. The assumed scale of production calls for a label *Region II*.

Third, for a still greater output $q_i > q_{i1}$,

$$q_{i1} = \text{max.} \ [q_i \mid t_{i+1}\phi_i(q_i) = t_i q_i] \tag{9}$$

we see $t_{i+1}\phi_i(q_i) > t_i q_i$ and location at or relocation toward the input site becomes feasible again. This output region corresponds to Region III in Figure 11-1.

But, why do smaller output in Region I and larger output in Region III require optimal location at input sites, whereas intermediate output in Region II requires location at the market site? To answer this question, recall that when output q is large enough to fall in Region III, the impact of decreasing returns related to it is so conspicuous that greater q requires increasingly greater amounts of input per unit of output. The transportation cost of input accordingly becomes dominant, and location at the input site definitely lowers this cost.

In Region II, production requires relatively small amounts of input per unit of output and accordingly warrants location at the market site to minimize transportation of output charged to customers. But very small amounts of output in Region I once more require relatively large quantities of input whose transportation can be minimized naturally at the input site.

Fourth, the fact that profit is increased under Regions I and III, but decreased under Region II, as the firm moves toward the input site, requires the cost curves depicted in Figure 11-1(b) to be shifted carefully in Figure 11-2. Given q_i, the average total cost ATC depends on firm i's location x_i. Thus, the ATC relations, that is, between $ATC(x_{i0})$ and $ATC(x_{i1})$, where $x_{i1} > x_{i0}$ are given by

$$ATC(x_{i1}) - ATC(x_{i0}) > 0, \qquad q_{i1} > q_i > q_{i0}$$

$$= 0, \qquad q_i = q_{i0}, q_{i1}$$

$$< 0, \qquad \text{elsewhere} \qquad (10)$$

where $q_{i1}, q_{i0} \in \{q_i \mid t_{i+1}\phi_i(q_i) = t_i q_i\}$.[4] Thus, the total cost, and therefore ATC in Figure 11-2, will be seen to stay higher or lower with greater x_i, that is, with location nearer to the input site, accord-

---

[4]The two critical values q_{i0} and q_{i1} may be readily identified by way of specifying a concrete form of the input requirement function. Consider, in particular, ϕ_i to be specified by $\phi_i(q_i) = [\alpha + \beta(q_i - \tau)^2]q_i$, $\qquad \alpha, \beta, \tau > 0$. Then the average total cost ATC is given by $ATC = [\alpha + \beta(q_i - \tau)^2][m_{i+1} + t_{i+1}(x_{i+1} - x_i)] + t_i(x_i - x_{i-1})$. Partially differentiate this with respect to x_i to obtain $\partial(ATC)/\partial x_i = t_i - t_{i+1}\alpha - t_{i+1}\beta(q_i - \tau)^2$.

Thus, insofar as $t_i \leq t_{i+1}\alpha$, the derived partial is never positive. For any q_i, relocation toward the market site x_{i-1} never proves profitable. This means that the assumed existence of Region II (along with I and III) requires that $t_i > t_{i+1}\alpha$; that is, the freight rate on output t_i must be sufficiently high relative to freight rate on input t_{i+1}. Assuming this relation and equating the earlier partial to zero yields $q_i = \tau \pm \sqrt{(t_i - t_{i+1}\alpha)/t_{i+1}\beta}$.

This equation indicates the two levels of output, $q_i = q_{i0}, q_{i1}$, at which relocation yields no change in ATC.

ingly as the firm's output q_i remains in Region II or Regions I and III.

Finally, the related shift in total marginal costs TMC appears to be somewhat more involved, but the two comparable TMCs can be readily stationed so that the areas under $TMC(x_{i1})$ and $TMC(x_{i0})$ are equal in Region I and Region II, but $TMC(x_{i0}) > TMC(x_{i1})$ in Region III. These conditions also imply that the first intersection of $TMC(x_{i0})$ and $TMC(x_{i1})$ in Region I should yield two equal totals for the two curves. Only under such specific conditions will the two corresponding ATCs intersect each other at $q_i = q_{i0}$, so that locational change at that level of output does not involve different total costs. Of course, to the left of q_{i0}, the location at x_{i1} is strictly preferable to x_{i0} for the unambiguous reason that the ATC is lower with x_{i1} or, equivalently, the area under $TMC(x_{i1})$ is less than for x_{i0}. Similar analysis holds for the curves in Regions II and III.

IV. Locational Choice under Conditions of Cournot Oligopoly

These findings allow a deeper probing into the firm's optimization behavior by introducing conditions of competitive entry. For this purpose, recall the optimization condition (5) introduced in Section II. The MR, which is to be equated with a given TMC for the first-order condition, is now subject to variation as more and more firms enter the market. To better appreciate the impact that this additional condition may have on the firm's locational decision making, attention will be confined to the TMCs of Figure 11-2, as stressed in Figure 11-3(a).

Suppose the firm's location is at x_{i0}, where $TMC(x_{i0})$ in Figure 11-3(a) provides the firm's cost condition at x_{i0}. The demand condition given by Equation (1), may, in turn, be represented by several alternative MR curves, with each MR being intersected by $TMC(x_{i0})$ in yielding a short-run (fixed-location) optimal output for the firm. However, the alternative equilibria, *each* reflecting a specific short-run market condition with a given degree of entry n_i, call for long-run locational and related output adjustments. Let us consider below the several possibilities on hand.

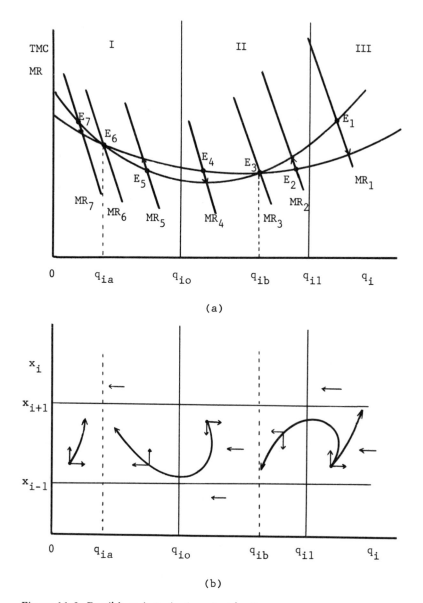

(a)

(b)

Figure 11.3. Possible trajectories (q_i, x_i) under Cournot entry.

Case 1. Equilibrium at E_1

This case represents a short-run equilibrium taking place in Region III in Figure 11-3(a). The market in this region may be considered highly monopolistic. Within Region III, the firm can increase profit with greater x_i; that is, relocation toward the input site x_{i+1} is warranted. This particular condition requires TMC with greater x_i to be stationed carefully, even exactly, in relation to TMC with smaller x_i, as in Figure 11-3. Evident from the figure is that relocation toward the input site (from x_{i0} to x_{i1}) should be accompanied by an *increase* in output q_i along the MR_1 curve, and a fall in the market price $f_i^{-1}(q_i)$ for that matter.

This chapter already has pondered the rationale for the firm to relocate toward the input site rather than the market site in this case; let us now consider an opposite case for comparison.

Case 2. Equilibrium E_2

This point, along with E_3 and E_4, belongs to Region II, Figure 11-3, under which greater profit is obtained by relocation toward the market site x_{i-1} since $\partial \Pi_i / \partial x_i < 0$. It is important to observe that the equilibrium in this region requires MR to be shifted downward below MR_1. If slight competition or a new entry lowered MR_1 to MR_2 to yield a short-run (fixed-location) equilibrium at E_2 in Region II, then the firm that had moved from x_{i0} to x_{i1} in Region III would be better off by moving back toward the market site rather than the input site. In this process, just opposite to Case 1, the firm output should be decreased not increased in the adjustment process along the curve MR_2. It warrants stress, however, that in this Region II case output does not always decrease as a consequence of relocation toward the market site. In fact, output increases if relocation takes place along with still greater entry reflected by the lower curve MR_4 than MR_3.

Given MR_3, relocation toward the market site takes place with no change in output. This result follows because TMC, which intersects MR_3, stays constant at $q_i = q_{ib}$, staying independent from location x_i, where q_{ib} in Region II, Figure 11-3, is given by

$$q_{ib} = \text{max.} \, [q_i \mid \partial(TMC)/\partial x_i = t_i - t_{i+1}\phi_i'(q_i) = 0] \qquad (11)$$

The ϕ_i' being U-shaped pursuant to Assumption C, the other q_i that yields constant TMC in Region I is correspondingly given by

$$q_{ia} = \text{min.} \, [q_i \mid \partial(TMC)/\partial x_i = t_i - t_{i+1}\phi_i' = 0] \qquad (12)$$

Case 3. Equilibrium E_5

Along with E_6 and E_7, this equilibrium point is in Region I, where relocation toward the input site again becomes feasible or optimal. Thus, if entry continues to shift MR down to MR_5, a short-run equilibrium is given by E_5, which in turn portends relocation away from the market site toward the input site. In the process output will be decreased. The subcases for different output effects are illustrated by equilibrium points E_6 and E_7.

In all of these situations, the firm tends to move toward either the market center or the input center, never to intermediate points. The dynamic adjustment process may be illustrated by a phase diagram in Figure 11-3(b), where the firm's output level and location are both subject to varying degrees of market entry and firm's optimizing behavior. Thus, starting from a monopoly demand condition f_i, it is possible to derive from Equations (5) and (6) the following differential inequalities under conditions of Cournot entry with n_i:

$$\left[\left(1 - \frac{1}{n_i e_i}\right) f_i^{-1}(n_i q_i) - t_i |x_i - x_{i-1}| \right.$$

$$\left. - t_{i+1}|x_{i+1} - x_i|\phi_i' \right]\partial q_i \geq 0 \qquad (13)$$

$$[t_{i+1}\phi_i - t_i q_i]\partial x_i \geq 0 \qquad (14)$$

where e_i stands for elasticity of market demand at x_{i-1}. Subject to the constraints (9) to (12), these inequalities define the direction of optimal adjustment for q_i and x_i from an arbitrary point (q_i, x_i).

While the effect of optimal adjustment upon (q_i, x_i) is not unidirectional, the impact of Cournot entry is. Since the individual MR_i

shifts downward with entry and nothing else changes inside the brackets of (13) and (14), the force of entry operates on q_i alone and unidirectionally as

$$\frac{\partial q_i}{\partial n_i} < 0 \tag{15}$$

The phase lines of Figure 11-3(b) can be derived from conditions (13) to (15) and illustrate how the ordered pair (q_i, x_i) can move over time and under Cournot competition. Note that although each phase line only shows a possible time path for (q_i, x_i), it always ends up with location x_i at either the input site x_{i+1} or the market site x_{i-1}. In any case, the long-run equilibrium output q_i can take any value within any region of output including Region III.

It is to be noted that any long-run equilibrium output in Region III requires the firm's profit to remain positive, any further entry making it negative. A strict "zero-profit" equilibrium requires the so-called Chamberlinean tangency equilibrium, which, if it occurs, takes place only in Region I or Region II. Henceforth, it will be assumed that the demand and cost conditions are such that a Chamberlinean tangency equilibrium, if not a strict one, is obtainable in either Region I or Region II, disregarding any long-run "minimum" profit equilibrium in Region III.

The question then is under what conditions competitive firms would concentrate at the market center in Region II *or* the input site in Region I. To resolve this matter of location per se, remember that the existence of Region II depends on the relative form or height of the two curves in Figure 11-1(a). Thus, the higher the curve $t_{i+1}\phi_i(q_i)$ relative to the curve $t_i q_i$, the smaller Region II will be. If, for example, $t_{i+1}\phi_i(q_i) > t_i q_i$ for any q_i, Region II will disappear. This means that firms invariably will concentrate at the input site, since the transportation cost of input per mile needed to produce a unit of output invariably exceeds transportation cost on a unit of output per mile. A necessary condition for the firm to locate at the market site is the existence of Region II, which in turn requires transportation cost of output to be sufficiently high that $t_i q_i > t_{i+1}\phi_i(q_i)$ for at least some $q_i > 0$.

Directly related to this is the condition that part of $ATC(x_{i0})$ in Figure 11-2 remain strictly below $ATC(x_{i1})$ for the same quantities

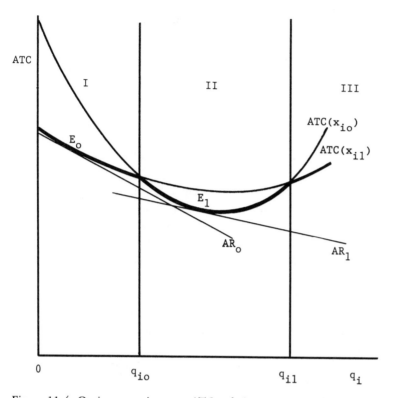

Figure 11.4. Optimum optimorum ATC and alternative Chamberlinean tangency equilibria.

of output q_i satisfying this inequality. Firm i's location x_i being equated alternatively with market site x_{i-1} or input site x_{i+1}, the *optimum optimorum ATC* may be specified or illustrated readily by the solid envelope curve in Figure 11-4. It follows that any Chamberlinean tangency is to be found on this envelope curve.

Remember now that, under Cournot competition, the individual firm demand shifts horizontally leftward as entry increases. Given a U-shaped ATC, it follows that the slope of the market demand for the relevant (lower) price range plays a decisive role in determination of the Chamberlinean tangency equilibrium in either Region I or Region II. To be specific, the flatter (not necessarily more elastic) the market demand is, the more likely the Chamberlinean tangency is to occur in Region II at the market site. Moreover, the firms at the market site will be seen to be producing at a greater scale, and lower costs accordingly, compared with the case of the alternative market condition with steeper demand. In this latter case, the firms tend to concentrate at the input site, producing in Region I a smaller amount of output individually,′ and inefficiently, that is, at a higher cost. Compare E_0 with E_1 in Figure 11-4.

Incentives therefore may exist for individual firms to deviate from their Cournot behavior. The upshot may be a smaller number of firms, each producing a greater amount of output, concentrating at the market center, relocating from the input site. These firms at the market site not only produce most efficiently and in greater quantity *individually* but also provide a greater industry output under conditions approximating perfect competition, all compared with high-cost producers concentrated at the input site.[5] In contrast, while atomistic firms each producing an extremely small amount of output at input sites *may* appear to be subjected to conditions of perfect competition, in fact they are not, at least in terms of efficiency in production. Not only are they remotest from perfect competitors, they also are most likely to be squeezed out of the industry unless protected by governmental interference. The variable treatment of the behavioral assumption itself, however, goes beyond the purpose of the present study and must be reserved for other writings.

We have so far assumed the mill prices of inputs to be constant. However, it is manifest both theoretically and empirically that the price of land inputs, among others, is highly sensitive to spatial concentration of economic agents. Thus, insofar as agglomeration at the market site gives rise to an increase in land rent, our $ATC(x_{i-1})$ is required to shift upward. This condition in turn clearly points to the feasibility of *intermediate location* or relocation of some firms away from the market center. However, even when the input price factor of *deglomeration* is assumed to exist, the basic tendency of market

[5] Cf. Ohta [10], where similar relations have been derived from assumptions fundamentally different from the present ones, namely, relations between long-run equilibrium subject to Löschian competition. The former equilibrium has been shown to yield a great many more firms producing less at higher prices compared with the latter equilibrium results. However, the previous model is not directly applicable to the analysis of spatial agglomeration of homogeneous firms at a point when market points are distributed uniformly over a linearly extended economic space.

concentration remains unchanged. This follows because the negative effect of agglomeration upon itself is derived from itself. Thus, agglomeration at the market site is to be offset only partly by the feasibility of an intermediate location, having lower land rent along with lesser concentration. The degree of concentration is required in fact to decrease monotonically with land rent as Chamberlinean tangency equilibria take place at each and every site x_i belonging to $[x_{i-1}, x_{i0}]$, where x_{i0} is a critical location with no differential rent and x_{i-1} is the market site, with highest land rent and greatest concentration. Thus, the basic contention regarding market concentration remains unchanged regardless of the assumption of fixed input prices.

In sum, consider a small number of monopolistic firms selling at a "point" market of given size. Suppose that the demand conditions are such that the firms opt to locate at the input site to enjoy monopoly profits. Entry is called for accordingly. Under conditions of Cournot competition, or its limiting case of perfect competition, the individual firm's optimal location eventually turns out to be the market site. Accordingly, it may be concluded that market competition is the fundamental factor promoting spatial agglomeration at the market center.

The competitive factor of agglomeration affects firms in industry i as well as firms in industry $i + 1$, $i + 2$, . . . and so on insofar as these industries are related vertically. Pursuant to the basic assumptions, firms in industry 1 are customers to firms in industry 2. Thus, if the former firms concentrate willingly at the market site x_0 under conditions of Cournot competition so will the latter firms, to be followed by firms in industry 3, 4, . . . n, all enticed toward the final market site x_0.

V. Division of Labor and Vertical Integration: Related Factors of Agglomeration

The preceding sections simply assumed n vertically related industries to produce the final good. Under certain well-defined conditions, further division of labor to increase the intermediate stages of production n may well enlarge the flow of the final good produced during a given period of time. To better appreciate the benefit arising from such a roundabout method of production based on division of labor, consider a given amount of subsistence fund S à la Böhm-Bawerk. Given S, assume that the same amount of output can be produced after a unit period of production. If the same S is divided into four parts and one of them is initially used as wage payment to workers to produce the same amount in value of an intermediate product, then the benefit from division of labor may be conceived in terms of the period of production being reduced, say, to one-half. With this assumed benefit of roundabout production, an $S/4$ subsistence fund is transformed into an $S/4$ intermediate product in the first half of the production period.

Assume further that at the beginning of the second half of the production period, the intermediate product equal in value to $S/4$ is combined with another quarter of the subsistence fund $S/4$ to produce the final product of equal value in input, again in a half-period. Thus, the value of the final product at the end of the unit period is equal to $S/2$.

Not only is this final product produced in the second half of the period, but another intermediate good is also produced out of a third quarter of the subsistence fund. Thus, at the end of the unit period, the $S/2$ final good, the $S/4$ intermediate good, and the remaining $S/4$ subsistence fund are all available.

It is important to note that, at the beginning of the second period, one-half of the $S/2$ final good now available can be used as wage inputs to be combined with the $S/4$ intermediate good also available to produce the new final good in equal value of inputs, that is, $S/2$. The other half of the old final good is to be used as wages for production of a new intermediate product of the same value $S/2$. All these new outputs will be available by the second half of the second period.

Related comments are in order.

First, with the input of three-quarters of subsistence fund S, the full amount S of final products can be produced continuously in every period thereafter.

Second, the remaining quarter $S/4$ of the subsistence fund has not been used up to maintain the flow of output S per period. Thus, only a smaller amount of subsistence fund is needed for production of a given level of output flow per period, if a greater number of intermediate stages of production can be allowed to precede the stage of production of the final consumption good.

Given n stages of production, the final good q_1 is to be produced by the inputs of an intermediate good q_2 and labor or $(1/n)^2S$ in terms of wages. However, since q_2 is to be produced likewise by the inputs of q_3, labor, and so on, it follows

$$q_1 = q_2 + (1/n)^2S$$
$$q_2 = q_3 + (1/n)^2S$$

$$\cdot$$
$$\cdot$$
$$\cdot$$

$$q_{n-1} = q_n + (1/n)^2S$$
$$q_n = (1/n)^2S$$

Hence, $\lim_{n\to\infty} \Sigma_{i=1}^n q_i = \lim_{n\to\infty}(1/n)^2S(1 + 2 + \ldots + n) = (1/2)S$ where Σq_i stands for the amount of subsistence fund needed for production flow of $nq_1 = S$ per period. Thus, as n approaches a large number, a given amount of subsistence fund can be transformed into a double amount of output flow per period. The increased number of firms (or stages of production) with enlarged economic activities tend, as demonstrated earlier, to congregate at the final market center.

Not only do firms seek greater specialization in production and specialized firms in related industries tend in turn to agglomerate spatially, incentives also exist for these highly specialized firms to consider vertical merger [4; 5].

This, however, should not be confused with action *against* division of labor or specialization in production. Vertical mergers in fact need not require exclusion of intermediate stages of production or distribution insofar as they are needed parts of efficient production of final goods.[6] Moreover, an increase in productive specialization for the

---

[6] In this connection, innumerable "unwarranted" stages of production and distribution are often alleged to characterize the Japanese economy, industrial organization in particular. A symbolic example mentioned to support this allegation is the so-called dark continent of distribution, which processes the world-famous Kobe beef with an almost incredible price tag of nearly $100 per pound. Time and again, the association of housewives and the like would run sales campaigns to bypass the intermediate channels, so far with no success.

sake of higher productivity may all the more require increased coordination of related activities.[7]

Insofar as vertical mergers yield greater final outputs, greater inputs are needed at all related stages of production. This means greater employment of workers, among other inputs, all needed at the already concentrated market and production center. The additional working population will agglomerate accordingly as the direct consequences of vertical mergers, which themselves may be prompted by spatial agglomeration of related firms. Thus, spatial agglomeration and industrial agglomeration are directly related to each other.

In conclusion, greater specialization in production and greater degree of vertical merger go hand in hand with each other and, most important, both go with spatial agglomeration.

VI. Concluding Remarks

Spatial agglomeration is a natural economic phenomenon. Moreover, it is a sign of economic prosperity, a product of profit incentives, spurred by active competition and supported by most effective industrial organizations promoting division of labor simultaneously with vertical coordination of the up- to downstream related activities, culminating in the production and marketing of the final good.

Accordingly, should urban agglomerations as presently seen be positively appreciated? K. Mera [8] has presented some empirical evidence seemingly in support of greater urbanization. However, he has not pointed out the problem of possible externalities related to it. Of particular interest in connection with a giant metropolis, such as Tokyo, is the question of possible excess agglomeration. What externality, if any, is related to it?

To answer this particular question, recall that the forces of agglomeration themselves tend to give rise to deglomerating forces such as rising land rents and prices. In fact, since the end of the Korean War,

---

[7] These cost-cutting aspects of vertical merger, however, are purposely disregarded by Greenhut and Ohta [4; 5] to reveal several other important effects of integration. In particular, Greenhut and Ohta show that what may be called the *market effects of vertical merger* help the final price to decline and *output to increase*.

Japan has experienced a sustained rise in land prices along with economic growth. While the present level of GNP is around sixty times what it was in 1950, land prices have skyrocketed by a factor of almost 200 during the same period. This is a startling result that the neoclassical theory, at least with fixed partial elasticity of production, can hardly explain, unless land input is assumed to have been steadily decreased over time. And indeed there have been two factors of critical importance to be carefully observed. One is the observation that the annual rate of increase in land price has invariably and substantially exceeded the rate of interest over time. The other is the fact that the property tax of the holding cost of land has been extremely low.[8]

Related to these is the background fact that land reform by the occupation troops cut up the land into pieces to be virtually given away to peasants, who have now become "petty" landowners and yet actual billionaires. These billionaires naturally have no incentives to sell their soil, which bears golden fruit in terms of capital gains. Neither do they have incentives, nor perhaps capabilities, to utilize optimally their high-opportunity means of production. It may be best for them to leave the land as it is, with no productive use. Moreover, these very peasants and others gifted with substantial equities may be in a position to finance additional purchases of land, which is believed to increase in value over time. The upshot is a sustained increase in blatantly underutilized land even within the metropolitan areas and the resultant overconcentration of population and industries in areas of substantially reduced availability. Apparently related to this worsening misallocation of productive resources, skyrocketing land prices and the notorious "rabbit hutch" housing conditions in Tokyo and other major cities in Japan is the insistent policy of subsidy in terms of a negligible property tax on, or low holding cost of underutilized land of accelerating market value. The detailed analysis of the impact of the property tax upon resource allocation and spatial agglomeration in particular must be reserved, however, for other writings.

---

[8] The tax rate on the land property in Japan is as low as $0.1-0.2$ percent of the market value. Moreover, landowners can be exempt even from this negligible property tax if they disguise themselves as engaging in agriculture.

References

[1]   Chamberlin, E. H. *The Theory of Monopolistic Competition.* Cambridge, Mass.: Harvard University Press, 1933.

[2]   Eswaran, M., Y. Kanemoto, and D. Ryan. "A Dual Approach to the Locational Decision of the Firm." *Journal of Regional Sciences* 21 (1981): 469–90.

[3]   Greenhut, M. L. *Plant Location in Theory and in Practice.* Chapel Hill, N.C.: University of North Carolina Press, 1956.

[4]   Greenhut, M. L., and H. Ohta. "Related Market Conditions and Interindustrial Mergers." *American Economic Review* 66 (1976): 267–77.

[5]   ———. "Vertical Integration of Successive Oligopolists." *American Economic Review* 69 (1979): 137–41.

[6]   Higano, Y. "On the Exclusion Theorem." *Regional Science and Urban Economics* 3 (1985): 449–58.

[7]   Louveaux, F., J. Thisse, and H. Beguin. "Location Theory and Transport Costs." *Regional Science and Urban Economics* (1982).

[8]   Mera, K. "On the Urban Agglomeration and Economic Efficiency." *Economic Development and Cultural Change* 21 (1973): 309–24.

[9]   Moses, L. N. "Location and the Theory of Production." *Quarterly Journal of Economics* 72 (1958): 259–72.

[10] Ohta, H. "Spatial Competition, Concentration and Welfare." *Regional Science and Urban Economics* 10 (1980): 3–16.

[11] ———. "Agglomeration and Competition." *Regional Science and Urban Economics* 14 (1984): 1–17.

[12] Sakashita, N. "Production Function, Demand Function and Location Theory of the Firm." *Papers, Regional Science Association* 20 (1968): 109–22.

PART IV

The Welfare Effects of Competition and Growth

12.

Spatial Competition and Optimal Location of Industries

I. Introduction

The discussion in Chapter 11 followed the classical (Weberian) school of location theory by assuming implicitly a "point" market rather than an "areal" market in dealing with plant location. The preceding chapters, however, avoided any postulate of point market (demand), as it seemed to limit the scope of "spatial" economics in the Löschian tradition. The present study must reconsider the basic postulate of the areal market as a path toward the general theory of spatial competition, location, and welfare. (Although Chapter 11 was a digression, this chapter is an extension of Chapter 10, using the background of Chapters 8 and 9.)

Related to the objective of this chapter is an observation that, in some industries, a number of firms are located virtually at a single point while a small number of firms are found in separate locations. These firms thus appear to be subject not only to *intra*local but also to *inter*local competition (Ohta [4]). Moreover, *inter*local distances seemingly vary from industry to industry, aside from varying numbers of firms concentrated *intra*locally. The present chapter presents a simple model of spatial competition to explain this locational complexity and derive conditions for so-called contestable markets characterized by zero-profit long-run equilibria. However, contestability ipso facto does not guarantee a social optimum, for it can be shown that certain *inter*local distances provide the firms with positive profit and society with maximum social welfare. In this sense, the present chapter is more normative than positive, as it demonstrates how contestable markets can be organized spatially to maximize social surplus.

Section II reviews a conventional model of spatial competition as a departure point. It begins with the conditions of Löschian competition in the short run and in the long run. With this review in mind, Section III poses the interesting question of whether greater competition or entry is always socially desirable. (The answer is negative.) Section IV will extend the model framework of Section III to consider a more complex situation mentioned earlier. Section V is a digression in the sense that it deals directly with a nonspatial model of Cournot competition. It is in part, however, an analytical simplification of Section IV and in effect focuses attention on intralocal competition by assuming *inter*local distances to be fixed (under conditions of Löschian competition). The focal point of analysis is whether *intra*local entry always increases social welfare. (The answer will again be negative.) Section VI concludes the chapter, summarizing selected findings of the analysis.

II. The Model of Löschian Competition: A Departure Point

Assume the following:

Assumption A. The basic demand density function is linear, identical, and distributed continuously along a circumference line.

Assumption B. All firms face identical cost conditions; each faces a given fixed cost upon entry at any market point. There are no other costs of production, relocation, etc.

Assumption C. All firms are subjected to Löschian competition.

Assumption D. The size of the firm is sufficiently small that an additional entry causes only an infinitesimal change (reduction) in the size of the firm's market area.

The Short-Run Equilibrium

Pursuant to these assumptions, we will first derive the short-run equilibrium in which each firm maximizes profit subject to the condition that its market area is fixed. The spatial (areal) demand Q_{x0}

that the firm faces subject to Assumptions A and C is defined tentatively by the aggregate (or integral) of the local demand:

$$Q_{x_0} = 2\int_0^{x_0} (a - m - x)dx \qquad (a > 0)$$

$$= 2\left(ax_0 - \frac{1}{2}x_0^2 - x_0 m\right) \qquad (m_0 > m > 0) \qquad (1)$$

where x stands for the distance variable (in terms of the *costs* per unit quantity to be shipped), x_0 for the fixed market radius, and m for mill price; m_0 is the *supremum* of mill prices that yield positive demand at every point in the entire market area $(0, x_0)$. As mill price rises to this critical level m_0, local demand from the firm's market boundary point x_0 vanishes. Thus, m_0 and x_0 are defined mutually by

$$a - m_0 - x_0 = 0 \qquad \text{or} \quad m_0 = a - x_0 \qquad (2)$$

As mill price exceeds this critical level m_0, only part of the firm's market area will be served. The market boundary point "naturally" (or noncompetitively) reduced by higher mill price ($m > m_0$) can be defined as x_n; at this point, the local demand vanishes; that is, $a - m - x_n = 0$. Thus, the market demand that the firm faces for $m > m_0$ can be defined as

$$Q_{x_0} = 2\int_0^{x_n} (a - m - x)dx$$

$$= (a - m)^2 \qquad (a > m > m_0) \qquad (3)$$

Combining Equations (1) and (3) yields the complete definition of the spatial market demand for the firm under Löschian competition:

$$Q_{x_0} = 2\left(a - \frac{1}{2}x_0\right)x_0 - 2x_0 m \qquad (m_0 \geqslant m > 0)$$

$$= (a - m)^2 \qquad\qquad (a \geqslant m > m_0) \qquad (4)$$

The firm's marginal revenue MR_{x_0} corresponding to (4) is given by

$$MR_{x_0} = a - \frac{x_0}{2} - \frac{1}{x_0} Q_{x_0} \qquad (Q_{x_0} > Q_0)$$

$$= a - \frac{3}{2} \sqrt{Q_{x_0}} \qquad (Q_0 \geqslant Q_{x_0} > 0) \qquad (5)$$

where Q_0 itself

$$Q_0 = (a - m_0)^2 \qquad (m_0 > a/3)$$

$$= x_0^2 \qquad (x_0 < 2a/3) \qquad (6)$$

The constraint on x_0 (or m_0) as specified in Equation (6) is needed whenever Löschian competition is assumed to be binding. Unless the firm's market radius is reduced to $x_0 < 2a/3$, the firm will behave as a spatial monopolist.

Profit maximization requires the marginal revenue to be equated to zero subject to Assumption B. Taking the zero of Equation (5) yields the profit-maximizing output $Q_{x_0}^*$:

$$Q_{x_0}^* = (a - m_0)(a + m_0)/2 \qquad (m_0 > a/3)$$

$$= (a - x_0/2)x_0 \qquad (x_0 < 2a/3) \qquad (7)$$

Substituting this result in Equation (4) yields the optimal mill price m^* (Greenhut [2]):

$$m^* = (a + m_0)/4$$

$$= \frac{1}{2}a - \frac{1}{4}x_0 \qquad \left(\frac{2a}{3} > x_0 > 0\right) \qquad (8)$$

The short-run equilibrium condition is illustrated by Figure 12-1, where AR_M depicts the average revenue curve for the spatial monopolist and AR_{x_0} the average revenue under Löschian competi-

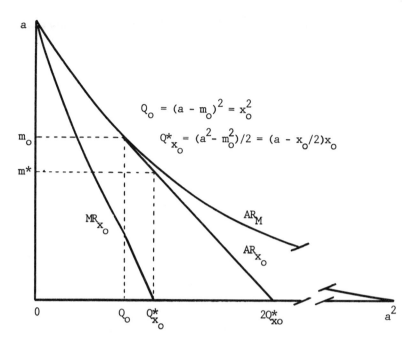

$$Q_0 = (a - m_0)^2 = x_0^2$$

$$Q^*_{x_0} = (a^2 - m_0^2)/2 = (a - x_0/2)x_0$$

Figure 12.1. Average and marginal revenues under Löschian competition.

tion, that is, the inverse of (4), and MR_{x_0} is the corresponding marginal revenue given by (5).

The Long-Run Equilibrium

The short-run profit of the firm under Löschian competition Π_{x_0} is given via Equations (7) and (8) as

$$\Pi_{x_0} = m^* Q_{x_0}^* - F \qquad (F > 0)$$

$$= \frac{1}{2}(a - x_0/2)^2 x_0 - F \qquad \left(x_0 < \frac{2}{3}a\right) \qquad (9)$$

where F is the fixed cost of entry. Note that $d\Pi_{x_0}/dx_0 > 0$ for any positive $x_0 < 2a/3$. Thus, as long as Π_{x_0} remains positive, new entry will be encouraged and the firm's own market radius x_0 tends to be reduced until the long-run equilibrium is finally obtained with $\Pi_{x_0} = 0$.

III. The Welfare Effects of Spatial Competition: The Question of Optimal Entry

An interesting question arises here: Is it socially desirable for an industry to *approach* the long-run zero-profit equilibrium? A similar question has been asked by Stern [5] and Bowes [1] in a spatial framework and by von Weizsäcker [7] and Suzumura [6] in a nonspatial (Cournot) framework of thought. The question is predicated on the models of spatial competition. In this connection it follows Holahan [3] to define the social welfare as the aggregate consumer surplus plus the producer surplus or industry profit.

Löschian Competition

Consider an individual customer's surplus CS_x at distance point x, which is defined as

$$CS_x = \frac{(a - m - x)^2}{2} \tag{10}$$

The aggregate consumer surplus CS_{x_0} created by one firm under Löschian competition is

$$CS_{x_0} = 2\int_0^{x_0} \frac{(a - m - x^2)}{2}\, dx$$

$$= (a - m)^2 x_0 - (a - m)x_0^2 + \frac{2}{3}x_0^3 \tag{11}$$

The social welfare SW_{x_0} is defined via (8), (9), and (11) as

$$SW_{x_0} = CS_{x_0} + \Pi_{x_0}$$

$$= \frac{26}{96} x_0^3 - \frac{6}{8} a x_0^2 + \frac{6}{8} a^2 x_0 - F \qquad (12)$$

The social welfare *per unit of area* SWA_{x_0} is then given by

$$SWA_{x_0} = \frac{13}{96} x_0^2 - \frac{3}{8} a x_0 + \frac{3}{8} a^2 - \frac{F}{2x_0} \qquad (13)$$

Differentiating (13) with respect to x_0 yields

$$\frac{d(SWA_{x_0})}{dx_0} = \frac{13}{48} x_0 - \frac{3}{8} a + \frac{2F}{4x_0^2} \qquad (14)$$

Equating (14) to zero yields two positive values of x_0, if the basic demand represented by its price intercept value a is sufficiently large relative to fixed cost F. The smaller of these is the optimal market radius, since it is easily seen that $d(SWA_{x_0})/dx_0 < 0$ for any x_0 slightly larger than the extremum.

Our question is whether this socially optimal market size x_0^* coincides with the long-run zero-profit equilibrium size x_{0L} under Löschian competition. The answer is no. To see this, note that the latter market size x_{0L} is given by equating (9) to zero. Thus,

$$\frac{1}{2} \left(a - \frac{x_0}{2} \right)^2 x_0 - F = 0 \qquad (15)$$

Subject to this condition, Equation (14) reappears as

$$\frac{d(SWA_{x_0})}{dx_0} = \frac{13}{48} x_{0L} - \frac{3}{8} a + \frac{[a - (x_{0L}/2)]^2}{4x_{0L}}$$

$$= \frac{8x_{0L}^2 - 15 a x_{0L} + 6a^2}{24 x_{0L}} \qquad (16)$$

While the sign of (16) is negative in the neighborhood of $x_{0L} =$

$2a/3$ (which is the maximum feasible market radius for a Löschian competitor), it can be seen to turn positive as x_{0L} is reduced below $x_{0L} = (15 - 3\sqrt{3})a/16$. Insofar as Löschian competition drives x_{0L} below this critical level, the social welfare per area starts declining with every additional entry. Löschian competition can thus become excessive unless entry falls short of the final stage of zero-profit equilibrium. In fact, when fixed costs are high enough to stop Löschian entry before the critical radius x_{0L} is reached, the sign of (16) remains to be negative, implying that further entry is needed for social optimum.

GO Competition

One may speculate that the perversity of "excess" competition can be ascribed to the peculiarity of Löschian competition, which tends to *raise* rather than lower FOB mill price. However, even under GO competition (Chapter 8), which always lowers mill price, the perverse negative effect of entry is shown to be unavoidable when fixed costs of entry are sufficiently small. To see this, consider the spatial market demand Q_{GO} under GO competition:

$$Q_{GO} = 2\int_0^{p_0-m} (a - m - x)dx$$

$$= (p_0 - m)(2a - m - p_0) \qquad (17)$$

where p_0 is the delivered price ceiling perceived by the GO competitor.

The profit Π_{GO} is then defined by

$$\Pi_{GO} = mQ_{GO} - F$$

$$= m(p_0 - m)(2a - m - p_0) - F \qquad (18)$$

where F is the fixed, and the only, cost pursuant to Assumption B. Using the first-order condition for profit maximization, we obtain[1]

---

[1] Since the first-order condition turns out to be a quadratic in m, two solutions are actually derivable. However, the smaller one can easily be seen to be the relevant

$$m^* = \frac{2}{3}a - \frac{1}{2}\left[\left(\frac{4}{3}a - p_0\right)^2 + \frac{1}{3}p_0^2\right] \tag{19}$$

The consumer surplus CS_{GO}, its average value (per unit area) CSA_{GO}, and the social welfare per unit area are in turn defined respectively as

$$CS_{GO} = 2\int_0^{x_0} \frac{(a - m - x)^2}{2}\,dx \qquad (x_0 = p_0 - m) \tag{20}$$

$$CSA_{GO} = CS_{GO}/2x_0$$

$$= \frac{1}{2}\left[(a - m)(a - p_0) + \frac{1}{3}(p_0 - m)^2\right] \tag{21}$$

$$SWA_{GO} = CSA_{GO} + \Pi_{GO}/2x_0 \tag{22}$$

Reducing (22) to a function of p_0, differentiating the result with respect to p_0, and then substituting the zero-profit equilibrium condition from (18) and (19) to eliminate F in the result, we obtain

$$\frac{d(SWA_{GO})}{dp_0} = \phi(p_0)/54\sqrt{}\left(p_0 - \frac{2}{3} + \frac{1}{2}\sqrt{}\right) \tag{23}$$

where
$$\phi(p_0) = 40p_0^3 - 122p_0^2a + 140\tfrac{2}{3}p_0a^2 - 60a^3$$
$$- (-18p_0^2 + 65p_0a - 45a^2)\sqrt{}$$

$$\sqrt{} = \left(\frac{4}{3}p_0^2 + \frac{8}{3}p_0a + \frac{16}{9}a^2\right)^{1/2}$$

Despite the messy appearance, the sign of (23) is tractable and can be shown to be positive when price ceiling p_0 is relatively low under related conditions of low fixed costs. However, the sign is reversed

solution, as in the text. (The larger one is irrelevant since it exceeds the monopoly mill price.)

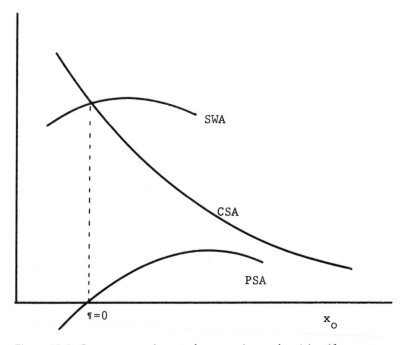

Figure 12.2. Consumer surplus, producer surplus, and social welfare per area.

when fixed costs are relatively high and higher equilibrium prices are needed accordingly.[2] This means that in the neighborhood of zero-profit equilibrium under GO competition, the social welfare (per unit of area) tends to increase with further entry when fixed costs are relatively large. Otherwise, entry must be discouraged for a social optimum, as in the Löschian case, and even in our present GO case.

The seemingly puzzling result derives from the fact that although greater entry may always raise the consumer surplus per area (especially under GO competition) and also reduce average transportation costs, the fixed costs of production and entry will increase by the

---

[2] The sign of (23) is tractable as follows: Note that the denominator of (23) is strictly positive over the domain $a > p_0 > 0$. Thus, the sign of (23) depends directly on the sign of its numerator. Note further that the basic form of the numerator is cubic in p_0, $\phi(0) = 0$, $\phi'(0) > 0$, and $\phi(a) < 0$. The cubic form of $\phi(p_0)$ therefore is positive in the neighborhood of O^+ while being negative in the neighborhood of a^-. Thus, the sign of $d(SWA_{GO})/dp_0$ depends on p_0; when fixed costs are relatively higher, equilibrium p_0 is required to be higher and $d(SWA_{GO})/dp_0$ tends to be negative accordingly and vice versa.

number of additional entries. Accordingly, there must exist some socially optimal degree of entry that need not be obtained exactly at the point where the firm's profit is completely wiped out.

The general relation between the social welfare per unit of area SWA, the consumer surplus per unit of area CSA, and the producer surplus (profit) per area PSA is illustrated by Figure 12-2. The SWA is the vertical sum of the downward-sloping CSA (as a function of the competitively circumscribed market radius x_0) and the upward-sloping PSA. As long as the positive slope of the PSA is steeper than the negative slope of the CSA at the point where profit vanishes, the SWA will slope upward at that point, as in the figure. The foregoing particular analysis of GO competition shows that the slope of SWA in the neighborhood of the zero-profit equilibrium depends on the size of the firms in terms of fixed costs. While relatively large firms warrant greater competition than they may wish, relatively small firms may be better protected from further entry by entry barriers!

IV. The Welfare Effects of Spatial Competition:
A Cournot-Lösch Model

So far we have assumed that at any stage of entry every firm is located apart from every other firm. (Relocation of existing firms upon new entry is completed instantly and costlessly.) The present section modifies this basic assumption. In particular, while Assumptions A and B of Section II will be preserved intact, Assumptions C and D are replaced by the following:

Assumption C'. Firms that *happen* to be located at the same local market point are subject to the Cournot type of competition.

Assumption D'. A firm is subject to Löschian competition with other firm(s) located at adjacent local market points.

Alternative Location Equilibria and Consumer Surplus

Pursuant to these assumptions, any stage of entry must be characterized by a uniform *and* discrete distribution of *intra*local concentrations of firms along the linear market. But, presumably, there may exist no unique level or combination of concentrations at a point *and* the *inter*local distance between any two adjacent firm concentrations may vary at any given stage of entry. However, there may be a unique combination (of concentrations) that maximizes social welfare. The present section initially seeks such a particular solution under conditions of long-run zero-profit equilibrium, the foregoing findings notwithstanding.

Consider a representative firm under Löschian competition located alone at an arbitrary point of the linear market. The market demand for the firm subject to Assumption A is then given by (4), repeated here as

$$Q_{x_0} = 2\left(a - \frac{1}{2}x_0\right)x_0 - 2x_0m \qquad (m_0 \geq m > 0)$$

$$= (a - m)^2 \qquad\qquad (a \geq m > m_0) \qquad (24)$$

where $m_0 = a - x_0$, and x_0 is the market radius (perceived as parametrically given), whereas m_0 is the critical level of mill price beyond which the firm's market radius must be reduced below x_0 to avoid negative (local) demand.

The inverse form of (24) represents a spatial market's (aggregate) demand for a given area $2x_0$, as illustrated by the AR_{x_0} curve of Figure 12-3. Given this market demand, Cournot competition and entry will take place under Assumption C' until the demand perceived by each individual firm $AR_{x_{0i}}$ shifts parallel leftward and finds itself tangent to the average fixed cost curve AFC, as in Figure 12-3. This same process is taking place in all other points of local concentration as well and yields the familiar Chamberlinean tangency equilibrium. The tangency conditions are given by

$$\frac{dm}{dQ_{x_{0i}}}\left(= \frac{dm}{dQ_{x_0}}\right) = -\frac{1}{2x_0} \qquad (x_0 \leq 2a/3) \qquad (25)$$

$$\frac{d(AFC)}{dQ_{x_{0i}}} = -\frac{F}{Q_{x_{0i}}^2} \qquad \left(F \leq \frac{4}{27}a^3\right) \qquad (26)$$

where $4a^3/27$ is the maximum possible fixed cost that may barely allow only one (monopoly) firm to enter the market. Equating (25)

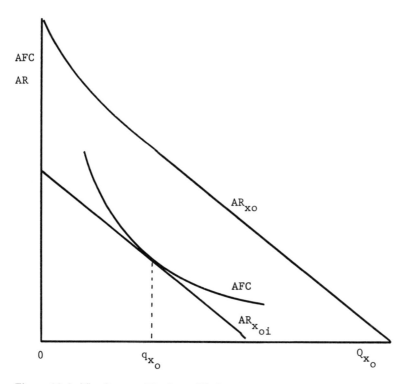

Figure 12.3. The Cournot-Lösch equilibrium.

and (26) yields the long-run equilibrium solution for the Cournot-Lösch type of spatial competition:

$$Q_{x_{0i}}{}^* = \sqrt{2Fx_0} \tag{27}$$

$$m^* = \sqrt{F/2x_0} \qquad (\text{via } m^*Q_{x_{0i}}{}^* = F) \tag{28}$$

where x_0 must be constrained so that $\sqrt{F/2x_0} < a/2$, since equilibrium mill price is always required to be smaller than the spaceless optimal price, which is $a/2$.

With this mill price the aggregate consumer surplus CS_x generated over the area $(2x_0)$ is computed as

$$CS_{x_0} = 2\int_{m^*}^{a-x_0}\left(ax_0 - \frac{1}{2}x_0^2 - x_0 m\right)dm$$

$$+ 2\int_{a-x_0}^{a}\frac{(a - m)^2}{2}dm$$

$$= a(a - x_0)x_0 - (2a - x_0)\sqrt{F/2x_0}x_0$$

$$+ \frac{F}{2} + \frac{x_0^3}{3} \quad (29)$$

The consumer surplus *per unit area* CSA_{x_0} is then given by:

$$CSA_{x_0} = \frac{a}{2}(a - x_0) - (2a - x_0)\sqrt{F/8x_0}$$

$$+ \frac{F}{4x_0} + \frac{x_0^2}{6}$$

$$= \left[\frac{1}{2}(1 - \theta) - (2 - \theta)\sqrt{\mu/8\theta}\right.$$

$$\left. + \frac{\mu}{4\theta} + \frac{\theta^2}{6}\right]a^2 \quad (30)$$

where we now use μ and θ as coefficients in $F = \mu a^3$ and $x_0 = \theta a$ such that $4/27 \geqslant \mu \geqslant 0$ and $1 \geqslant \theta \geqslant 0$.

We now differentiate (30) partially with respect to θ to obtain

$$\frac{\partial(CSA_{x_0})}{\partial\theta} = \left(-\frac{1}{2} + \frac{2 + \theta}{2\theta}\sqrt{\mu/8\theta} - \frac{\mu}{4\theta^2} + \frac{\theta}{3}\right)a^2 \quad (31)$$

The sign of this partial derivative presumably depends on particular values of μ and θ. However, it is meaningful to evaluate the sign within the relevant constrained domain for (θ, μ) that is given not only by (25), (26), and (28) as

$$2/3 \geqslant \theta \geqslant 0, \qquad 4/27 \geqslant \mu \geqslant 0 \qquad \text{and} \quad \theta \geqslant 2\mu \quad (32)$$

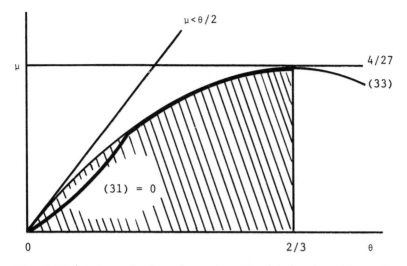

Figure 12.4. The optimal market radius (θ) of industries with varying costs (μ).

but also by the more binding requirement that the equilibrium industry revenue $m^*Q_{x_0}^*$ be greater than the individual firm's fixed cost $F = \mu a^3$. This condition is given via (24) and (28) by

$$m^*Q_{x_0}^* = [(2 - \theta)\theta - 2\theta\sqrt{\mu/2\theta}]\sqrt{\mu/2\theta} > \mu$$

$$\therefore \frac{(2 - \theta)^2\theta}{8} > \mu \qquad (33)$$

The constraints (32) and (33) on (θ, μ) are illustrated by the shaded area of Figure 12-4. The concave curve $\mu = (2 - \theta)^2\theta/8$ in this figure indicates the combination of the fixed cost μ and the market radius θ required for the local monopolist to obtain Chamberlinean tangency equilibrium under Löschian competition. An immediate question is whether this equilibrium is socially optimal in terms of consumer surplus per unit area CSA_{x_0}. The question is whether CSA_{x_0} may be increased by a larger market radius x_0 shared by a greater number of local firms under *intra*local Cournot competition. To answer this question, evaluate the sign of (31) at the boundary curve of (33). Thus, substituting $\mu = (2 - \theta)^2\theta/8$ in (31),

$$\frac{\partial(CSA_{x_0})}{\partial\theta} = \frac{23\theta^2 - 36\theta + 12}{96\theta} \qquad (1 > \theta > 0) \qquad (34)$$

By applying the familiar quadratic formula to this result, its sign can be positive or negative according to whether θ is less or greater than the smaller solution value of the quadratic equation on the numerator of (34); that is, $\theta = (18 - 4\sqrt{3})/23 \ (\cong 11/23)$.

The implication of this result should be clear. When the fixed cost μ happens to be relatively (or significantly) high, such that the required market radius (for the monopolist) is also high, a decrease in *inter*local competition with a greater market radius θ, which requires an increase in *intra*local competition via Cournot entry to maintain zero-profit equilibrium, will *lower* social welfare. Whereas *intra*local concentration of firms should be avoided, *inter*local competition should be sufficiently intense insofar as $\partial(CSA_{x_0})/\partial\theta < 0$. *Intra*local monopoly subject to *inter*local competition that tends to wipe out profit is the best that can be expected from a high-cost industry.

When fixed costs are relatively low, *inter*local concentration of *intra*local monopoly firms with smaller market radii should be avoided as *intra*local concentration of firms with more widely scattered production centers provides greater social welfare; that is, $\partial(CSA_{x_0})/\partial\theta > 0$.

The optimal combination of (θ, μ) obtainable in principle by equating (31) to zero is illustrated by the heavy lined curve in Figure 12-4.[3] Note, however, that where this optimal locus merges with the upper part of the constraint (33), the sign of (31) remains negative. The locus is nevertheless optimal *subject to the constraint*.

Maximization of Social Surplus (Welfare)

The foregoing analysis is concerned with the level of social welfare under conditions of long-run zero-profit equilibrium. It has already been shown that a smaller degree of *inter*local competition, which allows firms to earn positive profits, provides a greater *social* surplus, provided that fixed costs are sufficiently low. A new question now must be asked. Given locational equilibrium conditions that maximize consumer surplus, would a smaller degree of *intra*local compe-

---

[3] The author is indebted to M. Okamura for the underlying computation for (31).

tition yield a smaller or greater social surplus? Without loss of generality, this question can be framed in terms of the nonspatial model of Cournot competition because the degree of *inter*local Löschian competition is being treated as given.

The departure point is the Cournot equilibrium point E when market demand DD is linear, as illustrated by Figure 12-5. Consumer surplus (over a given area) is represented by the quasi-triangular area under DD above the price line p_0. A marginal exit will shift the firm's average revenue curve AR_i parallel rightward to AR_i'. An equilibrium price after exit is represented by p_1. (The optimum p_1 is given at the intersection of AR_i' and a straight line from the origin with the same slope as DD, AR_i, that is, b.) The industry profit is then given by the rectangular area equal to $(p_1 - p_2)Q_1$, where p_2 is the average (fixed) cost now lower than p_0 and Q_1 is the market demand quantity associated with the higher price p_1.

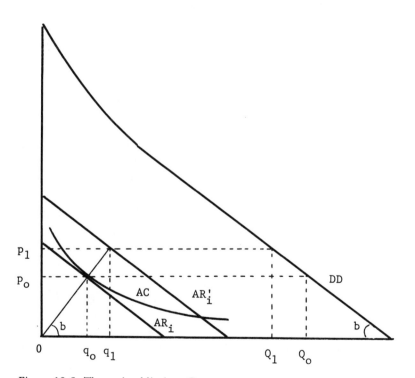

Figure 12.5. The optimal limit to Cournot entry.

The higher price reduces consumer surplus by an amount approximately equal to $(p_1 - p_0)Q_1$. However, this amount clearly is smaller than the increased producer surplus $(p_1 - p_2)Q_1$ by the amount $(p_0 - p_2)Q_1$. To be more precise, the net gain from reduced competition in terms of the aggregate social surplus is equal to $(p_0 - p_2)Q_1 - (p_1 - p_0)(Q_0 - Q_1)/2$. This quantity can be positive even if the shifted firm demand is as much as three times as large as the original AR_i in terms of the price intercept value, provided that the market demand is still larger. (See Section V of this chapter for details.) In this sense, the Cournot part of Cournot-Lösch competition is also excessive.

A final note is warranted on the generality of this last proposition. The net gain from reduced Cournot competition requires neither linearity in demand nor constancy of the marginal cost of production. As long as a market demand is sufficiently large relative to the individual demand that the firm *perceives* in the long-run zero-profit Cournot equilibrium, any marginal exit of firms is socially desirable regardless of the form of the demand or cost functions. This general result follows because, while the maximum possible reduction in consumer surplus is bounded and fixed, the amount of increased industry profit by reason of exit depends on the size of the market, which need not be bounded or otherwise small. Unlimited entry under Cournot competition is therefore generally excessive.

There must exist some degree of "optimal limit to *intra*local entry" insofar as Cournot competition is concerned. An optimal limit of this nature can be shown to be higher when market demand relative to the individual cost is larger. (The next section presents this contention with a proof based on linear demand and fixed cost.) In other words, the greater the market demand, the greater the warranted profit, and thus consumers are charged higher prices.

V. Optimal Limit to Entry under Cournot Oligopoly: A Digression

This section, as a final note, demonstrates that the so-called Cournot unlimited entry, which wipes out excess profit, tends to be "excessive" in the sense of reducing rather than increasing the social surplus.

Moreover, based on the calculation of an "optimal degree" of imperfect competition, a greater market demand relative to costs of production can be shown to warrant a higher profit to individual firms, and lower degree of competition, for that matter, for social optimum.

The analysis begins with two simplifying assumptions, both of which are relaxed in most of the arguments.

Assumption E. The market demand is a linear function of price alone.

Assumption F. Firms, including prospective entrants, are alike and subject to equal fixed costs of entry and production.

Any Cournot entry is known to shift the demand that the individual firm perceives leftward, parallel to the market demand.

Suppose a Cournot tangency equilibrium took place under conditions of the average cost and revenue given by

$$AC = \frac{F}{q} \tag{35}$$

$$AR_0 = a - bq \tag{36}$$

The equilibrium price p_0 and the quantity q_0 are then specifiable as

$$p_0 = a/2 \tag{37}$$

$$q_0 = a/2b \tag{38}$$

Now suppose AR shifted by an amount h to AR_1 because some firms exited. Then, the new equilibrium price or quantity set for each of the remaining firms is given by

$$p_1 = (a + h)/2 \tag{39}$$

$$q_1 = (a + h)/2b \tag{40}$$

The shaded triangular area in Figure 12-6 may be called the *deadweight loss* in consumer surplus, which is equal to

$$\Delta(CS) = (p_1 - p_0)(q_1 - q_0)/2 = h^2/8b \tag{41}$$

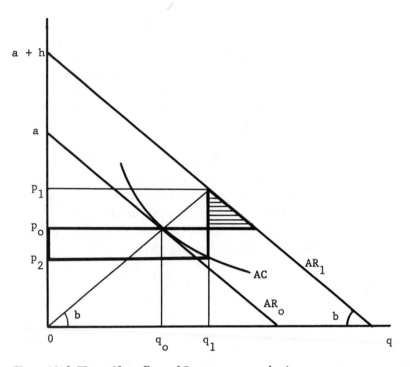

Figure 12.6. The welfare effects of Cournot entry and exit.

Aside from this loss, each firm now provides (or enjoys) profits that more than compensate for a reduction in consumer surplus. The excess surplus in this sense is $(p_0 - p_2)$ *per quantity served* by the whole industry. This amount $\Delta\pi$ is therefore at least as large as $(p_0 - p_2)q_1$. Thus,

$$\Delta\pi \geqslant (p_0 - p_2)q_1 = ah/4b \qquad (42)$$

It follows from (41) and (42) that the minimum net gain, in terms of social surplus, from arbitrary exit, which entails a shift in AR (by h in terms of the price intercept value) is

$$\Delta\pi_{min} - \Delta(CS) = h(2a - h)/8b \qquad (43)$$

This amount is nonnegative for any $b \leq 2a$. A direct implication of this result is that even if the market demand happens to be as small as AR_1 and with $b = 2a$, as many as two firms (out of three) can exit the industry without harm to the aggregate surplus. If the market demand is larger than $(AR_1 = 3a - bq)$, two or more firms can exit the industry and unambiguously increase the social surplus. In general, the larger the market demand relative to individual firms' costs, the larger the number of firms that can be enticed to exit from the zero-profit Cournot equilibrium industry in order to increase the social welfare. For this general result to hold, the market demand need not be linear; it need only be downward-sloping. Moreover, the firm's marginal cost MC need not be zero or constant. The firm's MC is required only to cut its MR from below for local stability of equilibrium. The reason for this generality and definitiveness in results is that although $\Delta\pi$, as equal to $(p_0 - p_2)Q$, can increase without limits as a monotonically increasing function of the market demand Q, the dead-weight loss in consumer surplus remains constant and finite, regardless of the size of the market demand, given p_0 and p_2.

Return now to Assumptions E and F in order to identify an "optimal limit" to entry. For this purpose, the b that maximizes the social surplus must be computed. It is important in this connection to define the "correct" net gain, not just the minimum one defined in (43), from the shift in b. Thus, (43) is replaced by

$$CNG \equiv \Delta\pi - \Delta(CS) = (p_0 - p_2)Q_0 - b^2/8b$$

$$= (p_0 - p_2)(nq_0) - b^2/8b$$

$$= \frac{2a^2nb - ab^2 - b^3}{8b(a + b)} \qquad (44)$$

where Q_0 (equal to nq_0) is the quantity of the market demand at $p = p_0$, and n is the number of firms under zero-profit equilibrium.

Differentiating (44) with respect to b yields

$$\frac{\partial(CNG)}{\partial b} = \frac{na^3}{4b(a + b)^2} - \frac{b}{4b} \qquad (45)$$

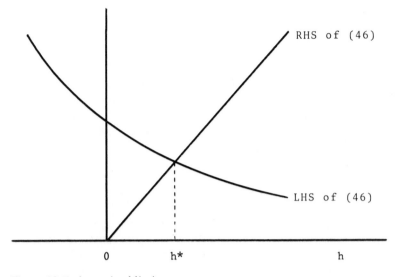

Figure 12.7. An optimal limit to entry.

Equating this result to zero yields

$$\frac{na^3}{(a + h)^2} = h \tag{46}$$

Thus, the h that maximizes the net gain from retreating from conditions of "excessive" zero-profit equilibrium can be obtained readily at the intersection of the two functions of h on the left-hand side and the right-hand side of (46). A diagrammatic solution of the optimal exit h is illustrated in Figure 12-7. Clearly, a higher n, that is, a greater market demand, implies a higher optimal h, which in turn implies a higher equilibrium price and profit and a lesser degree of competition, which are warranted to ensure social optimum (maximum aggregate surplus).

As an example, assume $n = 100$. Then the optimal $h = 4a$ and the optimal number of firms is $Q^*(p^* = 5a/2)/q^*(p^* = 5a/2) = 96/5 \cong 19$. Thus, as many as 81 firms out of 100 are excessive from the standpoint of social optimum. This seemingly surprising result is in fact quite understandable and reasonable in light of Assumption F, according to which one firm's unit cost decreases without limit as output is increased. Thus, from the standpoint of efficiency in production, one firm would suffice. Indeed, when economies of scale prevail the "first-best" solution in the sense of the marginal cost–pricing result is one firm.

Under conditions of imperfect competition à la Cournot, the optimal solution is only "second-best" in the sense that the dead-weight loss in consumer surplus can never be avoided. However, while this amount is relatively small and limited, the net gain from exit depends upon the size of the market demand, which can be infinitely large *regardless* of the form of the cost or demand functions, provided that the former is U-shaped and the latter slopes downward. For this reason, the conclusion that the greater market demand warrants greater limits to entry and higher prices for social optimum is fairly general.

VI. Conclusion

This chapter has presented simple alternative models of location to explain casual empiricism: In some industries, hundreds of smaller, independent firms are concentrated spatially in a small area (virtually at a point) to compete not only among themselves *intra*locally but also *inter*locally with firms in other spatially separate areas; in other industries giant firms are scattered sparsely, each seeming to monopolize a large market area; and in still other industries atomistic firms are dispersed evenly over a landscape.

Our model has shown that the size of the market demand relative to the costs in a given industry plays an important role in the optimal arrangement of firms over a market area where consumers are distributed continuously. In particular, it has shown that, given demand and cost parameters, certain degrees of not only *intra*local competition but also *inter*local competition help generate maximum social welfare. Perhaps most important, it was shown that such optimal locational arrangement involves positive (excess) profits for individual firms *under conditions of spatial,* that is, *imperfect, competition.* As long as perfect competition is nowhere to be found, the long-cherished paradigm of unlimited entry may warrant reconsideration.

References

[1] Bowes, M. "Profit-Maximizing versus Optimal Behavior in a Spatial Setting: Summary and Extensions." *Southern Economic Journal* 50 (1984): 680–89.

[2] Greenhut, M. L. *Plant Location in Theory and in Practice.* Chapel Hill: University of North Carolina Press, 1956.

[3] Holahan, W. "Welfare Effects of Spatial Price Discrimination." *American Economic Review* 65 (1975): 498–503.

[4] Ohta, H. "On Efficiency of Production under Conditions of Imperfect Competition." *Southern Economic Journal* 43 (1976): 1124–35.

[5] Stern, N. "The Optimal Size of Market Areas." *Journal of Economic Theory* (1972): 154–73.

[6] Suzumura, K. "Entry in a Cournot Market: Equilibrium versus Optimality." Discussion Paper Series No. 94, Hitotsubashi University, 1983.

[7] von Weizsäcker, C. C. "A Welfare Analysis of Barriers to Entry." *Bell Journal of Economics* 11 (1980): 399–420.

13.
Spatial Competition, Innovation, and Related Markets

I. Introduction

So far, the product market along with buyers (consumers) and sellers (firms) has been assumed, but the labor market has been neglected in the inquiry into spatial pricing. However, the consumers spatially dispersed over the firm's market area are prospective workers for the firm as well. A question might arise; would not some of the seemingly surprising results of spatial pricing have something to do with this analytically limited partial-equilibrium approach? With this question in mind, the present chapter develops a model of spatial pricing with specific reference to the spatial labor market. Widening the theoretical scope also allows examination of new questions, such as what happens to wages under various conditions.

Of particular interest in this connection is the impact of spatial competition or productivity changes (technical progress) on the spatial labor market as well as the product market.

This chapter discloses, among other things, that the so-called perverse effect of spatial competition remains intact in the generalized model as it reveals a rise in the mill price on one hand and a drop in the (real) wage rate as a consequence of Löschian competition. Moreover, the model also reveals a perverse effect of technical progress upon the local labor market. In particular, it will be shown that the greater the workers' willingness to work (i.e., the greater is the supply of labor for a given wage rate), the more likely the wage rate is to fall as labor productivity increases. Technical progress *can* be an enemy to workers even under the substitution conditions envisaged by Hicks [3] as being favorable to workers.

Section II sets forth the basic assumptions and the model of the chapter. Section III shows the basic framework and the mechanism of the model in a nutshell to emphasize the fundamental characteristic of the model: how it may be solved for equilibrium values and how they are interrelated. Section IV, in turn, examines the impact of spatial competition upon the regional product and labor markets. Similarly, Section V highlights the impact of innovation upon these markets. Section VI attempts to generalize the Section V analysis in terms of the form of assumed functions, followed by concluding remarks. [The Appendix, which follows Chapter 13, briefly sketches a simpler, yet more rigorously complete model of general equilibrium (than the text model) with one product and one factor under conditions of spatial competition.]

II. The Assumptions and the Model

Assume the following:

Assumption A. The local firm is subject to Löschian competition but otherwise is a local monopolist in selling its product.

Assumption B. The firm employs workers whose training is specific to that firm and who are distributed uniformly alongside an unbounded commuting route or loop.

Assumption C. Although the firm is a virtual monopsonist in the labor market, it behaves as a price taker in labor demand in tacit agreement with workers that they too behave as price takers in labor supply. Without such agreement or collusion the firm-specific workers may organize as a monopolistic union and confront the monopsonist firm. To avoid such a bilateral monopoly situation and at the same time maximize joint benefit require this particular labor-management relation to yield the Pareto optimal solution.[1]

Assumption D. The workers are homogeneous not only in their labor supply but also in their product demand. The labor supply of an individual worker-consumer is given by a linear function

---

[1] See Machlup and Tabor [4] and Greenhut and Ohta [1; 2] on the benefit of vertical merger by successive monopolists or oligopolists.

of his or her net real wage rate, net of the commuting cost. The individual demand for the product is, as described earlier, a linear function of the CIF price. In a more complete model of general equilibrium, the labor supply and the product demand must be related mutually in light of the Walras Law. In the present model of quasi-general equilibrium these functions are specified independently in order to introduce the cost of distance simply and directly into each specification.

Assumption E. The firm applies a variable labor input to other fixed inputs. Despite the existence of other fixed inputs, the output is a linear function of labor input alone.

All these linearity assumptions can be relaxed as in Section V with no radical change in the conclusions of this chapter. The linearity assumptions are adopted, however, to simplify exposition of the argument in concrete parameters.

The Model

Pursuant to Assumptions B and D, the following individual labor supply and product demand functions can be specified at any given point x distance units from the firm along the commuting route.

$$\ell_x = \alpha(w - kx) \qquad\qquad (w/k > x > 0) \qquad\qquad (1)$$

$$q_x = (a - m - tx)/b \qquad \left(\frac{a - m}{t} > x > 0\right) \qquad (2)$$

where ℓ_x is the quantity of labor supplied, w the real wage rate, q_x the quantity of product demanded at x, k the cost per unit of commuting distance, m the FOB mill price, and t is the freight cost of delivery per unit distance. The parameters α, k, a, b, and t all are positive.

The aggregate regional labor supply and product demand functions can be derived, respectively, from (1) and (2) subject to Assumption A. Thus,

$$L = 2\int_0^{w/k} \alpha(w - kx)dx = (\alpha/k)w^2 \qquad\qquad (w \leq kx_0)$$

$$= 2 \int_0^{x_0} \alpha(w - kx)dx = 2\alpha w x_0 - \alpha k x_0^2 \quad (w > kx_0) \quad (3)$$

$$Q = 2 \int_0^{(a-m)/t} (a - m - tx)(1/b)dx = (a - m)^2/bt$$

$$(m \geq a - tx_0)$$

$$= 2 \int_0^{x_0} (a - m - tx)(1/b)dx$$

$$= (2/b)(a - m)x_0 - (t/b)x_0^2 \quad (m < a - tx_0) \quad (4)$$

where x_0 is the market radius for the local firm, which is fixed parametrically under Löschian competition once rival firms' locations are fixed.

Several comments are warranted concerning Equations (3) and (4). First, the upper line of (3) indicates that the labor supply is determined uniquely as a quadratic function of the real wage rate alone, as long as it is kept below a certain critical level tx_0 associated with the Löschian market radius x_0. Not all individuals within this radius are willing to be employed at such low wages. The spatial labor market area (boundary) thus is defined naturally by wage rate rather than Löschian competition. Similar observations can be made about the upper line of (4). When mill price is sufficiently high, the firm's market area becomes smaller than the Löschian radius x_0. The quantity demanded decreases quadratically as mill price rises beyond the critical level, $a - tx_0$.

Second, Löschian competition becomes effective only under conditions of the lower specifications of (3) and (4), with x_0 sufficiently small. When Löschian competition is effective, both the regional labor supply and product demand curves become linear in terms of real wage rate and mill price, respectively. This result reflects the form of the individual labor supply and product demand functions, which are linear.

Third, and most important, the regional labor supply and product demand shift inward (outward) as effective Löschian competition becomes more (less) intense, that is, with a smaller (larger) market radius. This result follows from the following two related observations: that the linear portion of (3) or (4) is tangent to the convex part of these functions respectively at $w = kx_0$ and $m = a - tx_0$; and that the tangent becomes increasingly steep as the tangency point on the convex part of (3) and (4) moves away from the origin, that is, with greater market radius x_0.

Based on these observations, the regional labor supply (3) and the regional product demand (4) can be illustrated by Figures 13-1 and 13-2, respectively. In particular, these figures illustrate how the regional labor supply L_S and product demand Q_D shift leftward as effective Löschian competition reduces the firm's market radius from x_0 to x_0'.

At any given stage of Löschian competition, the firm must decide on the quantity of output Q and employment L subject to Equations (3) and (4) with a given market radius, for example, x_0. To solve this problem consider the firm's profit Π, which is defined by

$$\Pi = mQ - WL - F \tag{5}$$

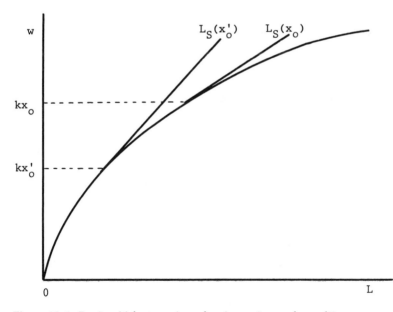

Figure 13.1. Regional labor supply under alternative market radii.

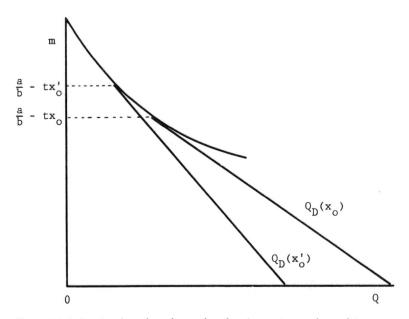

Figure 13.2. Regional product demand under alternative market radii.

where W is the money wage rate and F is the fixed cost. The first-order condition for profit maximization subject to (4) and Assumptions C and E is given by

$$\frac{\partial \Pi}{\partial L} = \frac{\partial \Pi}{\partial Q}\frac{\partial Q}{\partial L} = \left(a - \frac{tx_0}{2} - \frac{b\beta}{x_0}L \right)\beta - W = 0$$

$$\therefore \left(a - \frac{tx_0}{2} - \frac{b\beta}{x_0}L \right)\beta = W \qquad (6)$$

where the new symbol β stands for a constant marginal physical product of labor.

Note that the left-hand side of (6) is the marginal revenue product of labor to be equated with the right-hand side W, that is, the marginal nominal cost of labor. Thus, the right-hand side W being an exogenous parameter, Equation (6) represents the firm's demand function for labor. Recall in this connection that although the firm is a virtual local monopolist, it behaves as a price taker in labor demand pursuant to Assumption C.

Being defined in terms of the nominal wage rate, the labor demand function (6) can readily be put in real terms by dividing both sides by the mill price of the product. Since the mill price m is defined by (4) as a function of Q, which in turn is given by $Q = \beta L$, (6) is reduced to

$$\frac{[a - (t/2)x_0 - (b\beta/x_0)L]\beta}{a - (t/2)x_0 - (b\beta/2x_0)L} = w \tag{7}$$

where $w = W/m$ is the real wage rate. It can readily be shown that the regional labor demand function (7) is a concave, downward-sloping curve. Moreover, the price (wage) intercept value is β, whereas the quantity (employment) intercept value is $(a - tx_0/2) \times (x_0/b\beta)$. Thus, it follows that the regional labor demand curve shifts or is twisted inward (leftward) as the firm's market radius x_0 is

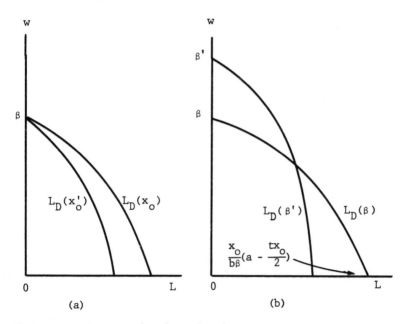

Figure 13.3. Regional labor demand under alternative shift parameters. (a) Shift in x_0, (b) shift in β.

reduced as a result of Löschian competition, as illustrated by Figure 13-3(a).

There is another important shift parameter in the labor demand: the labor productivity β. A rise in β not only twists the labor demand inward (leftward), but it pulls the price intercept value upward! The result is illustrated by Figure 13-3(b), which shows two labor demand curves intersecting under alternative labor productivities.

III. The Model in a Nutshell

It now is feasible to show in a nutshell how spatial equilibrium is obtained in the labor and product markets. For this purpose, it is necessary to initially utilize a so-called four-dimensional diagram with all four quadrants to illustrate how the variables are interrelated. With certain normalization and simplification procedures, the model then can be solved mathematically for equilibrium values.

Assumed in Figure 13-4 is a unique but arbitrary set of parameters. The first quadrant repeats Figure 13-2 and shows the regional product demand, or Equation (4), that the firm faces under Löschian competition. Related to this is the regional labor demand shown in the third quadrant. The curve there, in effect, is the derived demand, derived from the product demand via the production function shown in the fourth quadrant. This derived labor demand in the third quadrant intersects with the regional labor supply of Figure 13-1, which is now moved to the third quadrant of the figure. Thus, the model can be readily solved for the equilibrium real wage rate w^* and employment L^* at the intersection of these two curves. Equilibrium employment L^*, thus determined, determines in turn equilibrium output Q^* in the first and fourth quadrants. Directly related to equilibrium Q^* in the first quadrant is equilibrium mill price m^*. Finally, equilibrium money wage W^* is determined in the second quadrant by definition as a rectangular area of m^* by w^*.

In passing, note that in this general equilibrium framework with one product, the labor supply L_S and the product demand Q_D are defined *independently*. This is permissible only if there exists another market behind the model. In this respect, the present model requires the existence of a *money* wage rate, which implies the existence of a

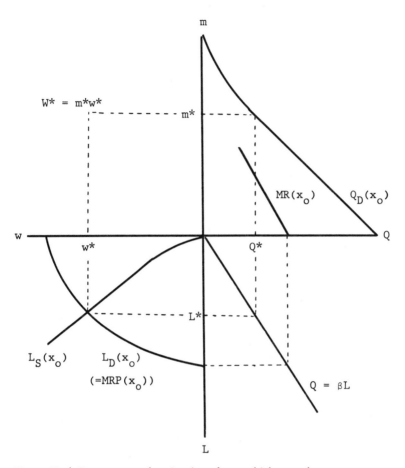

Figure 13.4. Interconnected regional product and labor markets.

money market, the equilibrium condition for which is deleted subject
to the Walras Law. Without money, the product price m must be
defined as *either* unity in terms of product *or* $1/w$. The latter is the
relative price of the product, relative to the real wage rate. With this
latter definition, the second quadrant of Figure 13-4 becomes a unitary rectangular hyperbola; that is, $m = 1/w$. It follows accordingly
that the Q_D in the first quadrant and $L_S(x_0)$ in the third quadrant
cannot be defined independently: One must be derived from the other
in conjunction with the second-quadrant–fourth-quadrant relations.

This approach, in effect, goes back to the prior analysis, developed in earlier chapters. The present chapter goes beyond them in widening the analytical framework as attention is focused on both the labor market and the product market.

The present model of spatial pricing may now be solved mathematically. In doing so, the computation is simplified by normalizing all function parameters to unity; that is, $a = b = \alpha = t = k = \beta = 1$. The regional labor demand and supply functions then are simplified respectively as

$$w = \frac{1 - x_0/2 - L/x_0}{1 - x_0/2 - L/2x_0} \tag{8}$$

$$L = 2wx_0 - x_0^2 \tag{9}$$

Substituting (9) in (8) yields[2]

$$w^* = \frac{3}{2} - \frac{1}{2}\sqrt{5 - 2x_0} \tag{10}$$

$$\therefore L^* = \left(3 - x_0 - \sqrt{5 - 2x_0}\right)x_0 \tag{11}$$

Substituting $Q^* = L^*$ back into the product demand function in turn yields

$$m^* = -\frac{1}{2}\left(1 - \sqrt{5 - 2x_0}\right) \tag{12}$$

where the equilibrium product price m^* must be nonnegative, which means that the firm's market radius x_0 is required to be less than 2 (mega miles, or million miles, or some other measure of distance).

---

[2] Technically, there are two solutions for x: $w^* = 3/2 \pm (1/2)\sqrt{(5 - 2x_0)}$. However, the solution that exceeds 3/2 is irrelevant because the normalization requires w^* to be less than unity, for the real wage rate cannot exceed average labor productivity; that is, $w \leq \beta = 1$. Without normalization of β to unity, the solution for w is given by $w^* = \beta + 1/2\beta + (1 - 1 - 1/\beta)x_0/4 - \sqrt{\{[\beta + 1/2\beta + (1 - 1/\beta)x_0/4]^2 + x_0(1/2 - \beta) - 1\}}$. This formula is derived from (3) and (7) with $a = b = \alpha = t = k = 1$.

The nominal wage rate $W^* = m^* w^*$ is given by

$$W^* = -\frac{1}{4}\left(1 - \sqrt{5 - 2x_0}\right)\left(3 - \sqrt{5 - 2x_0}\right)$$

$$= -\frac{1}{2}\left(4 - x_0 - 2\sqrt{5 - 2x_0}\right) \tag{13}$$

Finally, the profit for the firm is

$$\Pi^* = m^* Q^* - W^* L^* - F$$

$$= \left(3 - x_0 - \sqrt{5 - 2x_0}\right)^2 x_0/2 - F \tag{14}$$

The general form of this cubic function can be determined by observing the following: $\Pi^* = -F$ at $x_0 = 0$ or 2; and the derivative of Π^* with respect to x_0 can be shown to be zero at $x_0 = 1/2$. It follows that the maximum possible profit obtainable within the meaningful domain of x_0 is given at $x_0 = 1/2$. Moreover, profit decreases monotonically as x_0 diminishes due to spatial competition. Figure 13-5 illustrates these relations. The fact that the maximum Π^* is attained at $x_0 = 1/2$ means that the firm will choose this market radius under conditions of spatial monopoly. Any positive profit Π^*, however, tends to call for new entry, reducing under conditions of Löschian competition the firm's market radius below this optimal level until a zero profit equilibrium radius is attained at the intersection of the cubic curve $(\Pi^* + F)$ and the fixed cost line F of Figure 13-5. Thus, while the firm is unwilling to choose its market radius beyond $x_0^* = 1/2$, it may be forced to choose any market radius below it under various degrees of Löschian competition and/or levels of fixed costs. It follows that the economically meaningful domain for (14) is limited to $x_0 = [0, 1/2]$.

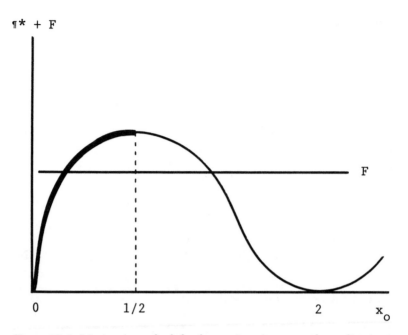

Figure 13.5. Maximum profit defined over the relevant market radius $x_0 =$ [0, 1/2].

IV. The Impact of Spatial Competition

It earlier was shown that spatial competition lowers the firm's profit. But what happens to other variables? This question can be answered simply by differentiating the relevant equations derived in the preceding section with respect to the market radius x_0 to see the resultant sign. Thus, from (10) through (13), the following is obtained:

$$\frac{dw^*}{dx_0} = 1/2\sqrt{5 - 2x_0} > 0 \tag{15}$$

$$\frac{dL^*}{dx_0} = 3 - 2x_0 - (5 - 3x_0)/\sqrt{5 - 2x_0} > 0 \tag{16}$$

$$\frac{dm^*}{dx_0} = -1/2\sqrt{5 - 2x_0} < 0 \tag{17}$$

$$\frac{dW^*}{dx_0} = 1/2 - 1/\sqrt{5 - 2x_0} \geq 0 \qquad (18)$$

where all the signs apply to the specified relevant domain $x_0 = [0, 1/2]$.

The positivity of $(16)^3$ implies that spatial competition tends to lower regional employment L^* (along with corresponding output Q^*). This should cause no surprise because, under the present model, a new entrant at a distance will take away or bid off part of the workers currently employed by the incumbent firm. Workers who have been commuting a long distance switch employers; the labor supply that the local firm faces shifts leftward accordingly. The wage rates, therefore, ought to have risen ceteris paribus. Nevertheless, as Equations (15) and (18) indicate, entry tends to *lower* real as well as nominal wage rates.

The unfavorable effects of spatial competition fall upon all workers who remain to be employed by the incumbent firm(s). Moreover, these same workers hit by lower wages are hit again by a rise in the mill price of the product upon any new entry with a resultant fall in x_0 as seen by (17). These adverse effects of spatial competition concur with, and actually are accounted for by, a downward shift in the regional product demand, which becomes increasingly inelastic with smaller market radii (under the present model of the linear basic demand function).

It goes without saying, however, that the workers who change employers after entry are mostly better off than before entry. Some workers change employers after new entry even if they are worse off than before. These "unfortunate converts" nevertheless are better off with new employers than with incumbent employers. In Figure 13-6, a heavy-lined spatial schedule of the net real wage rate is compared with a light-lined counterpart. If the former is generated by firms located at A and B, the latter is the result of a new firm entry at C. Workers located around C, over which the light-lined wage

---

[3] The sign of dL^*/dx_0 is positive for any relevant x_0, that is, $1/2 \geq x_0 \geq 0$. This follows because over the assumed domain L^* is a continuous differentiable function of x_0, $dL^*(0)/dx_0$ and $dL^*(1/2)dx_0$ are both positive, and $dL^*(x_0)/dx_0 = \{\sqrt{(5 - 2x_0)} - [(3x_0 - 5)/(2x_0 - 3)]\}(3 - 2x_0)/\sqrt{(5 - 2x_0)} = 0$ yields an extremum for L^* at $x_0 > 1/2$. Thus, L^* can be seen to be a monotonically increasing function of x_0 over the domain $1/2 \geq x_0 \geq 0$.

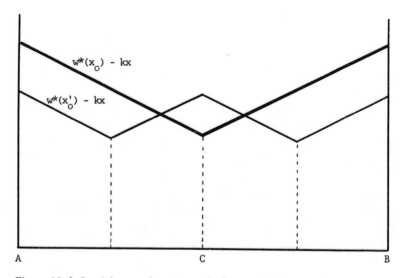

Figure 13.6. Spatial net real wage rates before and after entry at C.

schedule exceeds the heavy-lined one, are clearly better off after new entry and are "happy converts" while others are worse off and are divided into "unfortunate converts" and "unfortunate loyals" who should be readily identifiable in the figure.

While spatial entry may thus yield a distinct benefit to workers in the neighborhood of new firm location, it is also likely to yield a vast adverse effect upon workers in other chain-related areas. If there existed n incumbent firms under chain oligopoly à la Lösch, a new entry would benefit less than $1/(n + 1)$ of the total number of workers, a limited number around the entrant's location. However, most of the other workers can also be adversely affected by a resultant rise in mill price when a new equilibrium is attained with $(n + 1)$ firms, each monopolizing the same market radius after a due process of relocation. After relocation of any incumbent firm, half of its customers will be worse off simply because the firm moves away. The remaining half will find the firm to be nearer, but to the extent that mill price is higher after relocation, they should be less well off *and* the original half worse off to an even greater degree.

V. The Impact of Innovation

Now consider the impact of technical progress upon the variables of particular interest. For simplicity, evaluate the impact of a change in labor productivity β at the point of equilibrium obtained in Section III. Moreover, the evaluation is made at $x_0 = 1/2$, the maximum and most profitable market for the firm. Equations (10) and (11) must reappear accordingly, via (3) and (7), with $x_0 = 1/2$ and all other parameters but β being equal to unity, as follows

$$w^* = \beta + \frac{3 + \beta}{8\beta}$$

$$- \sqrt{\left(\beta + \frac{3 + \beta}{8\beta}\right)^2 - (3 + 2\beta)/4} \quad (19)$$

$$L^* = w^* - 1/4 \quad (20)$$

Differentiating (19) with respect to β and evaluating at $\beta = 1$ yields

$$\frac{dw^*}{d\beta} = 1 - \frac{3}{8\beta^2}$$

$$- \frac{[\beta + (3 + \beta)/8\beta](1 - 3/8\beta^2) - 1/4}{\sqrt{[\beta + (3 + \beta)/8\beta]^2 - (3 + 2\beta)/4}}$$

$$= -\frac{1}{16} < 0 \quad (21)$$

In light of (20), it follows

$$\frac{dL^*}{d\beta} = \frac{dw^*}{d\beta} < 0 \quad (22)$$

Thus, a rise in labor productivity as a result of innovation tends to lower, not raise, real wage rate and regional employment as well.

The fall in wage rate indicated by (21) shows only a short-run effect of innovation, in which the firm's market radius is assumed to be

fixed. However, although innovation is harmful to workers, it is
certainly beneficial to the firm, as it increases profits. However, as
seen earlier, profits or increases in profits tend to induce entry, which
in turn reduces the firm's market radius x_0. This fall in x_0 in turn, as
seen in Section IV, tends to further decrease real wage rates, which
have already been lowered by innovation. Thus, innovation can hit
workers twice: once by the innovation itself and once more by spatial
competition induced by innovation.

As the real wage rate declines, so does the regional labor supply
and hence employment, as indicated by Equation (22). Since the
firm's market radius is fixed and the number of firms under Löschian
competition also is fixed in the short run, the negative sign of (22)
implies that innovation tends to decrease aggregate employment as
well. However, whereas innovation-induced entry further lowers regional employment, entry itself makes a substantial contribution to
employment, at the point of entry at least. Moreover, declines in the
regional employment may be more than offset by an increase in the
number of employing regions so that the average employment *per unit
of distance* L^*/x_0 can increase. Indeed the derivative of this ratio with
respect to β evaluated at $x_0 = 1/2$, and $\beta = 1$ is reduced to

$$\frac{d(L^*/2x_0)}{d\beta} = \frac{\partial(L^*/2x_0)}{\partial\beta} + \frac{\partial(L^*/2x_0)}{\partial x_0}\frac{dx_0}{d\beta}$$

$$= -\frac{1}{16} - \frac{1}{4}\left(\frac{dx_0}{d\beta}\right) \tag{23}$$

where $L^*/2x_0 = w^* - x_0/2$ via (9), not to be confused with (20),
which requires x_0 to be a given constant, not a parametric variable.
Thus, as long as one unit of increase in β ends up with a decrease in
x_0 by more than 1/4 units, the sign of (23) becomes positive and
innovation helps to increase the aggregate employment or average
employment per area.

Allied with a β-related change in the regional employment L^* are
changes in the regional output Q^* and mill price of the product m^*,
which are evaluated, respectively, at $x_0 = 1/2$ and $\beta = 1$.

$$\frac{dQ^*}{d\beta} = \frac{\partial Q^*}{\partial L^*}\frac{dL^*}{d\beta} + \frac{\partial Q^*}{\partial \beta}$$

$$= \beta\left(-\frac{1}{16}\right) + L^* = \frac{3}{16} > 0 \tag{24}$$

$$\frac{dm^*}{d\beta} = \frac{dm^*}{dQ^*}\frac{dQ^*}{d\beta} < 0 \tag{25}$$

Thus, in the short run at least, innovation tends to increase the regional output Q^* and lower mill price m^*. Here, no perverse effects of innovation per se are observed insofar as the product market is concerned. However, in the sense that innovation tends to reduce the firm's market radius in the long run, it is not entirely unambiguous whether Q^* is higher and mill price lower with innovation after all.

The long-run impact of innovation upon the regional output Q^* is evaluated by

$$\frac{dQ^*}{d\beta} = \frac{\partial Q^*}{\partial L^*}\frac{dL^*}{d\beta} + \frac{\partial Q^*}{\partial \beta} + \frac{\partial Q^*}{\partial x_0}\frac{dx_0}{d\beta} \tag{26}$$

since Q^*, being βL^*, depends in the long run not only on L^* and β but also on x_0. The first two terms of the right-hand side of (26) are given by (24), while the third term, evaluated at $x_0 = 1/2$ via (3) and (7) with all parameters but x_0 equal to unity, is reduced to $(1/4)(dx_0/d\beta)$. It therefore follows that as long as a one-unit increase in β (say, by 0.1 from 1 to 1.1), reduces the firm's market radius x_0 by more than $3/4$ (from $1/2$ to $17/40$), the long-run impact of innovation upon the regional output Q^* is in the negative. Related to this decrease in Q^* is an increase in mill price m^*.

The average output per unit of distance is given by

$$\frac{Q^*}{2x_0} = \beta\left(w^* - \frac{1}{2}x_0\right) \tag{27}$$

By letting both β and x_0 be parametric variables, we obtain

$$\frac{d(Q^*/2x_0)}{d\beta} = \frac{\partial(Q^*/2x_0)}{\partial\beta} + \frac{\partial(Q^*/2x_0)}{\partial x_0}\frac{dx_0}{d\beta}$$

$$= \frac{3}{16} - \left(\frac{1}{4}\right)\frac{dx_0}{d\beta} > 0 \tag{28}$$

Thus, since $dx_0/d\beta < 0$, the long-run impact of innovation on the aggregate output clearly is positive.

These findings are summarized in Table 13-1, which assumes all parameters to be normalized as unity; that is, $a = b = \alpha = t = k = 1$. It also assumes initial β to be unity and initial equilibrium market radius x_0 to be 1/2. All these conditions in turn require $F = 1/16$. Table 13-1 then shows the impact of a change in β by $d\beta = 0.1$ upon the variables as listed. (Different combinations of parameters and/or different degrees of innovation *may* change some of the results of the table.)

That a particular set of parameters implies an adverse effect of innovation or spatial competition on workers does not in general prove it. The next section will focus attention upon more general conditions, upon the labor market in particular, under which such perversity can occur.

Table 13-1. The impact of innovation on various factors

Time Frame	Mill Price	Regional Output	Aggre-gate Output	Real Wage Rate	Regional Employ-ment	Aggregate Employ-ment
Short Run	Down	Up	Up	Down	Down	Down
Long Run	Up	Down	Up	Down	Down	Down

Note: The simulation underscoring this table is based on the following set of parameters: $a = b = \alpha = t = k = \beta = 1$, $d\beta = 0.1$, and $F = 1/16$.

VI. Innovation, Spatial Competition, and the
Labor Market: A Generalized Analysis

Consider the four-dimensional, back-to-back diagram of Figure 13-4, revised as Figure 13-7. Revision has been undertaken to relax the linearity assumption on the product demand, labor supply, and production functions. The original figure also has been transposed so that the labor market now appears in the first quadrant. Note that, even with such revision, the basic characteristic of marginal revenue product curves before and after innovation, which cross one another, remain unchanged. This occurs if (a) the regional marginal revenue curve slopes downward, having a finite horizontal intercept value, and (b) the marginal physical product of labor increases after innovation but is subject to the law of diminishing returns; that is, $d^2Q/dL^2 < 0$. It can be shown that, subject to these provisos, the two marginal revenue product (MRP) curves slope downward with distinct intercept values as in Figure 13-7.[4]

Against these crossing MRPs, which are the alternative regional labor demand functions, consider now a regional labor supply curve L_S or L_S'. If the labor supply happens to be L_S, the impact of innovation upon the real wage rate is seen, from Figure 13-7, to be negative, as it was before. However, if the labor supply is given by L_S', then the impact of innovation is reversed and is positive. In general, the lower the labor supply is, the more likely that innovation will be favorable to workers.

In summation, in an economy in which workers are more willing to work for a given real wage rate, relative to less willing workers, innovation tends to *lower* the wage rate. This negative effect of innovation upon workers is even aggravated over time. This follows because innovation awards the firm with a short-run profit, which in turn induces entry of new firms with a resultant curtailment of the firm's market radius. As seen in the text, this market area reduction tends to lower the real wage rate further under conditions of Löschian

---

[4]That the MRP slopes downward monotonically can be readily confirmed by differentiating it with respect to L. Thus, since $MRP = MR(dQ/dL)$, $d(MRP)/dL = [d(MR)/dQ](dQ/dL)^2 + MR(d^2Q/dL^2) < 0$. Note that both $d(MR)/dQ$ and d^2Q/dL^2 are negative by assumption, and MR is required to be nonnegative.

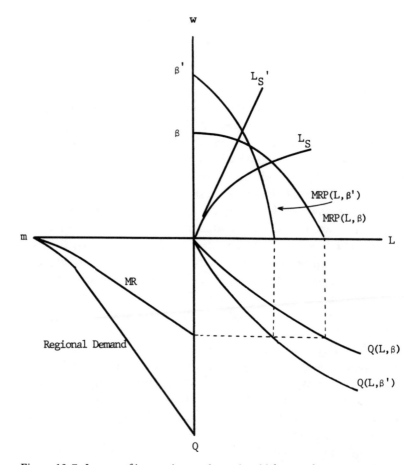

Figure 13.7. Impact of innovation on the regional labor market: a general case.

competition. On the contrary, the more reluctant the workers of the labor supply are, the higher the wage rate they can fetch and, more-over, the more likely the effect of innovation is to be favorable to them, at least in the short run. However, the long-run entry effect of innovation upon wages being negative, the net effect of innovation may not be so entirely rosy even in the eyes of these high-cost workers.

In any case, crucial to these results are the *MRPs'* cross-bound because of innovation. Such a perverse effect of innovation is definitive insofar as innovation raises the marginal physical productivity of labor on one hand and the regional product demand after innovation remains unchanged on the other. However, the latter condition will *not* hold unless the product demand and the labor supply are independent, as defined in the text. In a very simple model of general equilibrium with one product and one factor without money, innovation can be shown to shift the *MRP* curve outward *without* a cross. This possibility will be examined in the Appendix, which shows that the perversity *can* exist even under the crudest model of general equilibrium.

References

[1]   Greenhut, M. L., and H. Ohta. "Related Market Conditions and Interindustrial Mergers." *American Economic Review* 66 (1976): 257–77.

[2]   ———. "Vertical Integration of Successive Oligopolists." *American Economic Review* 69 (1979): 137–41.

[3]   Hicks, J. R. *The Theory of Wages.* New York: Oxford University Press, 1968.

[4]   Machlup, F., and M. Tabor. "Bilateral Monopoly, Successive Monopoly, and Vertical Integration." *Economica* 27 (1960): 101–19.

[5]   Nakagome, M. "The Spatial Labor Market and Spatial Competition." *Regional Studies* 20 (1986): 307–12.

[6]   Ohta, H., and H. Kataoka. "The Simplest Model of General Equilibrium." *Aoyama Journal of Economics* 33 (1982): 116–32.

Appendix

This appendix considers briefly the impact of innovation upon the regional labor and product markets within a framework of the simplest possible, one-product, one-factor model of general equilibrium. This is a spatial version of the simplest model of general equilibrium presented by Ohta and Kataoka [5].

This model is based fundamentally on the same assumptions set forth in the text. The only point of departure is that the existence of money is now explicitly disregarded. An immediate implication of this is that the price of a product now must be expressed in terms of *either* the product itself (in which case, the product price is unity) *or* the factor service. If the product price is to be expressed in terms of the factor service, and if the factor price is to be expressed in terms of the product, being denoted by w, then the product price m (FOB mill) must be given as $m = 1/w$.

This fixed relation between m and w plays an important role in deriving the regional product demand function from the regional labor supply function. To see this, consider the now familiar four-dimensional back-to-back diagram. The second quadrant of Figure A-1 shows the rectangular hyperbola representing the unitary w–m relation. The third quadrant depicts the regional labor supply curve L_S, the related marginal expenditure curve, and the marginal revenue product curve MRP, to be explained more fully. The fourth quadrant illustrates the production function applicable to the firm and the region under consideration. All these relations are based on the following system of equations,

$$m = 1/w \qquad (\text{A-1})$$

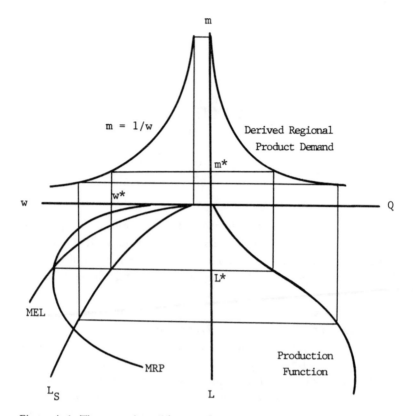

Figure A-1. The general equilibrium of related markets: short run.

$$L = L = L_S(w, x_0) \tag{A-2}$$

$$Q = f(L) \tag{A-3}$$

where, as seen in the text, $L_{S1} > 0$ and $L_{S2} > 0$, while the production function $f(L)$ is assumed to increase monotonically with L. The related AP and MP curves are assumed further to be hill-shaped to reflect partial scale economy.

From Equations (A-1) through (A-3) a negative relationship between m and Q can readily be derived, as in the first quadrant of Figure (A-1). This is what has been called the *derived regional product demand curve* Q_D.

Given the derived regional demand Q_D, the firm will determine its optimal employment via the production function (A-3). For this to be achieved the marginal revenue product curve $MRP = MR \times f'$ must be equated with the marginal expenditure on labor MEL under conditions of monopsony now assumed for the present analysis. Thus,

$$MR \times f' = w + (dw/dL)L \qquad\qquad (A\text{-}4)$$

where, while MR is unity in terms of output and hence is constant, f' is a hill-shaped function of L. In contrast, the right-hand side of (A-4) is a monotone-increasing function of L, given x_0. The equilibrium employment L^* then is determined at the intersection of these MRP and MEL curves. Related to this L^* are equilibrium wage rate w^* (on the labor supply curve L_S), output Q^*, and mill price m^*.

Insofar as these equilibrium values provide the firm with positive profit Π, new firms will be enticed to enter the market with the effect of lowering x_0. The long-run equilibrium requires this short-run profit to vanish. Thus,

$$\Pi = Q - wL - F$$

$$= L\left(\frac{Q}{L} - w - \frac{F}{L}\right) = 0$$

$$\therefore AP_L = w(L, x_0) + AFC \qquad\qquad (A\text{-}5)$$

where $AP_L = Q/L$ and $AFC = F/L$.

Solving (A-4) and (A-5) simultaneously yields the long-run equilibrium conditions illustrated by Figure A-2. The hill-shaped curve AP_L in the figure stands for the average product of labor while the U-shaped ATC curve represents the average total cost as it is a vertical sum of the regional labor supply, that is, variable average labor cost, and the average fixed cost AFC. The tangency point E between the two curves AP_L and ATC guarantees the long-run equilibrium (L^*, w^*) of spatial competition simultaneously satisfying equations (A-4)' and (A-5). Note in this connection that while the curve AP_L is fixed, the ATC curve is subject to variation as it depends upon the regional labor supply, which in turn depends upon the firm's market radius

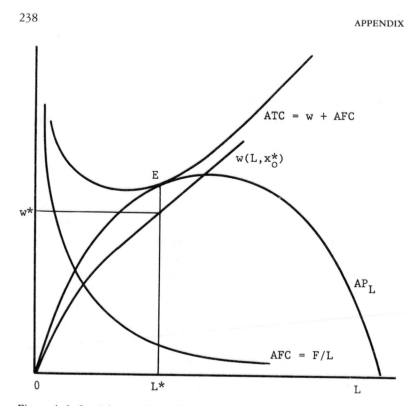

Figure A-2. Spatial general equilibrium in the long run.

x_0. With greater entry of new firms the market radius x_0 tends to be squeezed to yield what may be called the "porcupine effect" of spatial competition on the regional labor supply: the curve is twisted upward and leftward upon each rival encroachment. This porcupine effect yields a concomitant twist in the ATC, eventually generating tangency equilibrium.

The long-run tangency equilibrium E can occur on either the increasing or the decreasing part of the AP_L, depending upon the fixed cost level. When it is sufficiently high, it should be clear that no tangency at all is feasible, much less on the increasing part of the AP_L. However, if the fixed cost is sufficiently low, then the long-run tangency equilibrium is likely to occur on the increasing part of the AP_L. The underlying MP_L is also likely to slope upward in the neighborhood of equilibrium. These observations may be rephrased as Proposition A-1.

Proposition A-1. Firms in industries that require smaller (larger) fixed costs tend to operate economies (diseconomies) of scale under conditions of spatial competition (à la Lösch) in the long run, provided that the production function is hill-shaped in input L.

Alternatively stated, the marginal revenue product may decrease (or increase) in spatial competition if fixed costs are sufficiently low (or high). Thus, insofar as the regional labor supply becomes less elastic because of spatial competition (as in the present case, in which the wage rate for the individual labor supply is linear), the so-called perverse effect of spatial competition on wage rate (Nakagome [5]) is reinforced if fixed costs are sufficiently low to induce substantial entry, substantially curtailing individual firms' outputs. However, the perverse effect of spatial competition is weakened or possibly even reversed when fixed costs are sufficiently large. Summarizing these observations yields Proposition A-2.

Proposition A-2. Provided that the production function is hill-shaped in input and the elasticity of the individual labor supply increases with distance from the firm, spatial competition may yield a higher wage rate (and a lower mill price) initially, but further entry tends to reverse this trend eventually, lowering the wage rate and raising the mill price, unless inhibited by higher fixed costs.

To appreciate this proposition more fully, recall Equation (A-4), which can be rewritten as follows:

$$f' \equiv MP_L = w\left(1 + \frac{1}{\eta}\right) \qquad (A\text{-}4)'$$

where η stands for the elasticity of labor supply. Note that if MP_L decreases concomitantly with η because of spatial competition, then w must also decline necessarily. Even if MP_L increases when output is decreased, it is possible that wage rates will decline if η declines sufficiently to push up the right-hand side of (A-4)'. The perverse effect of spatial competition is thus confirmed under more general conditions than those in prior examinations.

We now turn our attention to the employment effects of innovation and subsequent spatial competition. When technical progress takes place to shift the production function upward, profit increases and regional employment may increase in the short run. But profit induces new entry, yielding a new tangency equilibrium on a new AP_L curve. This renewed tangency equilibrium after innovation may take place to the left of the original tangency point E. Thus, innovation *may* even decrease regional employment in the long run. However, greater entry means that a greater number of regions will be monopolized by individual firms. The aggregate employment therefore may increase even if regional employment decreased because of innovation, followed by further spatial entry. This question is to be examined more fully.

Given the individual labor supply $L_x = w - x$, Equation (A-2) is specified as:

$$L = 2x_0 w - x_0^2 \qquad (w > x_0) \tag{A-2$'$}$$

Assume that the average product curve is quadratic in L:

$$AP_L \equiv \frac{Q}{L} = \delta - (L - \gamma)^2 \qquad (\delta > \gamma^2) \tag{A-3$'$}$$

where the constraint $\delta > \gamma^2$ is needed to ensure that AP_L stays above the regional labor supply $w(L)$ in the neighborhood of the origin. Note that the present AP_L yields a hill-shaped curve with its maximum value of δ at $L = \gamma$.

Substituting (A-3)$'$ along with (A-2) into (A-4)$'$ yields:

$$-3x_0^2 y^2 + (4x_0 - .1)y - \frac{1}{2}x_0 - \gamma^2 + \delta = 0 \tag{A-4$''$}$$

where y is the transformed variable defined as the average employment per unit market area of the firm, that is, $y \equiv L/x_0$. This variable transformation proves to be very helpful because any change in the aggregate employment is directly related to y insofar as the total market area X is fixed and finite: the average employment per area y rises (falls) if and only if the total employment Xy rises (falls).

Equation (A-4)″ is the quadratic equation in y and is solvable in terms of x_0, given γ and δ. For purposes of simplification, assume $\gamma = 1$ and $\delta = 5/4$. The solution for optimal y is then given by:

$$y = \frac{4x_0 - 1 + (-6x_0^3 + 19x_0^2 - 8x_0 + 1)^{1/2}}{6x_0^2} \qquad \text{(A-4)}'''$$

which is the larger of the two solutions of (A-4)″. (This follows because the concave MRP underlying (A-4)″ exceeds the linear MEL also underlying (A-4)″ between the two solutions.) Equation (A-4)‴ thus provides the optimal solution for y which itself can be shown to be a concave, hill-shaped curve over the relevant domain of $x_0 = [0, 0.948]$. [The maximum distance $x_0 = 0.948$ is the optimal market radius for the spatial monopolist, which is determined by solving $(\partial\Pi/\partial x_0) = 0$ and $(\partial\Pi/\partial L) = 0$ simultaneously.] This means that while spatial competition tends to increase total employment initially, with relatively high x_0, further entry will eventually cause total employment to decline as x_0 approaches zero; the lower the fixed cost is, the smaller x_0 in equilibrium in the long run.

The hill-shaped curve $y^*(\delta)$ in Figure A-3 is derived from Equation (A-4)″ and is shown to shift upward upon innovation reflected by an increase in δ. This means that total employment can increase as a result of innovation, at least in the short run. However, the conditions of zero profit reflected by Equation (A-5) must prevail in the long run. Note that this equation requires y to be U-shaped in x_0, the curve of which, illustrated by $\Pi_0(\delta)$ in Figure A-3, is in turn shifted downward with innovation. It follows that the long-run equilibrium obtained at the intersection of these hill-shaped and U-shaped curves $y^*(\delta^+)$ and $\Pi_0(\delta^+)$ after innovation yields not only a much shorter market radius x_0, but it also *may* lower total employment per area y.

Figure A-3 illustrates these relations. Two notes are warranted. First, the right-most intersection points are irrelevant: any smaller x_0 yields a positive profit, hence warranting further entry, and reducing x_0 until the left-most equilibrium is attained at E_0 before innovation and E_1 after innovation. Second, whether or not total employment increases after innovation depends upon the elasticities or concavities of the intersecting curves in Figure A-3. The more concave the hill-shaped optimal employment curve is and the less convex

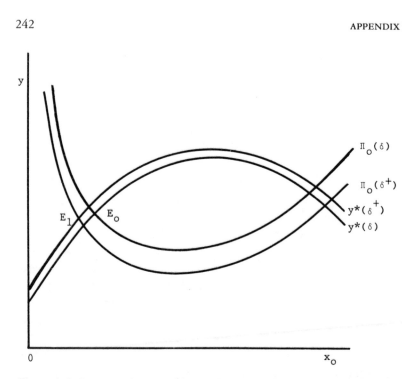

Figure A-3. Long-run impact of innovation on total employment and market radius.

the U-shaped iso-profit curve is, the more likely the equilibrium point E_1 is after innovation to be lower than the initial equilibrium point E_0. Total employment will be lower after innovation accordingly.

Now recall from Equation (A-2)′ that $w = (y + x_0)/2$. Thus, insofar as both x_0 and y are reduced after innovation in the long run, so is wage rate accordingly. Even if y did not decline, as long as the decline in x_0 exceeds a rise, if any, in y, wage rate must decline because of innovation. Thus, workers employed by the incumbent firms can be hit twice with reduced wages: by regular entry and then by innovation-induced entry.

The perverse effect of innovation upon the labor market can therefore remain invariant even under a simple, but rigorously defined model of general equilibrium with one product and one factor of production under conditions of Löschian competition.

Index

(Page numbers in italics indicate that an author's name appears on that page in a list of references.)

Spatial Price Theory of Imperfect Competition was composed into type on a Linotron 202 digital phototypesetter in eleven and one-half point Garamond with one and one-half points of spacing between the lines. Garamond was also selected for display. The book was designed by Jim Billingsley, composed by G&S Typesetters, Inc., printed offset by Thomson-Shore, Inc., and bound by John H. Dekker & Sons, Inc. The paper on which this book is printed bears acid-free characteristics for an effective life of at least three hundred years.

TEXAS A&M UNIVERSITY PRESS

COLLEGE STATION